PSYCHOLOGY RESEARCH PROGRESS

PSYCHOLOGICAL DISTRESS

RISK FACTORS, PATTERNS AND COPING STRATEGIES

PSYCHOLOGY RESEARCH PROGRESS

Additional books in this series can be found on Nova's website under the Series tab.

Additional eBooks in this series can be found on Nova's website under the eBook tab.

PSYCHOLOGY RESEARCH PROGRESS

PSYCHOLOGICAL DISTRESS

RISK FACTORS, PATTERNS AND COPING STRATEGIES

ANGELO COMPARE,
CLAUDIA ELIA,
ANTONIO GIULIO SIMONELLI
AND
FRANCESCO CATTAFI
EDITORS

nova publishers
New York

Library of Congress Cataloging-in-Publication Data

ISBN: 978-1-63485-405-4

Published by Nova Science Publishers, Inc. † New York

Contents

PREFACE

Psychological distress has become a very relevant and highly debated topic as a result of the increasing volume of information available. In fact, in the last decades, more and more research has been conducted in order to provide unique knowledge and shed new light on this important and sensible malady.

In a complex and variegated panorama of scientific research, this book is intended to clarify the most significant questions and to deepen the greater contents about psychological distress, analyzing its various aspects and focusing attentively on them.

Different facets will be addressed in order to accomplish this goal. Among them, personality characteristics that lead to vulnerability, psychological distress, and psychological patterns of acute stress response will be discussed in two different chapters in order to define the subject in a more general way.

On the other hand, the remaining chapters will treat more specific issues considered pivotal in several areas of psychological distress.

In particular, the aspects concerning psychological distress in sport athletes, cancer patients, posttraumatic stress disorder cases, adolescents, cardiac diseases and autistic children and their siblings will be expertly discussed.

Furthermore, this entire book is dedicated to investigate the issues relative to coping styles and strategies, distress assessment, and therapies or interventions able to improve the quality of life while also minimizing risk factors.

Chapter 1 - Personality and psychopathology have long been associated, however the mechanism that create this association are not well studied. Stress generation was examined as a potential mechanism to explain the association between personality traits, especially negative emotionality, and depressive symptoms. In addition, the moderating influence of cognitive vulnerabilities to potentiate the relation between stressors and depressive symptoms was investigated. This Chapter will presents as both dysfunctional attitudes and negative cognitive style interacted with additional stressors to predict prospective fluctuations of daily distress symptoms.

Chapter 2 - Until now, the fact that psychological factors have an influence on athletes' performance is commonly accepted in the sport psychology area.

Because of this, the thorough study of psychological factors that determine consequences on the result, have shed new light on how correct researches about this subject are important.

The individual reaction to stress, for example, is determined by the personality, although it presents common aspects regarding hormonal reactions. During a sport event circumstance, a stress stimulus will have consequences on the result. As for stress, a light anxiety level can help the performance, but if average levels are crossed, anxiety turns into a limit that compromises the subject's functions.

Self-esteem in sport is fundamental, it enables the athlete to give his best and the lack of it is one of the major obstacle that a champion could meet on his way.

Furthermore, it is important to underline that body and mind are in deep connection with each other.

So taking care of physical shape goes along with the mental and psychological balance achievement, which allows reaching a wellness state. This state, experimented by the athlete in sport performances, is known as the "flow".

In the application of appropriate intervention methods, the analysis of stress, anxiety and self-esteem and the knowledge of the athlete could be helpful. This statement is particularly true especially in crisis or low scores situations.

Managing the athlete's psychophysical state means being aware of his difficulties and his potential to develop techniques that allow an acceleration of the adapting processes and to turn a potentially "negative" situation into a "positive" one.

Chapter 3 - In oncology, psychological distress is expected during the entire disease trajectory, and beyond into the survival phase. It is a source of suffering on its own, but it may also interfere with treatment adherence, as well as with both health and well-being. These two reasons make psychological distress the 'core' psychological dimension in cancer care, and they are the main indicators for its routine monitoring and professional treatment. In the first section of the chapter, the features of psychological distress are defined: it is connected with other psychological dimensions and disease and/or treatment effects, and it is described in its evolution throughout the experience of illness. The second section offers practical guidance for psychological distress screening and for its management by means of a two-step psychological intervention. In this section practical advice for nurses, physicians, and health personnel is also provided. The last section is composed of three clinical vignettes, together with comments. The bio-psycho-social and patient-centered approaches frame all discourse in this chapter.

Chapter 4 - While a large percentage of the population experiences trauma, only 8-10% of those individuals develop posttraumatic stress disorder (PTSD) and other trauma-related mental health problems. Previous research has shown that female sex is associated with higher rates of negative mental health outcomes. Survivors of interpersonal violence (physical and sexual abuse or assault) report higher rates of PTSD than survivors of most other forms of trauma, such as death of a loved one or natural disasters. Among the possible explanations for these differences (including biological, social, cognitive, and behavioral factors), coping style has been suggested as an additional reason for increased mental health problems after trauma. Research has shown that avoidant coping is associated with increases in PTSD symptoms and other mental health outcomes. Yet there is a paucity of research examining the interplay among participant sex, trauma type, and coping style on PTSD symptoms and other trauma-related outcomes. A large sample of college student participants completed a survey study examining demographic information (including participant sex), trauma history, coping style, PTSD outcomes, and other mental health issues. The authors conducted a series of hierarchical linear regressions; the results indicated that female sex, interpersonal violence exposure, and avoidant coping styles were associated increases in PTSD symptoms and other negative mental health outcomes. Male sex and problem-focused coping seemed to buffer the effects of trauma on PTSD and negative mental health outcomes. The results confirm that being female and interpersonal violence exposure are both independently and in concert strongly related to PTSD while the influence of experiencing the death of a loved one seems to be important but mild. These findings support the assertion that problem-focused coping leads to desirable outcomes and avoidant coping leads to poor outcomes. Clinicians and first responders working with survivors of trauma should carefully assess for this constellation of risk factors (female sex, interpersonal violence, and avoidant coping), as individuals with these risk factors seem to be at a significantly high risk for negative outcomes. In addition, interventions that decrease avoidance coping and improve problem-focused coping will likely be useful for survivors of trauma.

Chapter 5 - In this paper the authors present a new rating scale for adolescent psychological distress based on an Italian population study carried out in a cohort of 31,661 adolescents, and analyzed with Rasch Analysis in addition to the traditional tests.

The Italian epidemiological survey on drug use in the school population was conducted by the Department of Anti Drug Policies in the first six months of 2014. It was based on a methodology of the European Monitoring Centre for Drugs and the Drug Addiction (EMCDDA - European School Survey Project on Alcohol and Other Drugs - ESPAD). The questionnaire and the survey procedures were taken from ESPAD and adjusted modified in order to address the specific characteristics of to the Italian school system.

The total population sample consisted on 31,661 15-19 years old students who attended Italian public high schools.

Among the items in the source scale the authors have selected nine items belonging to three dominions (Energy, Emotional Stability, Impulsivity and Risk-Taking) from which the authors expected the maximal indirect relation to wellbeing state and therefore as complement, to distress. To evaluate the psychometric properties of distress scale the authors carried out the homogeneity analysis or internal consistency of the scale, using the Crónbach's alpha coefficient, and analysis of the validity of the scale, using the Gamma coefficient of Goodman and Kruskal - index rank correlation. The data dimensionality was explored using Rasch Analysis and factor analysis.

The Cronbach's alpha obtained considering all items was to 0.694, making it quite satisfactory and meeting the standards criteria of acceptability. Rasch analysis confirmed the items validity and that the items distribution remains in the area of the tolerance defined.

A very good distribution emerges with a complete absorption of possible values along the scale range; neither ceiling or floor effect is observed.

Whereas the level of distress measured by the scale is higher the lower the score detected, it is observed a significantly higher level of distress in females than in males (52.59 vs 59.61).

For all psychotropic substances analyzed,significantly higher levels of distress in consumers than non-consumers have been found. In addition,the level of distress as measured by the scale appears to increase going from users of “soft” drugs to users of “hard” drugs: - 57.18 is the mean value obtained in the distress scale from the group of students who say they have never used any illegal drug; - 53.00 is the mean value obtained in the distress scale from the group of students who report use of cannabis at least once in their life; - 50.18 is the mean value obtained in the distress scale from the group of students who report use of cocaine at least once in their life; - 47.95 is the mean value obtained in the distress scale from the group of students who report use of heroin at least once in their life. This survey has detected several factors/conditions associated to the use of substances, which can be considered a reliable proxy of psychological distress: family background seems to be very important as well as the relationship with parents; this emerged as regards the presence of rules on behavior outside the home, the quality of relationships with prominent adult figures (particularly the father), their leadership role, and the family harmony.

Chapter 6 - The experience of childbirth and becoming a parent can become particularly distressing when newborn has a severe chronic disability, like Autism Spectrum Disorder (ASD). Families with autistic children face an overload of their adaptive capacities and crisis situations that can in turn lead to various negative psychological consequences on each parent, the couple, children, and the whole family. Indeed, parents of autistic children show high incidence of psychological distress and mental disorders (e.g., anxiety disorders, depressive symptoms). Evidence suggests that parents of children with ASD may benefit of comprehensive and flexible psychological interventions to reduce parental distress and promote the wellbeing and improve the quality of life of the family.

Chapter 7 - Parental mental stress is clinically common in families of autistic children and adversely affects the care of the child. Moreover, parents of autistic children frequently experience feelings of guilt, maladaptive coping styles, a lack of ability to forgive themselves and variations in mindfulness. However,it is unclear which of these dimensions is predominant in these families and their pattern of association with other components of this complex picture. While most notable in parents, this is also true of healthy siblings who intrinsically perceive more responsibility and often receive less attention than their afflicted brothers or sisters. The evidence available in the literature on the topic is quite controversial, revealing both positive and negative effects deriving from growing up with ASD siblings.

Demographic and psychological information on mental stress, feelings of guilt, ability to forgive, mindfulness and coping styles were collected through clinical interviews and self-report questionnaires in parents and siblings of autistic children. Artificial Neural Networks (Auto-CM system) were applied to parents data to highlight the associations among the variables under investigation.

Predominant dimensions in parents of autistic children indcluded low feelings of guilt, high levels of forgiveness and low levels of maladaptive coping responses. These three main dimensions were strictly related among themselves. While high parental mental stress was strictly related to high parental distress subscales, to high maladaptive coping styles, and to low self-forgiveness ability, conversely, low mental stress appeared to be marginal in relation to the other psychological dimensions.

This behavior is typical of complex nonlinear systems. The severity of the ASD was not related to parental psychological dimensions. The ADOS scores, both low and high, were in fact marginal in the connectivity map in relation to the other dimensions.

In siblings, the average distress scores level was extremely high irrespectively of ASD severity or family size. About one third of them were at risk of developing major depression. Distress appeared to be mainly related to difficulties in building a meaningful relationship with the ASD child and in managing the child's behavioral problems. In conclusione the interplay of psychological factors related to stress in parents and siblings of ASD children is complex. Understanding these relationships is the starting point to activating and enhancing parental resources essential to the wellbeing of both children and caregivers.

Chapter 8 - The World Health Organization states that cardiac diseases are the major cause of death worldwide. Evidence suggests that several psychosocial factors, including psychological distress and maladaptive coping strategies, may influence etiology and prognosis of cardiac diseases. Prolonged psychological distress may result in physiological dysregulations that, in turn, can promote the onset of a cardiac disease or negatively influence its prognosis. Moreover, psychological distress may lead to maladaptive behavioral coping responses (e.g., smoking, alcohol drinking, not adherence to medical treatments, etc.), which can indirectly be linked to the onset or worse prognosis of a cardiac disease. The importance to take into account these psychosocial factors in order to prevent their onset and improve the effectiveness of cardiologic rehabilitation programs will be discussed.

Chapter 9 - Near-Infrared Spectroscopy (NIRS) is a functional neuroimaging technique based on the properties of light that allows a non-invasive measurement of concentration changes in cortical hemoglobin. Developed in the last 40 years, NIRS can be used to detect non-invasively the activation patterns of cerebral cortex. Its use in the field of psychophysiology has constantly increased over time, thanks to some intrinsic advantages over other neuroimaging techniques.

Even so, one of the areas understudied using NIRS technology is stress responses. The exposure to both acute and chronic psychosocial stressors can lead to unfavorable health outcomes. Moreover, literature collected and meta-analyzed over time shows that the exposition to stressors hyperactivates right frontal areas of the cortex as well as neuroendocrine systems. Interestingly, these findings have been partly replicated by few NIRS studies, even though a number of methodological and practical issues have been raised.

The resolution of these problems could allow in future NIRS studies, to better explore the neurophysiological underpinnings of stress responses and even contribute to study the protective/risk factors of those physical and mental diseases exacerbated by stress.

Chapter 10 - Clinical Psychologists working in outpatient integrated care clinics can deal with particular psychological disorders including: psychological distress caused by infertility, premenstrual syndrome and premenstrual dysphoric disorder, postpartum depression, emotion dysregulation and eating disorder symptoms.

The present chapter will examine the role of psychologists in the assessment and treatment of these disorders.

In: Psychological Distress
Editors: A. Compare, C. Elia, A. G. Simonelli et al.
ISBN: 978-1-63485-405-4

Chapter 1

PERSONALITY AND VULNERABILITY TO PSYCHOLOGICAL DISTRESS

Claudia Elia, Antonio Giulio Simonelli and Angelo Compare
Department of Human and Social Science, University of Bergamo, Italy

ABSTRACT

Personality and psychopathology have long been associated, however the mechanism that create this association are not well studied. Stress generation was examined as a potential mechanism to explain the association between personality traits, especially negative emotionality, and depressive symptoms. In addition, the moderating influence of cognitive vulnerabilities to potentiate the relation between stressors and depressive symptoms was investigated. This Chapter will presents as both dysfunctional attitudes and negative cognitive style interacted with additional stressors to predict prospective fluctuations of daily distress symptoms.

INTRODUCTION: HISTORY OF THE RESEARCH ABOUT STRESS AND PERSONALITY TRAITS

The term stress was borrowed from engineering by Hans Selye in the 1930s and it is a measure of the internal forces acting within a deformable body.

Selye also defined stress as the result of an organism's failed attempt to respond properly to a physical change.

In the '70s, the transactional stress theory made by Lazarus and colleagues became the leading theory in the study of psychological stress and it kept this leadership even in the following years.

Personality is a key element of the transactional stress theory because it doesn't only concern the appraisal and coping of the stress but it selects and shapes stressful situations.

However it was pretty rare to find personality in this kind of research even though both Eysenck (1967) with his study on neuroticism and Friedman with his research on the type A personality showed that personality itself has a strong correlation with the stress and stress' outcomes.

Recently new research brought to light new insights concerning the effects of personality on stress.

This new framework, also known as the Five Factor Model (McCrae and John 1992) or the Big Five factors (John 1990), represents a major step forward in this kind of research.

Moreover the relationship between stress and coping was highly analysed in the field of personality psychology.

In particular, most of the research showed that personality dimension predicts increased emotional reactivity under a stressful situation.

These studies demonstrate that Neuroticism and Trait Anxiety are indeed significant predictors of increased anxiety and other negative affects under conditions of stress.

Generally speaking, personality researchers with an interactionist orientation analysed the interactions between situational attributes and personality disposition.

Interactional psychology outlines four principles: 1) behaviour has a key role in person-situation interaction; 2) the individual is an active, intentional agent in this process; 3) motivational emotional and cognitive variables determine the side of the person; 4) the psychological meaning a person ascribes to the situation is essential in determining behaviour (Endler 1975; Endler 1980; Endler and Edwards 1982).

Another branch of stress research in personality psychology concerned coping dispositions that were constructed as general response styles in hypothetical stress situations.

Examples of these coping dispositions are "repression- sensitization," "Monitoring-blunting," "Anger in," "Anger out."

Coping dispositions predict information processing, attentive orientation, emotional processing in demanding, ambiguity and anxiety in provoking or irritating situations.

Another line of the research is the one concerning Type A coronary-prone behaviour pattern and its relation to cardiovascular disease and this is due to the fact that Type A personality is characterized by time urgency, competiveness, aggression and hostility.

Another type of research is based on personality-related physiological reactivity to stress, as indicated by increases heart rate and blood pressure, excretion of stress hormones such as cortisol and catecholamines and changes in the immunological parameters.

Other research concentrates on the relation between trait anxiety and immunological parameters finding heightened reactivity only for those people who were exposed to long term stress (Ursin, 1984).

In the 1990s, there was a renewed interest in personality that brought to new research field.

According to Krohne, the stability and change are not mutually exclusive in the process model for both stable and unstable changes.

Unstable changes occur when the limits of the states of a system can not be defined while stable changes can be replicated easily.

So personality as a stable variable is a useful to predict stability and regularity in the system.

According to McCrae and Costa and according to the Health Psychology, trait measures should be included in stress research because stress is more apt to be influenced by enduring personality traits rather than appraisal and coping processes.

TRANSACTIONAL STRESS THEORY

In the 1970s, Lazarus and colleagues brought to light a new focus into stress research, and their theory of stress and coping soon became the most influential psychological stress model in the last few decades.

The main aspect of their theory is that stress is not part neither of environment nor of the person alone, but it is the result of the ongoing relationship between these two elements which Lazarus and Colleagues called transaction (Folkman and Lazarus 1988, Lazarus 1991, Lazarus 1993).

The meaning of transaction cannot be misunderstood with the meaning of interaction because they are two different constructs.

Interaction means that the two variables, environment and person, keep separate their own identities and they are statistically divided into portions of variance (Lazarus and Folkman 1984), whereas, transaction implies a newly created level of abstraction where both person and situation elements are united to form a new relational meaning.

Furthermore this transaction is mediated by appraisal and coping processes that determine the outcome of the stress process.

In the primary appraisal a person perceives harm, a threat of harm or challenge, while in the second appraisal person starts to analyse the possibility to use available options in order to cope with the situation.

After assessing the transaction as stressful, the coping process has to play a key role to manage the troubled person-environment relationship.

In this way, coping has two functions: 1) problem centered coping that is directed towards dealing with the conditions triggering stress; 2) emotion-centered coping that is directed toward regulating accompanying emotions.

As soon as coping changes both situation and person's well being, a new sequence of appraisal will start.

Moreover the coping strategies influence person's subsequent appraisal and thus the kind of intensity of the stress reaction. (Lazarus 1990)

Although Lazarus had worked with trait like constructs such as repression and dispositional denial, he put aside them when the transactional stress theory became increasingly developed.

The reason why he wrote off personality traits is because he thought that they were too static, too global, too reductionist.

He also lacked contextual referents because they were inadequate to capture the complexity and the variability of the stress process. (Lazarus 1990)

In addition he stated that trait like coping style and coping dispositions had no predictive value for adaptation to stress.

NEW RESEARCH ABOUT PERSONALITY IN STRESS

In the last few decades of the 20th century, new constructs have been considered the main aspects of personality and they are considered predictors of resilience, positive appraisal and effective coping.

Examples of this last statement could be personality traits such as Hardiness (Kobasa 1973), Optimism (Scheier and Carver 1985), Self –Efficacy (Bandura 1978), Sense of Coherence (Antonovsky 1993), Learned Resourcefulness (Rosenbaum 1990) and Hope (Snyder et al., 1991).

As a matter of fact, Hardiness is shown to predict better physical and mental health through the mediation of more challenging appraisal and better coping under stressful situations.

Same effects are visible in Optimism, which predicts superior mental and physical recovery after a coronary artery bypass surgery and better adjustment to the diagnosis of breast cancer.

However these studies paved the way for the introduction of personality in transactional stress research.

The new research underlines that these new constructs should be evaluated as well as Neuroticism and Extraversion that they has not been assessed yet.

Recent studies have demonstrated that Hardiness, Optimism, Hope, Self- Efficacy, Sense of Coherence and internal locus of control load heavily on Neuroticism and they charge personality factors such as Extraversion and Conscientiousness (Larsson and Kallenberg 1999).

These factors are part of the five factors model.

The Big Five and Coping

The five factor model or big five represents an important advancement in the field of personality psychology.

It provides a unified framework that creates a solid basis to the taxonomy of human personality.

Since 1980s the Big Five model was adopted due to the fact that it is the best comprehensive system of basic, independent personality factors.

It is a hierarchically system with five broad high order factors or domains at the summit which each integrate a number of narrow low- order traits.

The Big Five are Neuroticism, Extroversion, Openness to Experience (or Culture), Agreeableness and Conscientiousness.

Each factors is composed of several traits and facets, Neuroticism is made by traits of anxiety, angry, hostility, depression, self-consciousness, impulsiveness and vulnerability.

So several Big Five Factors correspond to long-established personality traits: Neuroticism and Extraversion are the pivotal elements in Eysenck's System (1967), while Agreeableness, for instance, is the negative pole of Hostility and Type A behaviour.

The Big Five Factors play a key role in the appraisal, coping and stress process.

Talking about neuroticism, those high on neuroticism are poor copers who choose ineffective strategies that may serve to inflame stressful situations.

In a study about coping with a broad set of stressors, those who have higher on neuroticism report lower levels of problem solving and higher levels of confrontation, escape avoidance and self blame.(Lee-Baggley et al., 2004)

Moreover those individuals reported also higher levels of interpersonal withdrawal as compared to those who have lower neuroticism.

Nevertheless, those high on Neuroticism are not only rigid copers, they lack the ability to cope using a given adaptive strategy.

The reason why they do not choose appropriate coping strategies is their high level of negative emotions.

In particular they tend to cope poorly with stress in close relationship, as a matter of fact they use maladaptive strategies when someone close to them is involved.

Instead, they increase their use of empathic responding when the stressful situation involves someone distant.

Individuals high on Neuroticism tend to experience stressful events as aversive and they react negatively.

This process to react is also known as "hyper-reactivity" (Suls, 2010) and it consists of a large change in negative effect in response to a stressor.

People with Neuroticism have four characteristics:

1) they tend to be more expose to stressful stimuli or they even create stressful situations (Bolger and Zuckerman, 1995)
2) They probably appraise stressors as threats instead of as challenges (Lazarus and Folkman, 1984; Suls, 2010)
3) After an event, they tend to remember this as stressful (Larsen, 1992)
4) They employ less productive coping strategies, especially emotion-focused coping (Bolger, 1990; David and Suls, 1999) or they use unproductive strategies that are damaging for themselves (Bolger and Zuckerman, 1995).

Concerning Extraversion, people who show higher levels of Extraversion appear to be effective and active copers so they are capable to use a variety of ways of coping including also cognitive reframing and active problem solving. (Lee-Baggley et al., 2004; Newth and DeLongis, 2004)

In one study it was reported that those higher on Extraversion probably have more benefit from engaging in cognitive reframing in comparison to those lower on Extraversion.

Regarding coping with family stressors, those higher on Extraversion tend to show engaging in compromise and accepting responsibility (Lee-Baggley et al., 2004).

Instead, higher levels of Openness to Experience are associated with lower levels of cognitive reframing in the daily process study of coping with pain (Newth and DeLongis, 2004).

However, O'Brien and DeLongis (1996) found cognitive reframing to vary across different types of stressors and they found also level of Openness to Experience to interact with type of stressor in predicting coping use.

Of course, those with high level of Openness to Experience tend to be adaptive, flexible copers able to engage with other and with those who are around and they have low level of distancing in coping with family stress (Lee-Baggley, 2004).

In addition they are more empathic in stressful situations concerning close others as compared to with noninterpersonal stressor (O'Brien and DeLongis, 1996).

Agreeableness has an interpersonal significance as a personality trait and it is strongly associated with ways of coping that are common.

According to O'Brien and DeLongis (1996), those higher on Agreeableness reported less faceoff coping and more support seeking than those with low level and they tend not to engage in self blame.

In the studies of Lee-Baggley and O'Brien and DeLongis, those higher on Conscientiousness show more empathic responding than those with low level.

So Conscientiousness people are characterized as hard- working and reliable and they use stoic distancing in order to facilitate task-directed efforts and minimize the interference of stress (Newth and Delongis, 2004).

Those higher on Conscientiousness showed less escape avoidance and self blame than those lower on Conscientiousness in coping with family stressors (Lee-Baggley, 2004).

Nevertheless, Conscientiousness interacted with stressor type in the prediction of self-blame, in particular the ones with high level were more used to use self-blame to cope with family situations.

To sum up, evidence shows that the Big Five dimension of personality interact with stressor type to elicit coping responses, and that people vary their coping style according to the needs of the situation.

So some may vary their behaviour more adaptively, for instance Openness, than others such as Neuroticism.

Nonetheless, the amount of empirical evidence to demonstrate the influence of personality on stress is still poor.

A few studies showed that Neuroticism is tightly related to the later occurrence of negative life events, even when these events are defined (Headey and Wearing, 1989; Magnus, Diener, Fujita and Pavot, 1993; Ormel and Wohlfahrt, 1991).

Extraversion and Openness to Experience are linked to favourable and unfavourable events (Headey et al., 1993), while for Agreeableness and Conscientiousness there are not evidence to prove their effects on stress.

The examination of stress producing mechanism could be considered one of the most promising ways to analyze the effect of personality on the ongoing of stress (Bermudez, 1999; Wiebe and Smith, 1997) and in particular there are three mechanisms useful to study this.

First of all, one mechanism lies in illusionary goal. In order to reach a utopian goal that goes far beyond their capacities, the possibility of the insurgence of stress become higher and higher.

People tend to set vary ambitious goals and hold on to them even when they fail (Bandura, 1992) and this is typical of a person with a Type A personality.

The key factor of this illusionary goal is Conscientiousness because the seeking of the goal is due to the presence of ambitious and perfectionism that are part of this Big Five element.

Second of all, risk behaviour is one of the mechanisms that makes people be prompt to the insurgence of stress (Bermudez, 1999).

People with a remarkable Extraversion or high Impulsiveness tend to have more stimulating and high risk attitude that inevitably brings to stress.

For instance, High Psychoticism and Conscientiousness are linked to healthy risk behaviour such as smoking and spontaneous sexual activities.

Another element in the risk behaviour is the sensation seeking that is a trait that includes boredom, susceptibility, thrill seeking and disinhibition and it predicts risky behaviours such as dangerous sport, reckless driving and the use of drugs.

Moreover Sensation seeking is connected to high level of Openness and low level of both Agreeableness and Conscientiousness.

The last mechanism is conflict behaviour in social interactions.

In this case, Agreeableness and low hostility are the main constructs of personality because people with high Agreeableness perceive other people as being more socially desirable and prefer integrating interactional style, avoiding actual conflicts in their relationship (Antonioni, 1999; Graziano, Jensen Campbell and Hair, 1996).

Instead, those high in dispositional hostility or type A are more inclined to interpret harmless behaviour of their interaction partners as provocative and to react with hostile, distrustful or openly aggressive behaviour and, of course, hostile people experience family conflicts more frequently and receive less social support (Smith and Christensen, 1992; Smith and Pope, 1990; Smith, Pope, Sanders; Allred and O'Keeffe, 1988; Watkins, Ward; Southard and Fisher, 1992).

The Big Five are very important in the appraisal process in particular Neuroticism and Trait Anxiety play a key role.

On the one hand High Anxiety person and high neurotic person tend to consider every day situation as threatening or damaging (Gallagher, 1990; Schroeder and Costa, 1984).

They tend to appraise their susceptibility to health risks as higher, irrespective of their actual risk behaviour (Vollrath et al., 1999).

On the other hand Conscientiousness, Agreeableness and Extraversion are related to lower appraisal of daily hassles and lower levels of perceived health risks.

Other studies tend to use different traits of personality such as Optimism or Self-Esteem as typical factors of appraisal.

However, the influence of personality traits should be considered separately from situation-specific appraisal.

As a matter of fact, Neuroticism is a predictor of a negative second appraisal over time and, according to Hemenover and Dienstbier, those who have high on Neuroticism have low appraisal.

The expectation of support is a key element of secondary appraisal. People who expected to receive support may be less at risk to be distressed in a stressful situation.

Some personality factors predict level of expectation and support, for example those with high Extraversion have a broaden network and more helpers and they are more trustful because these people would help them if needed, whereas, people with high level of Neuroticism or a High level of Hostility and low Agreeableness tend to have lower expectations.

The Big Five model of personality is also used to evaluate stress vulnerability (Costa, Somerfield and McCrae, 1996).

Neuroticism tends to predict negative affect and tense arousal in performance settings.

However, some studies demonstrate that the correlation between neuroticism and negative affects is quite neutral, whereas Extraversion is highly positive correlated to positive emotions and performance setting.

So people high on Neuroticism are more vulnerable because they tend to emphasize and sustain negative mood responses while those low on Neuroticism have more emotional stability.

Stress and Neurobiological Basis

Stress could modify the prognosis of a multiple set of psychiatric disorders such as schizophrenia, depression, PTSD and anxiety.

In both humans and animals, excessive or enduring stress could provoke structural and neurochemical alterations in several brain structures, in particular hippocampus, prefrontal cortex and amygdale.

It is not easy to identify behavioural or psychological factors (personality traits or hormonal responses to stress) that could help to predict individual psychopathological vulnerability or resistance to deleterious effects of stress in order to know the neurobiological characteristics beyond the stress itself.

Individuals differ in coping style and personality traits and this influence the way in which they are associated with resilience to stress or with stress induced depression.

The biological significance of neuroticism-anxiety as a predictor of stress-related disorders is supported by a link between this personality trait and basal cortisol level.

Moreover using the unpredictable stress model of depression, it was shown that there is an association between anxiety traits and both increased vulnerability to stress- induce depression like symptoms and response of the amygdale to the emotional cues (Sandi et al., 2008).

However, anxiety trait does not play a pivotal role in the link between stress and depression and therefore this means that personality traits do not explain entirely the variance of depressive symptomatology (Sandi and Richter-Levin, 2009).

Chronic stress is a known risk factor for the development of depression in general population (McEwen, 2004; de Kloet et al., 2005; Sandi and Richter-Levin, 2009).

Nevertheless not all the individuals are resistant to stress in the same way because the most of them shows a high vulnerability to stress.

This variation depends on both genetic factors and factors linked to the individual's life history that are the key elements that determine individuals' personality traits, coping styles and other behavioural and psychological characteristics involved in the connection between stress and psychopathology.

Evidence shows that anxiety and exploration traits are linked to stress-induced depression and high clucorticoid reactivity (Tyrka et al., 2008).

In order to analyze the effect on neurobiological structures, it was used the CUS protocol on rats.

The outcomes of the CUS protocol show that all the physiological (body weight gain, plasma, corticosterone), behavioural and neurobiological (activity in the amygdala) parameters are very high after two weeks of stress.

However, the activity of amygdala returns to normality after a longer stress exposure while the physiological and behavioural alterations become higher and higher after four weeks of stress exposure, except the activity of hippocampus that isn't affected by chronic stress at all because of his morphology.

For this reason, according to Castro, it is possible to claim that amygdala tends to be more vulnerable than hippocampus to the effects of stress even if amygdala shows higher reactivity to stress but a slower ability to recover from chronic stress than hippocampus which can recover after few days.

The data suggest also that individual vulnerability or resistance to stress is the result of the combination of anxiety and exploration behavioural traits because those with low anxiety and low exploration profiles are less vulnerable to stress exposure while those with high anxiety show higher levels of the behavioural, neurobiological and physiological parameters and they are more prompt to develop depression-like behaviours.

Neurochemically speaking, those who have high anxiety but low exploration profile show an enhanced plasma corticosterone levels in both amygdala and hippocampus after an acute stress exposure.

HPA axis dysfunction in depression is characterized by stress, hyperresponsivenss, an abnormal circadian secretory pattern and glucorticoid negative feedback resistance.

Regarding the immunological system, chronic stress could bring some changes, such as lack of cell trafficking, inhibition of mitogen- induced T cell proliferation, suppressed microphage function, inhibition of leukocyte function and so on.

Instead, acute stress enhance immunological responses, reactivated what chronic stress tend to shout down.

Resilience, Vulnerability and Allostasis

In order to predict and adapt to new experience, brain and body have developed coordinated and interacted mechanisms that have to be ready to face changes in the environment that could be threaten to survival.

The adaption made by body and brain leads to a readjustment that should help people to cope in the short term.

This ability to respond to and then to bounce back from stressor developed by environment is also known as resilience that concerns both resistance and recovery.

Of course brain seems to be the main element in the resilience because it has to control the allostatic system which affects the entire body and also responds to stressor by showing plasticity.

An element that contributes to vulnerability to stress is environment which could provoke adult psychopathology and abnormalities in HPA axis functions (Sanchez et al., 2001; Crawford et al., 2009; Neigh et al., 2009; Personen et al., 2010).

The differences in hypothalamic-pituitary-adrenal (HPA) axis have a pivotal role in vulnerability to stress (de Kloet et al., 1998).

As a consequence, vulnerability is linked to both immunocompetence and hyperresponsiveness of the HPA axis.

The ability to adapt to the environment could make individuals be vulnerable to stress or resilience.

This adaptation to environment's changes depends on the body and the brain, in particular the latter sorts relevant from irrelevant environmental inputs and pushes body system to respond to these stimuli.

These changes in the environment bring to psychological responses that are called allostatic responses.

In general the term allostasis represents biological mechanism employed to achieve stability of homeostatic system through active intervention by biochemical mediators resulting in adaptive plasticity in brain and body.

These responses are not negative but they play an important and positive role in order to help the organism to adapt to the environmental changes.

So allostasis can't be considered synonymous with stress but it represents the fact that stress might be helpful for survival.

Allostasis concerns the mediators of adaptation, such as cortisol, the autonomic nervous system, metabolic hormones and mediators that help to face stressors.

In the allostasis system, brain covers a pivotal role because neural activity which responds to the stressful experience, shows highly plasticity and endogenous activity in order to mediate the situation.

However, changes in these mediators (aminoacids, neutrophic factors and so on) could provoke changes in mental and physical vulnerability.

Besides the fact that brain is important for resilience because of its capacity of plasticity, the mediators of this process could cause damages if they are not controlled properly.

The most positive but in the same time most negative mediator in brain is the level of corticosteroids that could lead to some serious disease thanks to the fact that it is associated to neurotrophins.

In human body, a lack of resilience and a decreased capacity of plasticity are signs of depression and cognitive impairment caused by the inability to return to normal functions after stressful psychological or physical situations.

This means that when we are exposed to a tough stressful situation, our brain gets blocked and only external factors could help to restore the normal function.

As a matter of fact enduring situation of depression is risky for both hippocampus and prefrontal cortex because it could bring to atrophy.

Furthermore, in the allostatic process, when stress affects the system, the circadian disruption plays a fundamental role.

All the modulators of allostasis show rhythm of activity over the sleep-wake-cycle because some of them influence sleep deprivation because of the decreased of parasympathetic tone and the enhancement of corticosteroids and metabolic hormones that normally are low.

So, behind allostasis and the capacity of resilience in response to a stressor there is a highly functioning circadian timing system.

When the circadian timing system doesn't work well, there are damages regarding corticosteroids and HPA axis such as decrease cognitive flexibility and dysregulation of the metabolic system.

CORTISOL AND STRESS

It is already known that mood disorders are related to alterations of hypothalamic-pituitary-adrenal axis (HPA) function.

Recent studies state that different diagnostic subtypes of depression may be characterized by different types of stress system pathology, in particular, melancholic depression is connected with HPA axis down regulation (Gold and Chrousos, 2002).

However, HPA axis hyperactivity influences social phobia, panic disorder, generalized anxiety, obsessive-compulsive disorder and mixed anxiety-depressive disorder.

For instance, patients with PTSD show decreased basal cortisol levels but increased negative feedback regulation of the HPA axis (Yenuda 1997).

A bigger number of new data suggests that excess of cortisol secretion might determine mood symptoms in the major brain regions (Holsboer, 2000; Tsigos and Chrousos, 2002).

In addition, non affected family members of depressed often have an abnormal functionality of HPA axis and this means that glucorticoid abnormalities may represent genetic vulnerability factors that predispose to and exacerbate the course of mood disorders (Modell et al., 1998).

Beside the glucorticod abnormalities, personality traits play a key role in this context.

For instance, Neuroticism, Extraversion, Agreeableness and Consciousness are linked to depression and/or anxiety disorders.

Neuroticism is associated with social phobia, agoraphobia, panic disorder, obsessive-compulsive disorder and major depression.

Instead, Agreeableness is characterized by phobias while Conscientiousness is linked to phobic, panic and major depressive disorders (Bienvenu, 2004).

To analyze the relationship among stress, personality traits and levels of cortisol and levels of glucorticoid it was used the revisited NEO Personality stress test (Costa and McCrae, 1992) which consists of operationalizing five factors that represent the most basic dimensions of personality that have been identified in natural languages and in psychological questionnaires; each factor is differentiated into six facets.

The experiment conducted by Oswald et al. recruited 68 healthy adults, aged 18-30 years who had to do some specific medical exams (e.g., electrocardiogram, urinalysis and so on).

The first thing that they had to do was the Trier Social Stress Test (TSST) (Kirschbaum et al. 1993).

This test consists of an intravenous cather placed in a forearm vein for blood sampling and a pressure cuff on the arm in order to record vital signs and other information such as blood samples, heart rate and blood pressure.

Then it was told the participants that they would have faced a job interview for the position of hospital administrator and they would have been speaking for five minutes in order to convince the commissioners that they were their best choice for this job.

They were also told that after the job interview they would be asked to perform a 5 minutes arithmetic challenge that would have been judged on speed and accuracy.

The job interview was set in a room with two commissioners; one had to ask the participant his/her qualifications for the job while the other one had to record it using a video camera.

After it, they had the math problem which consists of a four digit number to repeat and then they had to do some operation on this number; if they made a mistake they had to do it again.

At the end of all, they had to stay in another room quiet because they needed to recorder their blood pressure and heart rate.

Moreover participants had to fill the self-report measures of personality, psychological distress and anxiety.

These measures consist of revised NEO Personality Inventory, Brief Symptom Inventory and State Trait Anxiety Inventory.

The Revised Neo Personality Inventory (Costa and McCrae, 1992) is a 240-item questionnaire that measures the five major factors personality: Neuroticism, Extraversion, Openness to Experience, Agreeableness and Conscientiousness.

These traits were represented by six facets subscales that help to have a deeper analysis.

They were measured by a 5-points Likert scale ranging from "strongly agree" to "strongly disagree" and these items are statements that describe general tendency.

Instead, the Brief Symptom Inventory (Derogatis and Melisaratos, 1983) consists of 53-item self report, clinical rating scale.

It is more a measure of current psychological symptoms rather than of personality and therefore the individuals have to respond how much they were distressed or bothered during the past weeks.

The last, the State-Trait Anxiety Inventory is a 40-item self rating scale that measures state and trait anxiety.

It consists of 20 statements that assess temporal or transitory feelings of anxiety and the participants have to answer about how they feel in that moment.

Concerning the gender, the outcomes show that females reported greater psychological distress and anxiety than males (see Table 1).

Table 1. Subject Characteristics[a]

	Males	Females	*p*
Sample size	43	25	
Age (years)	21.7 (2.8)	21.4 (2.8)	
Race, no. (%)			0.0209
Caucasian	34 (79.1)	15 (60.0)	
African-American	4 (9.3)	9 (36.0)	
Asian	5 (11.6)	1 (4.0)	
Education (years)	14.6 (1.7)	14.3 (1.8)	
BSI Global Severity Index	0.16 (0.2)	0.30 (0.2)	0.0148
STAI Trait Anxiety	28.7 (7.6)	33.3 (8.2)	0.0250
NEO Neuroticism Factor	43.8 (8.4)	45.4 (8.6)	
NEO Extraversion Factor	52.3 (9.0)	51.0 (7.3)	
NEO Openness Factor	52.6 (9.2)	57.4 (12.4)	
NEO Agreeableness Factor	49.7 (9.8)	46.7 (11.6)	
NEO Conscientiousness Factor	54.0 (10.9)	50.7 (11.2)	

[a]Values represent means and standard deviations or absolute numbers.

Table 2. Relationship between Neuroticism and Cortisol TSST Responses Over Time*

	Sex-adjusted models z (p)	Sex-by-trait interaction models z (p)	Males only z (p)	Females only z (p)
Neuroticism	0.18 (0.857)	1.46 (0.144)	1.46 (0.145)	−2.11 (0.035)
Sex	−2.99 (0.003)	1.86 (0.068)	—	—
Sex*Neuroticism	—	−2.65 (0.008)	—	—
Anxiety (N1)	0.00 (0.996)	1.10 (0.273)	1.10 (0.272)	−1.83 (0.068)
Sex	−3.08 (0.002)	1.48 (0.139)	—	—
Sex*Anxiety	—	−2.27 (0.023)	—	—
Anger Hostility (N2)	−1.31 (0.189)	0.11 (0.912)	0.12 (0.907)	−2.00 (0.045)
Sex	−2.70 (0.007)	0.64 (0.525)	—	—
Sex*Anger	—	−1.38 (0.168)	—	—
Depression (N3)	−1.70 (0.090)	−0.39 (0.697)	−0.37 (0.715)	−2.51 (0.012)
Sex	−3.15 (0.002)	1.07 (0.696)	—	—
Sex*Depression	—	−1.76 (0.078)	—	—
Self-Conscious (N4)	−0.58(0.562)	0.71 (0.476)	0.71 (0.477)	−2.08 (0.038)
Sex	−2.96 (0.003)	1.23 (0.218)	—	—
Sex*Self-conscious	—	−2.02 (0.044)	—	—
Impulsiveness (N5)	0.93 (0.351)	1.23 (0.217)	1.23 (0.219)	0.06 (0.955)
Sex	−3.72 (0.000)	0.35 (0.723)	—	—
Sex*Impulsiveness	—	−0.90 (0.368)	—	—
Vulnerability (N6)	−0.14 (0.886)	0.49 (0.624)	0.49 (0.621)	−0.93 (0.354)
Sex	−3.11 (0.002)	0.40 (0.69)	—	—
Sex*Vulnerability	—	−1.09 (0.276)	—	—

*Separate models were conducted for the Neuroticism factor and each of the facet subscales.
Each model also includes terms for baseline cortisol, time and $time^2$.

Table 3. Relationship Between Extraversion and Cortisol TSST Responses Over Time

	Sex-adjusted models z (p)	Sex-by-trait interaction models z (p)	Males only z (p)	Females only z (p)
Extraversion	0.62 (0.539)	1.97 (0.048)	2.07 (0.039)	−1.72 (0.086)
Sex	−2.96 (0.003)	1.75 (0.081)	—	—
Sex*Extraversion	—	−2.39 (0.017)	—	—
Warmth (E1)	1.48 (0.140)	2.46 (0.014)	2.49 (0.013)	−0.50 (0.620)
Sex	−2.86 (0.004)	0.51 (0.613)	—	—
Sex*Warmth	—	−0.97 (0.334)	—	—
Gregariousness (E2)	−0.39 (0.695)	0.25 (0.799)	0.35 (0.727)	−1.11 (0.268)
Sex	−3.23 (0.001)	0.23 (0.819)	—	—
Sex*Gregariousness	—	−0.86 (0.392)	—	—
Assertiveness (E3)	−0.42 (0.676)	0.03 (0.975)	0.01 (0.992)	−0.98 (0.327)
Sex	−3.12 (0.002)	0.06 (0.956)	—	—
Sex*Assertiveness	—	−0.69 (0.490)	—	—
Activity (E4)	2.57 (0.010)	2.67 (0.008)	2.67 (0.008)	0.43 (0.671)
Sex	−2.55 (0.011)	0.86 (0.390)	—	—
Sex*Activity	—	−1.41 (0.158)	—	—
Excitement (E5)	−1.47 (0.141)	−0.05 (0.961)	0.20 (0.841)	−4.39 (0.000)
Sex	−3.30 (0.001)	2.24 (0.025)	—	—
Sex*Excitement	—	−3.12 (0.002)	—	—
Positive Emotion (E6)	2.00 (0.046)	2.35 (0.019)	2.36 (0.018)	0.21 (0.835)
Sex	−3.07 (0.002)	0.16 (0.873)	—	—
Sex*Positive Emotion	—	−0.76 (0.447)	—	—

*Separate models were conducted for the Extraversion factor and each of the facet subscales.
Each model also includes terms for baseline cortisol, time and time^2.

Moreover during the experiment higher levels of cortisol were recorded and this proves that psychological stressors influence the activation of physiological stress responses.

This was particular remarkable for those participants with higher pre-stress cortisol because the level of their cortisol strongly enhanced during TSST.

Looking at the data regarding the relationship between personality and cortisol, Openness to Experience is tightly correlated to cortisol responses, in particular during the NEO test, but there was no interaction, for example, between Openness to Experience and gender.

Instead, either Neuroticism or Extraversion show correlations between gender and personality traits and further data suggest that Neuroticism is negatively linked to cortisol responses to the TSST in female rather than males, while Extraversion is the other way round.

According to the Table 2, females have negative relationship between neuroticism and cortisol due to the presence of Anxiety, Anger Hostility, Depression and Self-Consciousness.

Instead, Table 3 shows that males have positive relationship between Extraversion and cortisol because of Warmth, Activity and Positive Emotions.

Agreeableness and Conscientiousness are not related to cortisol levels at all.

During the TSST it was recorded an increase of cortisol levels but the differences in response to psychological stress are linked to differences in personality traits and not to physiological factors.

Those with Openness to Experience had lower cortisol responses during TSST and those who scored higher in Openness to Experience tended to be reflective concerning healthy psychology functioning, including aesthetic sensitivity, attentiveness to inner feelings, preferences for variety, intellectual curiosity and independence of judgement.

Personality traits are correlated with HPA axis responses to stress and this is proved by the fact that those individuals with lower self-esteem, less hardiness or level perceived sense of control have lower basal or provoked adrenocortical activity than individuals without these characteristics.

People high on Neuroticism have high level of cortisol that combined with dexamethasone-corticotropin-relasing hormones provokes changes in the activity of HPA axis.

Furthermore, Neuroticism is linked to enhancing salivary cortisol level and low plasma cortisol.

Individuals high on Neuroticism have higher levels of anger and depression and in particular this is typical of women and this means that gender plays a key role in the relationship between stress and personality.

To sum up, cortisol is linked to high somatic anxiety, high depression and a low sense of mastery (Grossi et al., 1998) and also personality traits influence affective reactions to stress and other events.

Stress and Cortisol: Type D Personality

To sum up once again, exaggerated biological reactions to stress have generally been viewed as maladaptive, as a matter of fact individuals with exaggerated cardiovascular stress responses are more prompt to develop cardiovascular disease due to hypertension, systemic atherosclerosis, left ventricular hypertrophy, coronary calcification and increased cardiovascular disease mortality.

Moreover exaggerate cortisol reactivity has been associated with coronary artery calcification, increased hypertension and cardiovascular disease risk.

Social threat is considered one of the key elements in stress increased reactivity because it increases cardiovascular responses to stress and therefore Social-evaluative threat is the cause of the activation of HPA axis.

An increase of cardiovascular and cortisol reactivity to speech stress task was seen under conditions of increasing social-evaluative threat as a consequence of increasing audience size during a speech stressor.

Type D, "distressed," personality is characterized by the tendency to inhabit emotions in social situations and to be more prone to experience high levels of negative emotions that cause a tight correlation with the development of cardiovascular disease.

Evidence shows an association between type D and increased risk of mortality in patient with coronary artery disease as well as increased risk of developing coronary heart disease in healthy population.

A pivotal role in the Type D personality is played by social nature of stress tasks.

Type D individuals tend to inhibit emotions in social situations and this brings to an exaggerated cardiovascular and cortisol stress reactions.

However it was shown that there is no difference between type D and no type D individuals regarding blood pressure and heart rate stress responses.

According to the data brought by Bibbey, Carroll, Ginty and Phillips, non type D individuals in the social and non social conditions showed massive cardiovascular reactions, whereas Type D individuals in the social conditions were characterized by higher systolic blood pressure, diastolic blood pressure and heart rate reactions than the counterpart.

Moreover, type D individuals show a higher level of cortisol reaction than the non type D individuals.

They also seem to be more reactivity to social-evaluative threat, but they do not react to nonsocial tasks.

Type D individuals have higher cardiovascular and cortisol reactivity mainly when they are exposed to stress tasks in social evaluative threat. When the stress exposure is non social, the type D individuals are similar to the non type D concerning cardiovascular activity.

In addition type D individuals consider social tasks highly stressful because they might have a cognitive bias toward interpreting threat and this might enhance their vulnerability to perceive social stress.

Evidence of this last statement is the presence of two components of type D personality: social inhibition and negative affectivity.

These two elements are linked to unique brain activity patterns in response to perceived socially threatening stimuli.

There is even a correlation between Type D personality and increased risk for cardiovascular disease, morbidity and mortality.

Neurobiologically speaking, there are dysregulation of sympathetic-adrenal-medullary system (SAM) and HPA axis.

For this reason they tend to suffer from coronary artery calcification, hypertension and cardiovascular disease due to a massive cortisol activity.

Furthermore type D individuals have an interpersonal sensitivity trait that concerns their way to evaluate social situations negatively.

Individuals high in interpersonal sensitivity are vigilant and sensitive to others' evaluation and, adopt defensive behaviour such as social inhibition to avoid social assessment.

So people who have high interpersonal sensitivity might be more prompt to develop cardiovascular disease when they are exposed to a stressful situation over time.

Some studies suggest that Type D personality could be consider as a continuous variable with high or low extremes that they are the causes of the maladaptive social behaviour typical of this personality.

Stress and Age

A characteristic that might influence the reaction toward stressful event is Age, as a matter of fact, adults and young adults react differently.

To analyze the effects of age on stress, sample contains young, midlife and older adults.

Older adults report less negative affects than midlife and young adults and they even show less intensive emotional reactions.

Some studies hypothesize that older adults are less reactive to stress than younger adults.

According to Diehl et al. older adults show greater control than young adults when they have to face a stressful stimuli.

This means that age might help to cope better and help to regulate emotions.

According to Lawton and Schultz the repletion of negative effects might decrease the possibility of triggering these effects in the future.

The enhancement of the threshold for experiencing negative effects due to repeated activation is also known as “dampening” effects (Diener, Colvin, Pavot and Allman, 1991).

However, some research report that this “dampening effect” could cause an increased reactivity in adulthood.

Repetition of negative effect activation may lead to sensitization and this is because of changes, in the aging brain, that may alter the way of experiencing emotion.

As mentioned before, amygdale and the limbic system become more sensitive due to the aging.

This sensitivity might lead to easier activation of negative effect when a stimulus such as stressful one is faced.

These heightened sensitivity is similar to the “Kindling effects” that is a process where the repeated exposure to some stimuli causes sensitization (Gilbert, 1994; Kendler, Thorton and Gardner,2001).

Moreover,“Kindling effects” are typical of chronic pain, drug abuse, epilepsy, traumatic stress, anxiety and depressive episodes.

Current studies state that personality and context play a key role in the gathering of negative effects experienced in daily life.

In the experiment conducted by Mroczeck and Almeida, age is inversely correlated with daily negative effect, daily stress and Neuroticism.

Young adults tend to report more daily stress and negative affect than adults and they have high level of Neuroticism.

Nevertheless young adults are less reactive to daily stress than older people because of the kindling effect.

The outcomes of their experiment showed that older people have a stronger association between daily stress and negative affect than younger adults even though high neuroticism older adults displayed the greatest stress reactivity.

When stress was high, older adults reported higher levels of negative affect than did younger adults and they are also more prone to experience negative affect when they have to face stress rather than younger and midlife adults.

However, there is a huge paradox concerning daily stress, negative affect and neuroticism.

Heightened stress reactivity among older adults coexist with lower levels of daily negative affect, daily stress and neuroticism.

So age seems to be negatively correlated with these three elements because it makes experience less stress and less negative effects.

Nevertheless, when stress occurs adults tend to react with higher levels of negative affect than younger adults.

To sum everything up, age and neuroticism play a key role in moderating the relationship between negative affect and daily stress.

Older people reported more negative affects on days when stress is high than younger adults.

Moreover people high on Neuroticism showed stronger relationship between daily stress and negative affect.

TASK-INDUCED, EMOTIONAL INTELLIGENCE AND PERSONALITY

Task induced stress concerns many domains of applied psychology.

Generally speaking, task may be stressful even without the presence of environmental stressors and this is due to the presence of factors intrinsic to the task such as time pressure, overload of attention and monotony.

There are also some differences in vulnerability, because some individuals appear to be highly resilient even though they have to face a tough challenge whereas other people are sensitive to even modest demands (Costa et al., 1996; Suls, 2001).

In order to predict subject's stress response, it might be useful to measure Emotional Intelligence which is a set of interrelated abilities for identifying, understanding and managing emotions both in the self and in others.

The core elements of emotional intelligence are related to resilience and adaptability in stressful environments.

However, task induced is a multidimensional account that is necessary for disturbance of motivation and cognition.

According to Matthews, the Dundee Stress questionnaire (DSSQ) might be helpful in order to assess multiple constructs connected with disturbance.

The DSSQ underlines the presence of three factors that influence the way in which a person experience a stressful situation:

1) Task engagement that concerns energy, task motivation and concentration.
2) Distress, which refers to negative affects and to cognition and lack of control.
3) Worry which regards various forms of self-referent.

Speaking of Emotional intelligence, the main point of this kind of measure is to identify, to assimilate, to understand and to manage emotions.

The outcomes, emerged from the experiment conducted by Matthews and all, report that Emotional intelligence showed incremental validity in predicting pre task distress, post task distress, worry and avoidance coping.

Moreover, the different tasks provoke different patterns of change in the state because it was shown that distress responses appear to be ubiquitous to high workload tasks.

In theory, emotionally intelligent individuals should be more tolerant of stressful environments because of their greater ability to adapt to circumstances and because of their ability to handle negative emotions and cognitions successfully.

POSTTRAUMATIC STRESS DISORDER

Research shows that personality traits account for high comorbidity among disorders and also individual differences in personality traits underlie variations in psychopathology.

The DSM-5 includes a new model of personality traits that consists of five higher order dimensions: negative affect, detachment, antagonism, disinhibition and psychoticism.

This model was used to study the posttraumatic stress disorder and its relationship with other disorders.

The internalize subtype of PTSD is characterized by high negative emotionality, low positive emotionality and highly comorbid with depression, panic, schizoid and avoidant features.

Instead, the externalizing subtype of PTSD is characterized by a lack of constraint and it is highly comorbid with substance use disorders, antisocial personality disorder and borderline personality disorder (Miller et al., 2008; Wolf, 2012).

The distress typical of PTSD people is emphasized by the presence of major depression (Cox et al., 2002; Miller et al., 2008; Slade and Wilson 2006).

After an analysis conducted by James et al. on 185 US veterans who suffer from PTSD, divided into two groups, PTSD group and control group, it was seen that PTSD and control veterans are quite distinct at the level of maladaptive personality trait facets.

Using the PID-5 domain score, the PTSD group showed a reduction of antagonism, high psychoticism, detachment and disinhibition and negative affect.

Compared to the control group, the only facets that are similar are attention seeking, deceitfulness, grandiosity, manipulativeness (also known as antagonism), risk taking (disinhibition) and submissiveness (negative affect).

Five of those last six elements are linked to externalizing psychopathology and this means that the external features seem to be limited in the PTSD group, in particular antagonism (12,7%) whereas those facets concerning the internalizing dimension are greater in the PTSD group than the control group.

In general, the PID-5 were high in the PTSD group and some features were more relevant in the PTSD group than others.

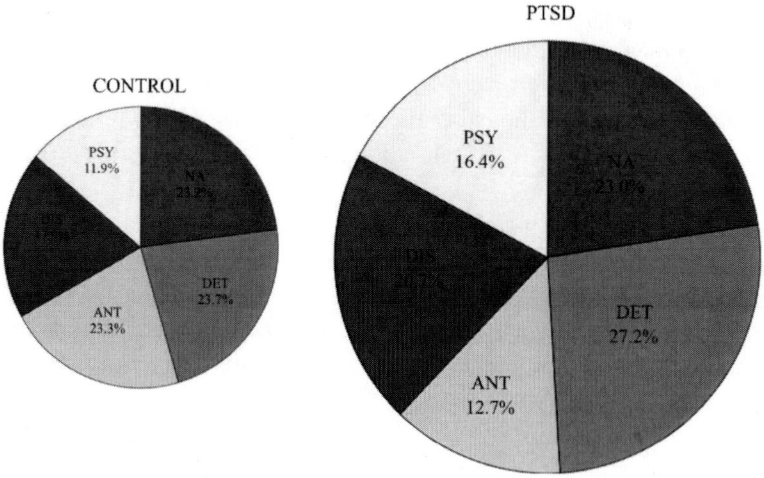

Figure 2. PID-5 domain score profile composition of control and PRSD groups.

For instance, both detachment and psychoticism were the most dominant features of the group because of their characteristics.

Detachment domain is characterized by a withdrawal from interpersonal interactions and a limited hedonic capacity that is joint with an association between PTSD and depression.

Analyzing both groups, negative affect was roughly equivalent in PTSD and control group, while antagonism is lower in the PTSD group rather than control group.

Instead, disinhibition in the PTSD is higher than in control group and this is due to the fact that this kind of domain includes problematic substance use, interpersonal violence, risk taking and self-destructive behaviour.

The difference between antagonism in the PTSD group and control group is remarkable and unpredictable.

The chart shows that control group tends to be more antagonistic than the PTSD group.

However, the PTSD profile is characterized by detachment and negative affect followed by dishinbition, psychoticism and lastly antagonism.

Neurobiologically speaking, hypercortisolism could be correlated to post traumatic stress disorder even if it is not the main factor of PTSD and it is more related to other type of pathology (Heim et al., 2008).

CONCLUSION

A Consequence of Stress: Burnout

Burnout is a tripartite syndrome that includes feelings of emotional exhaustion, depersonalisation and lack of personal accomplishment and it is a response to chronic stress in jobs where individuals work with other people (Maslach, Jackson and Leiter, 1996).

Emotional exhaustion refers to feelings of being emotional overextended and a strong reduction of one's emotional resources.

Depersonalisation refers to a negative heartless and detached attitude towards the people that work with the individual.

Reduced personal accomplishment is accessible through a person's negative self-evaluation in relation to his or her job performance.

The manifestation of burnout is a function of stressors brought about at both personal and environmental-organisational level.

According to the transactional model, burnout is the result of interaction between triggering environmental variables and intra-personal traits (personality characteristics) which contribute to the manifestation or not of burnout.

Burnout seems to be the complex interaction between individuals and issues in the job environment.

For instance, teachers suffer from burnout because of the stress enhanced due to the lack of social recognition, the size of the class, isolation, fear of violence, lack of classroom control, role ambiguity and limited professional opportunities.

Stability in individual characteristics helps to face the negative events in a better way and it can facilitate or not the adaptation process and the psychological and physiological health outcomes (Kaplan, 1996).

To study the burnout process it was used the five factors model of personality.

According to Zellars et al. Neuroticism predicts emotional exhaustion, Extraversion and Agreeableness predict depersonalisation and Openness to Experience and Extraversion predict personal accomplishment.

According to Bolger and Eckenrode (1991) Extraversion and Neuroticism are associated with current mental health status.

In addition Neuroticism predisposes individuals to experience negative life event, while extraversion predispose the other way round.

Workers higher in positive affectivity, so high on Extraversion, experience less burnout.

As a consequence, those high on Neuroticism experience emotional exhaustion and depersonalization.

Instead, individuals high on Agreeableness show more nurturing behaviours, they are more sensitive and humanistic and thus they are less likely to depersonalize others.

They also perceive greater personal accomplishment due to the fact that they are dedicated and idealistic.

On the contrary, those high on Openness to Experience tend to have more problems concerning coping because on one hand they are open to experience something news, but on the other hand they are felt threatened by change.

For instance, in a study conducted about the percentage of teachers' burnout, it was clear that neuroticism was the main cause of burnout.

Emotional exhaustion was easily predicted by feelings of stress, misbehaviour, neuroticism, time constraints, extraversion, conscientiousness, role ambiguity and administrative status.

So burnout is strictly correlated to job stressors and personality characteristics.

Emotional exhaustion and depersonalization are linked to the environmental stressors whereas personal accomplishment to personality variables.

Neuroticism is the main predictor of burnout, Conscientiousness is the key for the development of depersonalization and personal accomplishment.

So people high on Neuroticism tend to show more negative emotions, emotional instability and stress reactions and thus they become more prone to burnout and to develop psychopathology.

Depersonalization was predicted by greater levels of stress arising and low Conscientiousness and it is also a defensive seclusion when emotional resources are not enough to face the situation.

Nevertheless both Extraversion and Conscientiousness are connected with low burnout and feelings of enhanced personal accomplishment.

Those who have high levels of Conscientiousness and Extraversion and low Neuroticism are more prone to have feelings of increased personal accomplishment and therefore of low burnout.

Conscientiousness is linked to involvement, persistence and reflects the individual's need for achievement.

As a matter of fact it is related to punctuality and organization and having high level of Conscientiousness means success at.

Instead, Extraversion is associated with sociability and high interpersonal relationships and this means less probability to burnout while, Openness to Experience does not predict burnout.

REFERENCES

Bibbey, A. PhD; Carroll, D. PhD, Ginty, A.T. PhD; Phillips, A.C. PhD. Cardiovascular and Cortisol Reactions to Acute Psychological Stress Under Conditions of High Versus Low Social Evaluative Threat: Associations With the Type D Personality Construct. *Psychosomatic Medicine*, V 77, 599-608 (June 2015).

Bolger, N., Eckenrode, J. Social relationship, personality and anxiety during a major stressful event. *Journal of Personality and Social psychology, 61* 440-449 (1991).

Castro, J.E.; Diessler, S.; Varea, E.; Marquez, C.; Larsen, M.H.; Cordero, M.I.; Sandi, C. Personality traits in rats predict vulnerability and resilience to developing stress-induced depression-like behaviors, HPA axis hyper-reactivity and brain changes in pERK ½ activity. *Psychoneuroendocrinology* 37, 1209-1223 (2012).

Costa, P.T., Jr. Work and personality: Use of the NEO-PR-R in industrial/ organizational psychology. *Applied Psychology: An international review, 45* 225-241 (1996).

Cox, B.J.; Clara, I.P.; Enns, M.W.; Posttraumatic stress disorder and the structure of common mental disorders. *Depress Anxiety 15* 168-171 (2002).

De Kloet, E.R.; Joëls, M.; Holsboer, F.; Stress and brain from adaptation to disease. *Nat. Rev. Neurosci.* 6, 463-475 (2005).

DeLongis, A.; Holtzman, S. Coping in Context: The Role of Stress, Social Support, and Personality in Coping. *Journal of Personality* 73, Blackwell Publishing (6 December 2005).

Diehl, M.; Coyle, N.; Labouvie-Vief, G. Age and sex differences in strategies of coping and defense across the lifespan. *Psychology and Aging*, 11 127-139 (1996).

Diener, E.; Colvin, C.R.; Pavot, W.G.; Allman, A. The psychic costs of intense positive affect. *Journal of Personality and Social Psychology* 61, 492-503 (1991).

Endler, N.S.; Edwards, J.; Stress and personality. *Handbook of stress: theoretical and clinical aspects* 36-48 (1982).

Eyesenck, H.J.; Eysenck, M.W.; *Personality and individual differences*. New York:Plenum Press (1985).

Folkman, S.; Lazarus, R.S.; Coping as a mediator of emotion. *Journal of Personality and Social Psychology* 54, 466-475 (1988).

Gilbert, M.E; The Phenomenology of limbic kindling. *Toxicology and industrial health* 10, 343-358 (1994).

James, L.M; Anders, S.L.; Peterson, C.K; Engdahl, B.E.; Krueger, R.F; Georgopoulos, A.P. DSM-5 personality traits discriminate between posttraumatic stress disorder and control groups *Ex Brain Res* 233, 2021-2028 (2015).

Kaplan, H.B. Psychosocial stress from the perspective of self theory. *Psychosocial stress: Perspective on structure, theory, life-course, and methods* 175-244. (1996).

Karatsoreos, I.N.; McEwen, B.S. Psychobiological allostasis: resistance, resilience and vulnerability. *Trends in Cognitive Sciences,* December 2011, Vol.15, No.12.

Kendler, K.S.; Thorton, L.M.; Gardner, C.O.; Genetic risk, number of previous depressive episodes and stressful life events in predicting onset of major depression. *American Journal of Psychiatry* 158, 582-586 (2001).

Kokkinos, C.M; Job stressors, personality and burnout in primary school teachers. *British Journal of Educational Psychology* 77, 229-243 (2007 The British Psychological Society).

Maslach, C., Jackson, S. E, Leiter, M.P. *Maslach burnout inventory manual*. Consulting Psychologist Press (1996).

Matthews, G; Emo, A.K.; Funke, G.; Roberts, R.D.; Zeidner, M.; Costa Jr, P.T.; Schulze, R. Emotional Intelligence, Personality, and Task-Induced Stress. *Journal of Experimental Psychology: Applied* 2006, Vol.12, 96-107.

McEwen, B.S.; protection and damage from acute and chronic stress: allostasis and allostatic overload and relevance to the pathophysiology of psychiatric disorders. (2004).

McRae, R.R.; John, O.P.; An introduction to the Five Factors Model and its applications. *Journal of personality 60* 175-215 (1992).

Miller, M. W.; Fogler, J.; Wolf, E.J.; Kaloupek, D.G, Keane, T.M. *The internalizing and externalizing structure of psychiatric comorbidity in combat veterans*. J Trauma Stress (2008).

Mroczek, D.K.; Almeida, D.M. The Effect of Daily Stress, Personality, and Age on Daily Negative Affect. *Journal of Personality* 72, Blackwell Publishing 22 April 2004.

Oswald, L. M.; Zandi, P.; Nestadt, G.; Potash, J.B.; Kalaydjian, A.E.; Wand, G.S. (2006) Relationship between Cortisol Responses to Stress and Personality. *Neuropsychopharmacology 31*, 1583-1591 11 January 2006.

Sandi, C.; Richter-Levin, G.; From high anxiety trait to depression: a neuro cognitive hypothesis. *Trends Neurosci.* 32, 312-320 (2009).

Stiller, A.L.; Drugan, R.C.; Hazi, A.; Kent, S.P. Stress resilience and vulnerability: The association with rearing conditions, endocrine function, immunology, and anxious behaviour. *Psychoneuroendocrinology* 36, 1383-1395 (2011).

Suls, J. Affect stress and personality. *Handbook of affect and social cognition* 392-409 (2001).

Tyrka, A.R.; Wier, L.M.; Price, L.H.; Rikhye, K.; Ross, N.S.; Anderson, G.M.; Wilkinson, C.W.; Carpenter, L.L.; Cortisol and ACTH responses to the dex/CRH test:influence of temperament. *Horm. Behaviour.* 53 (4), 518-525 (2008).

Vollrath, M.; Personality and stress. *Scandinavian Journal of Psychology* 42, 355-347 (2001).

In: Psychological Distress
Editors: A. Compare, C. Elia, A. G. Simonelli et al.
ISBN: 978-1-63485-405-4

Chapter 2

THE PSYCHOLOGICAL DISEASE IN SPORT: STRESS, ANXIETY, SELF-ESTEEM AND WELLNESS OF THE ATHLETES

Giulia Di Blasi*[*]*, Angelo Compare, Claudia Elia, Antonio Giulio Simonelli and Francesco Cattafi
Università degli Studi di Bergamo, Bergamo, Italy

ABSTRACT

Until now, the fact that psychological factors have an influence on athletes' performance is commonly accepted in the sport psychology area.

Because of this, the thorough study of psychological factors that determine consequences on the result, have shed new light on how correct researches about this subject are important.

The individual reaction to stress, for example, is determined by the personality, although it presents common aspects regarding hormonal reactions. During a sport event circumstance, a stress stimulus will have consequences on the result. As for stress, a light anxiety level can help the performance, but if average levels are crossed, anxiety turns into a limit that compromises the subject's functions.

Self-esteem in sport is fundamental, it enables the athlete to give his best and the lack of it is one of the major obstacle that a champion could meet on his way.

Furthermore, it is important to underline that body and mind are in deep connection with each other.

So taking care of physical shape goes along with the mental and psychological balance achievement, which allows reaching a wellness state. This state, experimented by the athlete in sport performances, is known as the "flow".

In the application of appropriate intervention methods, the analysis of stress, anxiety and self-esteem and the knowledge of the athlete could be helpful. This statement is particularly true especially in crisis or low scores situations.

[*] Università degli Studi di Bergamo, 2, S. Agostino, 24129, Bergamo, Italy. giulia.diblasi@yahoo.it.

Managing the athlete's psychophysical state means being aware of his difficulties and his potential to develop techniques that allow an acceleration of the adapting processes and to turn a potentially "negative" situation into a "positive" one.

INTRODUCTION

In the last decades, a large amount of research has been conducted into anxiety and stress of the athletes.

In particular, Mahoney and Avener (1977) demonstrated that winning athletes show a lower level of anxiety than those who lose. Moreover, those more anxious make more effort during competitions so they get more fatigued, this increased weariness is also due to less effective motor patterns.

Landers (1982) showed how psychophysiological activation (arousal) is lower in the athletes with better performances then in the less able ones.

Furthermore, Mahoney and others highlighted how top athletes have personality traits and self-regulation ability that allow them to get an optimal control of their arousal and a better concentration skill focused on the task and the context.

Tennenbaum-Furst (1985) also verified that best athletes usually attribute their results to themselves rather than to external causes, contrary to the less capable ones.

While these studies can stimulate researches about possible intervention modalities (e.g.: stress release techniques, cognitive reorganization, biofeedback, self-efficacity growth, etc.), many others studies about personality did not prove to be very effective in giving useful indications to specialized staff in applying this knowledge on athletes of individual sports working in groups.

As a matter of fact, the intervention on athletes competing individually (e.g.: high jump, run, discus, etc.) needs to be different for those competing in teams.

SECTION 1. THE STRESS

1.1. Definitions

Stress is differently experienced, this difference is based on different personality.

Many researchers, coming from different frameworks, dealt with stress: physiologists were the first ones, then cognitive psychologists added their representations and formulations of this process to physiologists' work.

In 1915, the physiologist Cannon studied the psycho endocrine relations of emotions (fight-escape).

In addition, in 1935, Selye described the General Adaption Syndrome and defined stress as the combination of non-specific responses of the organism; a happy event will cause stress reactions just as a negative one will, therefore is not important the pleasant or unpleasant aspect, but the stress agent.

H. Laborit (1979) defined three automatic reaction forms to stress:

- Escape: the subject tries to escape.
- Fight: the subject tries to dominate.
- Inhibition: the subject submit.

Then, Steptoe stated that stress is a transaction between men and environment.

Folkman and Lazarus (1984) sustained that stress is the response to an imbalance between the situation and the ability to face it.

Bensabat, in his book “le stress c’est la vie” (1989), claimed that it’s not possible to live without stress.

1.2. Stress Biology

While facing stressful situations the individual presents an ensemble of biological, hormonals and nervous reactions that correspond to an activation of the sympathetic system, the hypothalamus-hypophysis-adrenal axis and the central nervous system that allow the individual to mobilize the energetic resources to survive.

General Adaption Syndrome

The stress model “General Adaption Syndrome”, created by Selye in 1936, is a model found on the biological elements based on experiments on animals.

This syndrome develops in three phases:

- A warning phase
- A resistance phase
- An exhaustion phase

1. *The warning phase*: it is the initial phase, during which the organism gathers all of its resources indispensible for the immediate action. This process is accomplished mostly secreting hormones that can provoke appropriate changes in certain organic functions.

In this phase, an intense adrenaline production (catecholamine) and a fast increase of the cardiac rate can be observed.

2. *The resistance phase*: the duration of every stress reaction is due mainly to this phase that lasts until special quickness and ability of action are required. It depends on perceptions based above all on psychological factors.

In this phase, the activation of the hypothalamus- hypophysis-adrenal axis (axis HPA) has an essential role, during which a complex program, either biological and behavioral, is implemented and sustains a response to stressor. The crucial event is the over production of cortisol which leads to an immune system drop.

3. *The exhaustion phase*: when the “danger” is perceived to be over or when the stress energy begins to lack, the conclusive phase starts. Its aim is to make sure that the organism gets the necessary rest time.

From a biochemical point of view, the beginning of the exhaustion phase is characterized by a rapid decrease of the adrenal hormones (the catecholamines adrenaline and noradrenaline and in particular the glucocorticoid cortisol) as well as the energetic reserves.

The consequence is a depressive action that reverses the organic processes of the stress reactions to bring the organism back to a normal functionality. The stimulation effect of the sympathetic nervous system is replaced by the calming one of the parasympathetic nervous system. Thanks to this one's activation the normal blood inflow of the digestive system, of the brain and of the skin is re-established (H. Selye, 1956).

Cerebral Structures Involved with Stress

When an individual faces a stressful situation, different structures of the central nervous system such as the limbic system, the reticular formation, the hypothalamus and the hypophysis, take part in the stress reaction in order to adapt. (F. Bear; W. Connors; A. Paradiso, 2009).

The Hypothalamus acts on the regulation of the glucose, lipid and water metabolism.

It is a regulator of the vegetative functions and it establishes different functions regarding the endocrine secretions and the sympathetic nervous system. It also controls the hypophysis secretions.

The hypothalamus has nervous connections with the limbic system and it is involved in several functions: cognitive, memorization and emotional and motivational analysis. It allows assimilating information on the bases of the subject's past life and also allows a moderated response to the stress situation.

The neocortex permits a personalized analysis of the situation on a emotional and cognitive level and a personal response to stress.

The Sympathetic System

In stressful situations, the hypothalamus is stimulated and the sympathetic nervous system begins to work releasing noradrenaline and adrenaline.

- Adrenaline: it is very important on situations of psychological stress. Its secretion depends on the emotional intensity. It stimulates immediately reaction providing the energy to face and act
- Noradrenaline: its intervention comes decisive in case of focus and vigilance.

The subject in a stressful status rapidly perceives the variations of environment.

The organism faces the situation increasing and redistributing oxygen and blood to the organs.

The increase of the oxygen rate in the brain and in muscles makes sure that a decrease in the zones not concerned by stress (digestive tract, skin, limb extremities) occurs.

The major physiological changes are:

- Increase of cardiac rate and blood pressure
- Increase of respiratory amplitude and rate
- Vasoconstriction and skin perspiration
- Increased muscle tone
- Dilatation of pupils
- Increase of glycaemia

Low-term stress results are healthy, but the repetitive hormonal secretions provoke a chronic stress status and biological damages (cardio-vascular and digestive).

Hypothalamus-Hypophysis-Adrenal System

In the following phase, once the warning status is over, the hypothalamus-hypophysis-adrenal system is activated and it secretes cortisol.

The hypothalamus secretes CRF (cortico releasing factor) which secrets (ACTH) that, through blood, stimulates cortico-adrenal glands that secret glucocorticoids (cortisol).

The glucocorticoids facilitate sugars production that convey necessary energy to the organism.

They facilitate the action of the catecholamines and have a global effect of counter regulation during the response to stress.

Other hormones and neurotransmitters are involved in stress: the growth hormone, estrogen, insulin, testosterone, serotonin, thyroid hormones, acetylene, dopamine and endorphins.

1.3. Stress Psychology

The personal stress reaction is established by the personality that takes in the event in its own way, although it presents common aspects regarding the hormonal reactions.

These hormonal reactions follow various intensities, influence by the environment and circumstances.

Because of this reason, stress needs to be faced not only by a physiological point of view but even by a psychological one as well.

Positive Stress

Positive stress enables to face problems activating the required energy to find the solution. It is a natural reaction of adaptation to life events. (Ideal stress, Bensabat (1989) and successful stress, Crocq, (1999)).

Negative Stress

An intense and sustained stressful status leads to a physical and psychic energy decline that can cause maladjustment reactions and pathologies.

The negative stress can be divided into hyper stress determined by overstimulation (problems, excessive work etc.) and into hypostress determined by understimulation (disinterest, inactivity, depression, demotivation).

Rivolier (1989) so distinguishes:

- Positive or adequate stress zone, also known as "optimal activation zone": wellness and balance status characterized by appropriate stress reactions.
- Negative or inadequate stress zone: discomfort inefficiency or illness. This status is characterized by inadequate reactions to stress of two types: hyperstress or hypostress (Picture 1).

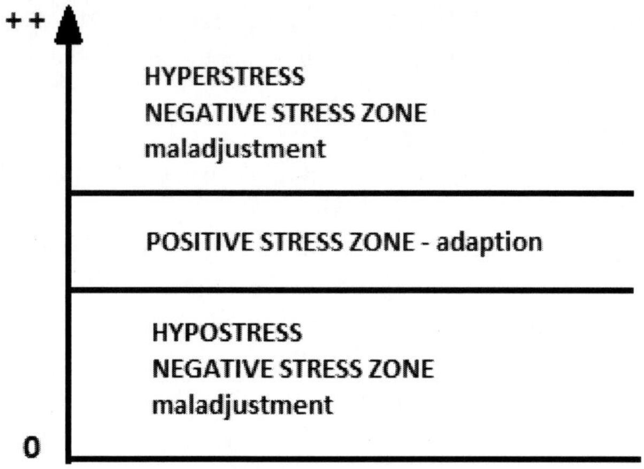

Picture 1. *Positive and negative stress:* the horizontal line symbolizes the adequate stress zone. This line is placed more or less high on the axis depending on each person. When it is placed higher the subject needs to be encouraged to act; for those where the positive stress zone is lower, they are overwhelmed by events. Furthermore the length of the line varies for each individual: sometimes it is wide (it takes a lot to disturb the individual), sometimes it is tighter (to other individuals it takes a certain amount of stress to act but they are quickly overwhelmed).

Cognitive Stress Concept

Lazarus (1966-1976), in his model of the "double evaluation" of stress states that relations depend on the individual cognitive evaluation that the subject makes of the problem.

Cox e Mackay (1978) keep count of the subject's resources and add to Lazarus's theory the importance of perception in the evaluation of problems.

Coping Strategies in the Stress Process

Lazarus e Launier (1978) elaborated the concept of coping as: "the ensemble of cognitive and behavioral efforts used to control, reduce and tolerate the internal and external needs that threaten or overcome the subject's resources".

Dantzer distinguishes action strategies from defense ones, other theories unlikely distinguish three coping types:

1. Problem centered coping, that aims to control and modify the stressful situation;
2. Emotional oriented coping, that tries to reduce emotional tension;
3. A social point of view oriented coping

1.4. Stress Factors

A stress factor, or stressing agent, is a condition that the subject faces and has to adapts to.

The stress factors are numerous and we can divide them into:

Individual Factors

- Personality and coping mechanism
  - Intelligence;
  - character;
  - temperament.
- Previous experience and belief:
  - Self-confidence;
  - satisfaction/dissatisfaction;
  - motivation;
  - incomprehension;
  - future uncertainty;
  - stressing agents.
- Environmental factors:
  - Lifestyles (career, family, working life, etc.);
  - Health practices (nutrition, alcohol, drugs, sleep etc.);
  - Social interaction (social conflict, work conflict etc.);
  - Physics conditions (weather, noises, cold/hot etc.).

1.5. Stress Reactions

In a stress status, everybody has a certain number of reactions; these are classified in three big categories that are in constant interplay.

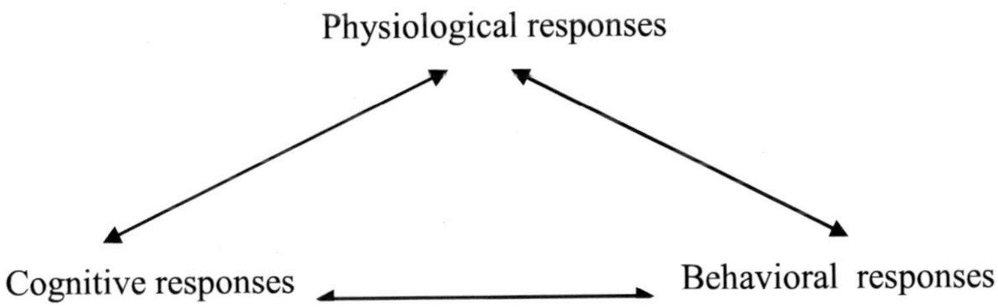

Picture 2. Three-dimensional mould of stress responses by Lang.

The more intense the physiological reaction are, the more important the cognitive reactions will be, provoking adequate or inadequate behavioral reactions; the stronger the thoughts are, the more they will fuel physiological reaction, that will have an influence on the behavioral ones (Picture 2).

Body and mind are connected to give stress responses, physiological responses cause behavioral ones and mental stress generates physiological responses that have influences on behavior.

We can categorize stress reactions in adequate and inadequate.

The adequate ones lead to physiological and cognitive-behavioral responses with brief term positive solutions, like:

- Increased attention;

- Good error handling;
- Optimism;
- Serenity;
- Emotional stability;
- Assuming responsibility;
- Good work organization;
- Harmonious professional and personal relations

Inadequate responses, instead, lead to physiological reactions and psycho-cognitive-behavioral problems, that determine physical and psychological issues, like:

- Muscle tension
- lump in one's throat;
- closing stomach sensation;
- cramps;
- diziness;
- migraines;
- hypertension;
- concentration disorder;
- ability decrease;
- performance decrease;
- indiscipline;
- memory disorders;
- hyperactivity.

The aforementioned points, are resumed with the Laborit and Fradin's model:

Stress status	Physical symptoms	Emotional symptoms	Cognitive symptoms
Lost	Reddening Dry throat Agitation Sleeplessness Staring	Trembling, afraid Agitation shame Anxiety	Difficulty in organizing thoughts and actions Afraid to being hurt Fear of threaths
Fight	Tension in the neck Backache Fixed expression into interlocutor's eyes	irrittablity Aggressiveness Anger	Need to be right Feeling of superiority Impatience Susceptibility
Inhibition	Weakness Teary-eyed Look downward	Discouragement Sadness Negative view Feeling of pressure	Feeling of inferiority Self-evaluation Decrease of pleasure

1.6. Stress and Performance Connection

A stressful stimulus will have consequences on performance. Several authors have studied the connection between stress and performance.

This connection take into account a great deal of factors:

- Factors connected with the action to accomplish (difficulty level, complexity, aptitude required) and with the contest (professional or emotional);
- Personal factors (personality, ability and motivation).

The optimal performance is obtained by an activation level (stress intensity) nor too weak, neither too strong, everybody has its own "optimal performance zone".

In hyperstress the "drop" is harsh and rapid, therefore it's important to know the positive stress zone and, most of all, not to cross the guard line, or the performance will a sink.

It is essential then, to know one's own limits.

SECTION 2. STRESS AND ANXIETY

The concept of stress and of anxiety often is mixed in both causes and remedies.

Facing a so perceived threatening situation, a warning psychological condition is implemented.

The reaction can be explicated with a normal protective adaptation, but if it have last through time, it can lead to physiological modifications that can later cause psychosomatic illnesses.

On a psychological level, instead, tension, fear and irritability emotions are felt; the warning level grows, developing an anxious personality.

Anxiety is various and complex, because it expresses a deep discomfort of the human who is trapped into fighting tensions: on one hand there is the desire to do something, to accomplish one's potential, to be and to show off; on the other hand there is the tendency to quietness, to inactivity and not to make decisions (Dragoni G., 2014).

Anxiety is, as well as stress, a vital phenomenon and not necessarily an illness. There are two anxiety signs:

- State anxiety, the anxious condition connected with a momentary state, caused by real events or symbol-situations that happen under certain circumstances.
- Trait anxiety, the enduring anxious situation of the subject that usually reacts in an anxious way under different circumstance; anxiety has became a stable trait of personality.

2.1. Anxiety in Sport Activities

Anxiety is one of the leading emotional states in athletes too.

Before competition, many people experiment pre-competition anxiety: they lack of sleep the night before, they forget some clothing item, they check many times their bag, they often used the bathroom, minor pains appear, they change emotions, they chat a lot or on the contrary they get really quiet.

Many expressions of anxious state are distinguished: fear, anguish, general anxiety state, panic, and phobia.

It looks like body and mind are in the warning and excitement state.

A certain amount of activation is useful to the success of a performance; if it is too low we call ourselves "turned down", if it is too high the subject gets in a confused state; in both cases the performance is compromised.

As for stress, a light level of anxiety helps with the performance, but if normal limits are crossed, then anxiety becomes an illness and compromises the subject's functions.

It is important, then, to keep the anxiety level on average values; in this way, the athlete is at the top of his physical and psychological abilities, ready for a demanding performance.

The symptoms linked to anxiety can be physiological, behavioral, emotional and cognitive ones.

Anxiety cannot only be the result of a failure, but also of a success: a failed performance can cause anxiety; furthermore, both anxiety and failure can be influenced by other causes.

It seems anyways, that the connection anxiety-failure is ambivalent and that it develops following a cyclic process: from anxiety to failure and from failure to anxiety.

2.2. Competitive Anxiety

In the specific sport sector, a typology of anxiety known as "competitive anxiety" was noticed and it shows in specific competitive situations and it can be expressed as trait anxiety (stable) or state anxiety (passing) (Dragoni G., 2014).

It is fundamental the athlete's behavior in competitive situations, saw as events faced with tension, with the brought in question of one's own abilities, with insecurities and fear rising.

This situation is experienced by many athletes close to an important competition. Thoughts like: "will I make it? What are the difficulties? etc." come to their minds.

These doubts catch especially on an insecure and unconfident personality, creating an aptitude to live many occasions with anxiety. The consequences are unsatisfying results and quitting.

When considering an athletes behavior regarding a specific competition two dimensions of anxiety are noticed:

1. Cognitive anxiety: with negative expectations and worries for the result; it has a great impact on the performance because the focus ability and the self-efficiency perception decrease.
2. Somatic anxiety: it is related to the concerns for one's own body and the emotional aspects in view of the competition; the level of this kind of anxiety is high up to the performance, then it decreases and it does not interfere much with this result.
3. Physiological anxiety: it also exists a useful anxiety (normal), it is the "activation", focus, vigilance, warning anxiety; the Americans call it "arousal".

The performance abilities are rapidly reduced when the activation (arousal) it's too low (lack of focus), or too high (anxiety).

2.3. Athlete's Anxiety

Anxiety is not continuative; it tends to rise through time. It does not start from zero, as there is always a little bit of anxiety in everyone (trait anxiety).

So anxiety (situational) increases (state anxiety) Approaching the competitive commitment (anxiety state).

The rising development of pre-competitive anxiety can be divided into two phases A and B.

In an athlete the A period goes from the days before the competition up to the day before it. During this time, the athlete is quiet calm, available to learn new techniques and tactics suggested by the trainer, approachable to conversation, focused on the competition just to optimize the training.

The phase B goes from the night before to the competitive event. An uneasiness is noted which provokes sleeplessness, emotional incontinence, lack of appetite.

Some athletes reach the maximum level of anxiety before the worm up with symptoms of cold sweating, trembles, retching. The level of anxiety naturally depends also on the subject's personality. Who is naturally anxious (trait anxiety) suffers independently from the competition.

SECTION 3. STRESS FACTORS IN SPORT

a) Physical Stress

In sport activities, a physical stress situation happens when the human performance limits are crossed. In this case, the professional sport practice lead to an overload determined by sport schedules and the high number of competitions that leave few time to rest.

The physical stress involves many physiological, metabolic and central and autonomic nervous system mechanisms.

b) Psychological Stress

The pressure that weights on an athlete is determined mainly by both economical and emotional interest that sport creates.

Psychological stress is an important component in success and optimization of the performance.

In top-level sports, the athlete undergoes various pressures that change depending on the momentary situation.

Stress Factors

Individual:

- Sex;

- Technical level: implies several levels of responsibility, it is related to environmental requests;
- Role;
- Social relationship: with staff and family

Teamwork:

- Goal setting: brief term (e.g., one game by time), medium term (e.g., winning the first round) and long term (e.g., winning the championship) planning. The performance improves when the aims are mildly difficult (Kyllo, Landers, 1995), because of these reasons:
  - The first refers to the link between ability and goals, if an athlete evaluates not being skillful enough to reach them, he will hardly be motivated to commit to a frustrating activity (e.g., the team goes to a game against the favorite without its most important players because they are injured).
  - The second is about the relation between the difficulty of the goal and the psychological dimension, the self-confidence or self-efficacy.
  - Therefore, the self-efficacy directly influences the perception of the hardness of present and future tasks.
  - The third factor relates to poorly motivational or too easy goals (e.g., competing against an inferior team).
- Opponent: the performance depends on the teammates and on the opponents.
- Surrounding Organization of the club: communication and organization among the staff within the director.
- External pressures: from the sponsors, mass medias, society and fans.

Resulting from the training:

- logistic: e.g., type of soil, lights, material
- weather conditions: e.g., rain, snow, etc.

Resulting from the competition:

- Important game: the finals, fight for salvation, scores are games in which is necessary to get an optimal anxiety level (arousal). In these occasions, it is hard to control fear (e.g., a missed goal can be due to inability of controlling one's own actions).
- Away game: e.g., atmosphere and fans.

This stress factors can lead, in the athlete, to a serious of psychophysical symptoms (e.g.: anxiety, depression, demotivation, isolation from the team, tiredness and muscle tension) and behavioral (eating disorders, sleep-wake cycle alterations, alcohol abuse and doping) which are designed to cause poor efficiency, arguments among the team, absenteeism, tendency to injury.

The trainers must keep count of the psychological stress when they are planning the training because it acts on the psyche and on the physiological efficiency of the athlete.

SECTION 4. SELF-ESTEEM

The psychologist William James (1842-1910) was one of the first to study a particular phenomenon: some people poorly gifted seemed to be very confident, while those highly respected by many people are more self conscious.

Still, nowadays many magazines, TV programs and self-help books suggest some "receipts" and advises to improve one's own self esteem, giving the illusion of a solution that fits everybody, forgetting that it is the individual component that characterizes us as human beings.

Self-esteem is something very simple and very personal; it's just an esteem, an evaluation. Some authors maintain that self-esteem originates between the image that everybody has of his self and the image of what they would like to be.

From this point of view, the further "what we are" is from the "what we would like to be", the more we feel like people of low esteem the more we feel dissatisfaction towards ourselves (Pope A.W, 1992).

Then, self-esteem is a component of our psychological wellness and it works like a special lens that magnifies or minimizes one's personal sources.

Who experiments low self-esteem does not feeling comfortable enough with their own value and skills so he avoids to choose and act because of an excessive fear of making mistakes, experimenting higher self-consciousness and difficulty to get out of the problematic situation to seek for a solution.

As a consequence when they live failure they suffer more, because they associate the event exclusively to their failing even if their tendency to experiment success belittle it.

Furthermore, who experiments low self-esteem lives the sensation of losing control of their own emotions feeling often missing strength and determination to reach their goals.

It's important to consider self-esteem as a warning spy; when it decreases it warns us that we are reaching for wrong goals neglecting our real needs.

4.1. Self-Esteem in Sport

Self-esteem is fundamental in sport, it enables the athlete to give their best and make good long term performances. If the goal to which the athlete aims is realistic it certainly can lead to an improvement of the performance and increase his personal satisfaction to reach the fixed goal.

If, otherwise, he is insecure and he doesn't trust himself, the defeat will be more feared and closer.

The lack of confidence is the biggest obstacle that the champion can find on his way as it forbids him to get the best out of the performance.

From various sport activities champions it's deduced that: the successful athletes don't compete to show themselves as superior, but to be aware of who they truly are and what goals they want to reach. This makes them know and accept their potentialities and above all, their limits.

Moreover, when a champion is confident on his success his possibilities will increase without having to seek for external approval and satisfaction.

Sport especially deals with competitive self-esteem:

Many great athletes are perfect during training sessions obtaining great performances, but during an important competition they don't get the same results.

A champion doesn't only need to be confident most of the time, but he also needs to trust himself when competing. The competitive self-esteem is not built in one day but it something that is developed after many years of practice and after having obtained several successes, and that can resist at high stress and competitive levels.

Being very confident in sport comes from having a positive image of ourselves.

SECTION 5. WELLNESS IN SPORT

5.1. Wellness Concept

Wellness is a good quality of life. It means to "feel good in one's own skin", doing a harmonious activity that involves both body and soul (Dragoni G., 2014).

A linked concept to wellness is quality of life. It has many definitions.

Firstly, the one from World Health Organization (Dragoni G., 2014)): "health is not only the absence of illness, it's a complete psychophysical, mental and social state of wellness". Therefore, the individual is considered as an entity constituted by a body and a mind linked and incorporated into each other.

The research of the last years of the century developed several studies about this subject, each with specific objectives and areas. Shalock's (1991) multidimensional model identifies, as parameters to grant a good quality of life, personal characteristics, life conditions and the perception that the others have towards problems.

On the contrary, other studies, for example Noris and Murrell's (1987), consider the type of environment from which it is possible to get wellness and the possibility to have personal relationships that allow participation in social life from where the individual self efficacy comes from.

Egerton's (2002) following studies expanded the number of factors, mainly the personality ones. The quality of life, indeed, is also built on the achievement of values, prefixed and reached aims, as well as the satisfaction of the individual's personal needs through the development of its own capabilities and the actuation of its own abilities.

Wellness is reachable keeping an aware and deliberate approach to get the best out of one's own physical and psychic health.

Exercising helps sustaining and keeping wellness through the development of aerobic skills, muscular mass, alimentation, lifestyle, care of the environment and security.

5.2. Wellness and Exercise

The careful athlete is familiar with his own abilities, measurement systems, factors that affect the performance and can discover his potential. He understands the relation between physical shape, mental stability, state of health and wellness too.

Psychophysical form is constituted by physiological and psychological aspects linked to sensations and emotions. Being in shape means to have a good state of health, that enables great sportive performances. The athlete "in shape" perceives a sensation of deep physical and psychological wellness during the activities he does during the day.

All of those who do sport know that it is necessary to take care of mental health as much as physical health.

The second one deals with calories, cardiac rate, training schedules, stamina and muscles. The first one is psychological and is about sensations and emotions that can improve or worsen the athletic result.

It is clear then, that there is a circular relation between body, mind and health. If the muscles are relaxed, the pain is reduced and nervous tensions go away. If mind is relaxed, muscles will be too.

The sportsman knows that less tension corresponds to better focus, trust in one's own sensorimotor potential, awareness of one's own skills, self-control and eventually, to a development of a good self image and better athletic results.

From these points, it is deduced that mind and body are in deep connection. Taking care of physical shape goes along with getting a good mental and psychological balance, it is essential, then, taking care of the psychological factors that warn us of discomforts as anxiety, dissatisfaction, inferiority complex, panic moments.

The best wellness state experienced by the athlete is called with the noun "flow", or acknowledge flow. It corresponds to an optimal psychological state, a certain state of grace in which mental conditions are the most favorable to get an optimal performance.

Sport psychology takes as model the "flow" to analyze the excellent performance situation, the peak performance, during which an athlete scores better than his standard.

The flow experience gets the performance ready and leads to the peak performance.

The athlete who keeps this state has higher possibilities to make the most of his potential.

If he will be able to analyze his experience during the "flow", monitoring his psychophysical state in occasion of such a great and rewarding performance will get him useful information for the pursuing of the training.

We consider then, the flow status as an integral moment between mind and body. After these phase it might be necessary to improve focus and attention, or to reconsider the goals and perhaps reset them, or to structure better the psycho-bodily techniques.

The better the athlete can feel and develop the flow state, keeping in mind the external environment and his psychic states, the more an optimal performance will be probable.

5.3. The Athlete's Wellness

The athlete's wellness is determined by various factors:

a) Physical shape:

The correct training, an appropriate amount of work and the appropriate rest time lead to a balanced training verifiable by the relation testosterone-cortisol.

b) The technical-tactic state:

The athlete is in a balanced state when he accepts and recognizes his strengths and weaknesses. This will enable him to get the best out of his qualities.

c) The psychological state:

It is determined by internal factors such as personality, and external factors due to several components, the main ones are relationship with teammates and coaches.

The relationship with the trainer is one of the most important aspect and it depends principally by the trainer personality and the training techniques he uses.

Alimentation

The modern alimentation has established an individualization based on the athletes characteristics.

Nowadays the tendency is to reduce sugar and the use of a zone diet.

A psychological approach to vary individual habits is important.

Sleep

Sleep management is fundamental for the recovery. Therefore, it is correct to set sleep qualitatively.

Psychological techniques help the athlete to lower stress and anxiety levels and permits to him to have a reviving sleep.

CONCLUSION

On the basis of what was previously said, it is clear how the mental and psychological aspects are fundamental for the accomplishment of a good sportive performance.

The analysis of stress, anxiety, self-esteem and the knowledge of the athletes, individually or as part of a team, could be a major help to apply appropriate methods of intervention, especially in crisis and low scores situations. From a modern point of view, the work done on an athlete shouldn't be separated between physical and psychological, but one single psychophysical training, focused on the individual.

A sport psychologist should therefore be an integrating member of the staff of every sport club, taking care of stress management, team dynamics, learning and self-esteem.

The importance of studying connections between stress, anxiety and the psychophysical performance of the athlete makes it necessary to consider it as a fundamental part of training.

The research of specific techniques that enable the improvement of the wellness state of the athlete is, then, a task that psychology of sport must confront.

A lot is known about technique-tactic and physical preparation, but just few actually consider how greater the impact of psychological preparation is.

Ultimately, managing the psychophysical state of the athlete means: being aware of his difficulties and his abilities, developing techniques that permit faster adaptation processes and turning a potentially "negative" situation into a "positive" one.

In order to reach this goal, there are four different approaches:

a. *physiological approach:*

It consists of acting on physiological reactions through breathing and relaxing techniques.

b. psycho-cognitive approach:

Its aim is to modify the cognitive evaluation of requests and resources to facilitate the perceived control, using the mental reprogramming.

c. behavioral approach:

It is about changing inadequate behaviors, giving the subject additional competences to find a new acting strategy.

d. global approach

It integrates the three previous approaches.

REFERENCES

Bear F., Connors W., Paradiso A. (2009). *Neuroscienze esplorando il cervello*: Elsevier.

Bensabat S. (1989). *Le stress c'est la vie*. Paris: Fixot.

Cox T., Mackay C.J. (1978). *Stress*. London: Macmillan

Crocq L. (1999). *les traumatismes psychiques de guerre*. Paris: Odile Jacob.

Dragoni G. (2014). *Vincere con la mente*: Elika Editrice.

Egerton M. (2002). *Family transmission of social capital: differences by social class, education and public sector employment*. Social Research Online.

Folkman, Lazarus R.S. (1984). *Stress, appraisal and coping*. New York: Springer pub co.

Kyllo, L. Blaine; Landers, Daniel M. (1995). *Goal setting in sport and exercise: A research synthesis to resolve the controversy*. Journal of Sport & Exercise Psychology, Vol 17(2), 117-137.

Laborit H. (1979). *L'inhibition de l'action*. Paris: Masson.

Landers D.M. *Arousal, attention and skilled performance: further considerations*. Quest. 33, 271-83 (51982).

Lazarus R. S. and Launier R. (1978). *Stress-related transactions between person and environment*. In L A Pervin and M Lewis (Eds), (1978). *Perspectives in Interactional Psychology* (pp. 287–327). New York,: Plenum.

Lazarus R.S. (1966). *Psychological stress and the coping process*. New York: Mcraw-Hill.

Mahoney M. J., Avener M. (1977). *Psychology on the elite athlete an exploratory study*. Cogn. Ther. 135-41.

Norris F.H., Murrel S.A. (1987). *Older adult family stress and adaptation before and after bereavement*. Journal Gerentology.

Pope AW, McHale S, Craighead WE, (1992). Migliorare l⅃autostima. Trento, Erickson.

Rivolier J. (1989). *L'homme stressé*. Paris: Puf.

Selye H. (1956). *Le stress de la vie*. Paris: Gallimard.

Shalock, R.L. A multivariate investigative study of the correlates of quality of life. *Journal on Developmental Disabilities*, 3(2), 59-73.

Tennenbaum G., Furst D. (1985). *The relationship between sport, achievement responsibility, attribution and related situational variables*. Int., J. of Sport psychology. 16, 4, 254-69.

BIBLIOGRAPHY

Andre C., Legeron P., Lelord F. (1995). *La gestion du stress*. Paris: Bernet-Danilo.
Bandura A. (2000). *Autoefficacia: teoria e applicazioni*. Trento: Erikson.
Bruchon, Schweitzer M., Dantzer R. (1994). *Introduction à la psychologie de la santé*. Paris: Puf.
Kendall P.C., Norton Ford J. D. *Psicologia clinica*. Ed: Il Mulino.
Lazarus R.S. (1991). *Emotion and Adaption* London: Oxford University.
Legeron P. (2001). *Les stress au travail*. Paris: Odine Jacob.
Le Scanff C., Bertsch J. (1995). *Stress et performance*. Paris: Puf.
Paulhan I., Bourgeois M. (1998). *Stress et coping, les stratégies d'ajustement à l'adversité*. Paris: Puf, collection Nodules.
Rivolier J. (1992). *Facteurs humains et situations extrêmes*. Paris: Masson.
Salvini A., Guicciardi M. (1988). *La psicologia dell'atleta*. Milano: Giuffrè.

In: Psychological Distress
Editors: A. Compare, C. Elia, A. G. Simonelli et al. ISBN: 978-1-63485-405-4

Chapter 3

PSYCHOLOGICAL DISTRESS IN CANCER PATIENTS: FROM RECOGNITION TO MANAGEMENT

Barbara Muzzatti, Francesca Bomben, Cristiana Flaiban, Sara Mella and Maria Antonietta Annunziata**
Unit of Oncological Psychology, Oncology Referral Center,
National Cancer Institute, Aviano, Italy

ABSTRACT

In oncology, psychological distress is expected during the entire disease trajectory, and beyond into the survival phase. It is a source of suffering on its own, but it may also interfere with treatment adherence, as well as with both health and well-being. These two reasons make psychological distress the 'core' psychological dimension in cancer care, and they are the main indicators for its routine monitoring and professional treatment. In the first section of the chapter, the features of psychological distress are defined: it is connected with other psychological dimensions and disease and/or treatment effects, and it is described in its evolution throughout the experience of illness. The second section offers practical guidance for psychological distress screening and for its management by means of a two-step psychological intervention. In this section practical advice for nurses, physicians, and health personnel is also provided. The last section is composed of three clinical vignettes, together with comments. The bio-psycho-social and patient-centered approaches frame all discourse in this chapter.

Keywords: cancer, emotions, oncology, psychological distress, psychological intervention

INTRODUCTION

Cancer is not rare. In 2012, there were 14.1 million new cancer cases worldwide and 8.2 million deaths (www.globocan.iarc.fr). The incidence of cancer is said to increase in the near

* Correspondence to: annunziata@cro.it.

future, particularly due to the aging population. Cancer is a disease that puts the body to the test since it requires aggressive treatment, with significant side effects, frequently prolonged over time.

Cancer is now a disease which is becoming more and more curable, but it is still perceived by public opinion as an experience to be suffered and still closely related to death.

It is a disease that involves the whole person and life experience; this emerges in clinical practice as well as from patients' stories, the patho-biographies. The construct of psychological distress is pivotal in the psycho-social component of the disease experience, and in understanding how it supports the promotion of health and the curing of disease (see the World Health Organization's (WHO) definition of 'health,' 1948).

Balint (1969) established a patient-based medicine practice, not a disease-based medicine practice, thus starting the valorization of patients as interlocutors and actors in their own care rather than just being a passive recipient of it.

In 1976, Engel invited us to reject the biomedical approach in favor of a holistic and multidimensional approach, taking into account the complexities of the human being and the conjunction of all the bio-psycho-social dimensions. In 1993, the WHO stressed the concept of quality of life and coupled it with the concept of health.

As will be clear at the end of this chapter, recognizing and managing psychological distress (both as a specialist and supportive intervention, and a psycho-educational intervention) represents the application of patient-centered and bio-psycho-social approaches and, at the same time, is a form of sensitization to holistic care by all operators in charge of taking care of cancer patients.

In theory, the present chapter aims at defining, characterizing and quantifying the wide construct of psychological distress; in practical and operational terms, instead, this chapter intends to improve understanding, recognizing and managing psychological distress. For this reason, a psychological intervention aiming first at welcoming and legitimizing the multidimensionality of the disease experience and second at addressing a structured specialistic intervention is here described, along with some suggestions to not-psychologist members of the caring staff.

What Is Psychological Distress and How to Recognize It

Definition and Features

The term "psychological distress" indicates: "a multifactorial unpleasant emotional experience of a psychological (cognitive, behavioral, emotional), social, and/or spiritual nature that may interfere with the ability to cope effectively with cancer, its physical symptoms and its treatment. Distress extends along a continuum, ranging from common normal feelings of vulnerability, grief and fears, to problems that can become disabling, such as depression, anxiety, panic, social isolation, and existential and spiritual crisis [...]" (National Cancer Control Network - NCCN, 1999).

The word 'distress' was intentionally chosen in order to avoid the stigmatizing terms of psychiatry, or psychopathology, and the adjective 'psychological' defines it as a personal state, conferring the emotional, cognitive, relational, social and existential content starting from the disease of the body.

Therefore, psychological distress includes all negative subjective experiences elicited by cancer and/or its treatments along the whole disease process which, as is known, can be very long and have different outcomes. It is, then, a reactive and situational suffering that may complicate the natural process of adaptation and reaction that follows dramatic events.

The NCCN definition also refers to a heterogeneous range of the possible nature of this suffering (cognitive, emotional, relational, spiritual, etc.) and/or to their concomitance. The third relevant element of the definition regards the extreme variability of distress in terms of intenseness. The term 'distress,' in fact, includes all levels of unpleasant emotional experiences, from those which are expected (as consequences of the disease, the treatments and the side effects), to those that are more acute and could represent interference with subjective functioning. Psychological distress is not a psychopathological disorder even if, like psychopathology, it must not be overlooked, since mood, anxiety and coping are important aspects in oncology (Mitchell et al. 2012; Smith, 2015).

As reported by Annunziata and Muzzatti (2012), the psychological distress must be differentiated in other psycho-social dimension of cancer such as body image-related problems (Annunziata, Giovannini, and Muzzatti, 2012), sexual difficulties (Hordern, 2008), cognitive limitations (Vardy et al. 2008; Soussain et al. 2009), post-traumatic growth (Calhoun and Tedeschi, 2006; Sawyer, Ayers, and Field, 2010), and cancer-related fatigue (Stone and Minton, 2008).

Considering the sudden, pervasive and demanding nature of cancer, it is not surprising that patients may experience feelings of grief, uncertainty, preoccupation, demoralization, fear, anxiety, and/or anger. Recognizing and monitoring psychological distress means monitoring emotions and eventually intervening so that they do not become chronic, thus crippling and interfering with psychosocial functioning and/or result in full-blown psychopathology (van't Spijker, Trijsburg, and Duivenvoorden, 1997; Holland and Alici, 2010). In addition, we must be aware that clinically significant distress is associated with maladaptive coping, reduction in quality of life, more unmet needs, more problems, poor adherence to treatment, abnormal illness behavior, longer hospital stays, longer rehabilitation phases, family dysfunction, psychosocial morbidity, impairment in social relationships, risk of suicide, and possibly a shorter survival (Ballenger et al. 2001; Bringman et al. 2008; Grassi and Riba, 2009; Hamer, Chida, and Molloy, 2009; Annunziata, Muzzatti, Bidoli, and Veronesi, 2012; VanHoose et al. 2015).

In general, psychological distress is reported as a unique index or as the presence of anxiety/depression states (Mitchell, Kaar, Oggan, and Herdman, 2008; Vodermaier, Linden, and Siu, 2009; Luckett et al. 2010; Mitchell, 2010; Muzzatti and Annunziata, 2012). However, it must be noted that the NCCN definition of psychological distress is not limited to these two states and that other negative emotions (such as rage and anger) often play a role in the well-being and functioning of cancer patients (Annunziata and Muzzatti, 2013).

Extent of the Phenomenon

In North America and Western Europe, the prevalence of psychological distress is comprised between 22% and 45% (Zabora et al. 2001; Carlson and Bultz, 2003; Carlson et al.

2004; Keller et al. 2004; Gil et al. 2006; Sellick and Edwardson, 2007; Strong et al. 2007; Dolbeault et al. 2008; Grassi et al. 2013; Meggiolaro et al. 2015; VanHoose et al., 2015).

The two more studied aspects of psychological distress are anxious and depressive states: depressive states prevalence is comprised between 9% and 21% (Keller et al. 2004; Gil et al. 2006; Strong et al. 2007; Annunziata et al. 2012; Linden, Vodermaier, Mackenzie, and Greig, 2012), anxiety prevalence was comprised between 10% and 48% (Stark and Housel, 2000; Stark et al. 2002; Keller et al. 2004; Gil et al. 2006; Strong et al. 2007; Annunziata et al. 2012; Linden et al. 2012).

Even though there is variability in the data regarding the literature, it must be considered that anxiety and depressive states in cancer patients are usually higher than in the general population (e.g., Hinz et al. 2012).

Many different reasons may explain the wide range that comprises the psychological distress values and those of its anxious and depressive components, including personal factors (for example, gender or age) and cultural factors related to the tendency to share one's own personal experiences. The different values may also be influenced by the stage and type of disease, the different treatment facility of referral (for ex. ward or outpatients clinic/office), the way the data collection was conducted (for ex. interview or self-filling questionnaire), or type of assessing tool employed.

In the following paragraph we list the socio-demographic and clinical factors more frequently associated to psychological distress and its components.

Factors Associated with Psychological Distress

Psychological distress seems to be associated with both socio-demographic and clinical factors. Among the socio-demographic factors, gender, age, and marital status are the most studied. In particular, distress seems to be higher in women with respect to men (e.g., Herschbach et al. 2004; Strong et al. 2007; Dolbeault et al. 2008; Herschbach et al. 2008; Grassi et al. 2013), even though Carlson et al. (2004), for example, did not report gender-related differences. It also seems to be more common in younger patients (Osborne, Elsworth, and Hopper, 2003; Herschbach et al. 2004; Strong et al. 2007; Tuinman, Van Nuenen, and Hagedoorn, 2015). Moreover, patients who do not have a partner (i.e., singles, divorced, widowed) show more psychological distress respect married patients (Tuinman et al. 2015).

Many clinical factors (among which disease, stage, good general state of health, and comorbidity) also concur in determining psychological distress in oncological patients. Therefore, distress seems to be associated with the type of diagnosis: its prevalence, in fact, is higher in lung cancer, cerebral tumors, Hodgkin and non-Hodgkin lymphomas, head and neck, pancreas and breast cancers patients (Zabora et al. 2001); it is higher in breathing system and gynecological tumors (Herschbach et al. 2008); in breast and soft tissue tumors (Herschbach et al. 2004) (see also: Carlson et al. 2004).

The most distress-related treatment is chemotherapy, while patients report radiotherapy and surgery to be as stressful as not being treated at all (Herschbach et al. 2008).

Patients who obtain a diagnosis at an advanced stage of disease show higher levels of distress, especially in the presence of metastasis (Herschbach et al. 2004). Moreover, distress levels are higher when the disease is active rather than in the remission phase (Carlson et al.

2004; Strong et al. 2007), and this may characterize the long-term survivorship phase (Mitchell et al. 2013; Muzzatti and Annunziata, 2014).

Finally, there are still further factors associated with the psychological distress such as worse physical functioning, increased pain and fatigue, previous psychiatric disorders, poor communication between patients and therapeutic team, and lack of social support (Ballenger et al. 2001; Stark et al. 2002; Hann et al. 2002; Lueboonthavatchai, 2007; Dolbeault et al. 2008; Hill et al. 2011).

The data on the two main components of psychological distress is less univocal. Depression is reported as gender-associated with higher values in women by Carlson et al. (2004) and Linden et al. (2012) but as non gender-related by Sellick and Edwardson (2007) and by Annunziata et al. (2012). It is reported as age-related (higher in older patients according to Sellick and Edwardson, 2007 but higher in younger patients according to Linden et al. 2012) but it was not found to be age-related at all by Annunziata et al. (2012). Higher values were found by Sellick and Edwardson (2007) in widowers, while Annunziata et al. (2012) reported no variations dependent on marital status.

As regards anxiety, Sellick and Edwardson (2007), Annunziata et al. (2012), and Linden et al. (2012) reported higher values in women, while Carlson et al. (2004) did not endorse gender-based differences. Differently from Annunziata et al. (2012), Sellick and Edwardson (2007) reported an association between both anxiety state and age and anxiety and marital status (see also Linden et al. 2012).

Moreover, both depression and anxiety are more intense and wide-spread among lung, hematological and gynecological cancer patients (Sellick and Edwardson, 2007; Linden et al. 2012). In addition, in a longitudinal study assessing anxiety and depression at one, six and 12 months from diagnosis, anxiety decreased over time, whereas depression increased (Linden et al. 2015). In the same study, about one third of initial classifications based on distress levels changed from one assessment to the next supporting the usefulness of constant and prolonged distress monitoring

Despite the significant heterogeneity of research data (for which some explanations were given in the preceding paragraph), it is possible to conclude that psychological distress (even in its separate components of anxiety and depression states) is a recurring aspect of the cancer experience that can emerge in any phase of the disease or can persist in different phases of the disease, long-term survivorship included.

The most severe diagnosis and prognosis are usually associated with higher distress, as well as the female gender (these data are also confirmed for the general population). The young, due to a number of evolution tasks still to accomplish, but also the old – due to less resources and concomitant aging processes, result to be vulnerable to cancer-related distress.

Since the disease path often requires different treatments which have different side effects (short-term, long-term or late effects) it is understandable that psychological distress changes over time with different evolutions. In other words, it is possible for distress to decrease in intensity as a result of an occurred adjustment, or that it increases as a response to new challenges of cures and symptomatology. Therefore, it is relevant to promote a useful screening of distress and to help patients to recognize, manage and reduce it.

In the following section, we describe a short, two-step intervention for recognizing and managing distress in inpatients. Some practical guidance for physicians, nurses and non-psychologist healthcare personnel will also be given.

SCREENING AND MANAGING PSYCHOLOGICAL DISTRESS

Nowadays, psychosocial care is considered a fundamental aspect of quality oncological care (Adler, 2008) and, in particular, constant monitoring and management of psychological distress is widely recommended (NCCN, 2014). Unfortunately, less than 10% of the cases are actually recognized and referred to mental health services (Kadan-Lottick et al. 2005). This lack of recognition of distress causes problems for patients in making therapeutic decisions, adhering to treatments, and making complementary medical appointments, and it also causes problems for the oncological team, in terms of stress and length of appointment times (Carlson and Bultz, 2003; NCCN, 2014).

Knowing all this, we have developed a short intervention for recognizing and managing psychological distress that has become routine practice in our Institute. In the following paragraph this intervention will be illustrated (see also Annunziata et al. 2013), while in the following section three clinical cases will be discussed.

Recognizing and Managing of Psychological Distress: A Brief Intervention

In 2009 in our cancer institute a two-step report and managing distress routine activity was started.

The main aim of the intervention consists of helping patients to acknowledge and integrate emotions as natural aspects of their disease experience, so that their multidimensional (bio-psycho-social) wellbeing can become an achievable goal. In other words, the intervention is directed at encouraging cancer patients to also pay attention to their emotional states, and start considering them as objects for care just as much as their bodies. The intervention objectives can be specified as follows: (1) to encourage/normalize awareness of the importance of emotional aspects of the cancer experience. (2) to provide psycho-education to patients on the importance of psycho-social care in promoting wellbeing; (3) to introduce the patient to the Institute's psychology service and to promote its usage.

All new inpatients (i.e., those who are in the diagnostic phase or are receiving their first treatment) of both medical and surgical divisions are offered this intervention by a trained psychologist.

The intervention consists of two consecutive steps: psychological distress screening followed by a clinical interview.

In the first step (the psychological distress screening), a psychologist contacts the patients and presents the intervention as a routine practice of the Institute, which measures and monitors emotions, just like routine checks of blood pressure, temperature, pulse, breathing and levels of pain. The psychologist delivers and accurately describes the screening instruments in order to ensure proper autonomous completion, and informs patients that the results will be discussed in a subsequent colloquium.

The administered instruments (i.e., the Hospital Anxiety and Depression Scale – HADS by Zigmond and Snaith, 1983, and the Distress Thermometer and Problem list – DT and PL by Roth et al. 1998, See Box 1 and 2) offer both a global psychological distress measure and an anxiety and depressive states measure.

Patients are contacted when they first enter the hospital division. The intervention is usually proposed the day after admission. Because of the complexities related to the operative phases (e.g., pre-operative anxiety, post-surgery physical conditions), in the breast surgery division the activity is proposed the day after surgery whereas, in the general or gynecological oncological surgery division, it is proposed three days after the operation.

The first step does not require any specific written agreement from participants because it is included in the Institute's standard clinical practice. The patient, however, may refuse both the psychological distress screening and the clinical interview.

The second step (the clinical interview) takes place the same day, if the distress screening has been performed in the morning, or the next day, if the screening has been conducted in the afternoon.

When distress is absent or mild, patients are encouraged to express any potential needs, and are encouraged to contact the oncological psychology unit at any time in the future if they feel the need to speak to someone.

When the psychological distress is moderate or severe, the objectives become more complex. In particular, patients are encouraged to understand the disease experience through speaking about its personal meaning, and to acknowledge and understand the emotions they expressed. They are also made aware of suffering and its causes, given information which could be useful in the practical management of cancer, for example where information materials can be found about insurance and pension information, or information about volunteer organizes), and, ultimately, patients can be motivated to participate in a more structured professional intervention.

The psychological interview is conducted in a non-directive way and based on client-centered therapy as developed by Rogers (1951). Acceptance of the other as an individual, absence of judgment about the issues being discussed, and empathy, the ability 'to see through the patient's eyes' are the main elements of the interview and these that allow an understanding of the patient's actual disease experience by the psychologist. Both verbal and non-verbal communication are used, together with paraphrasing.

The positive response from an evaluation of a sample of 484 oncological patients for a preliminary version of this clinical activity has been described elsewhere (Annunziata et al. 2013). In particular, there was a low percentage of patients who refused screening, as well as a negligible percentage who did not wish to have the results of their screenings returned to them. Together with the high scores given to the intervention as far as usefulness and effectiveness in a feedback questionnaire built ad hoc, this all points to the positive reception of this activity. Moreover, the fact that the clinical interview encompassed so many different issues seemed to highlight to the usefulness of this experience for patient well-being. In fact, aside from anxiety and depression symptoms, many other issues came up during the clinical interview. 'Some patients spoke about issues with different types of relationships. Others expressed the need to speak more about the illness and its medical and practical aspects (even with a provider who was not directly involved in therapy management and medical communications). Patients discussed the actual impact of the illness on their functioning on the job, in the family, etc. They spoke about other current or past stressful life events, of body image, of the future and death, of spirituality, and also of the difficulties they encountered in communicating with healthcare providers' (Annunziata et al. 2013).

Box 1. Hospital Anxiety and Depression Scale (HADS)

The Hospital Anxiety and Depression Scale (HADS, Zigmond and Snaith, 1983) is one of the most frequently used in oncological settings as well as for other medical conditions (e.g., cardiology, brain injury, general medicine). Originally, it was designed to screen emotional suffering of patients in non-psychiatric settings by detecting the two most frequent distress expressions: anxious and depressive states. Since it is specific to patients with organic disease HADS excludes somatic symptoms of psychological distress (e.g., headache, weight loss, insomnia) that could be caused by the illness itself (including its treatments) rather than being psychological distress expressions. Furthermore, severely psychopathological symptoms are not covered by HADS to improve sensitivity to medical conditions.

It is composed of 14 items: 7 measuring anxiety state and 7 measuring depressive state. For each item, respondents are asked to indicate which of the four options (rated 0-3) comes closest to describing how they have been feeling.

Box 2. Distress Thermometer and Problem list (DT and PL)

The Distress Thermometer (DT) and Problem List (PL) is the tool recommended by the NCCN for the routinely screening of the distress in oncology.

The DT is a visual analogue tool asking participants to rate their level of distress in the week prior to the interview on a scale from "0 no distress" to "10 extreme distress." It is usually administered together with a list of 36 problems (PL) patients may experience. The problems are grouped into 5 categories: practical problems (5 items), relational problems (3 items), emotional problems (6 items), spiritual/religious concerns (1 item), and physical problems (21 items). Each problem is rated in a yes/no format.

Bio-Psycho-Social and Patient-Centered Approaches as Milestones in Recognizing and Embracing Psychological Distress

The above-described intervention requires the actions of a psychologist, a professional member of the team in charge of care, specially trained in managing the psycho-emotional aspects of patients. However, psychological distress is not an aspect of the cancer experience that only belongs to the psychologist. Although the treatment of psychological distress needs the professional competence of a clinical psychologist, it is also true that all members of the care staff have to recognize it in terms of its manifestations, effects, associations, and prevalence from the view of the comprehensive care of the patient. It is, in fact, important that physicians, nurses and other healthcare professionals involved in patient care are aware of how psychological distress is experienced in itself, as well as how it can interfere with the treatment in terms of therapeutic adherence and emotional complications. The health professional, the physician, and the nurse build a relationship with patients as people and the bio-psycho-social complexity of their disease experience. It is, therefore, important to recognize, welcome, legitimize, and cope with the emotional component of the cancer experience as a real and natural component by itself.

Confirming the natural and normal quality of possible psychological suffering related to cancer is beneficial to patients since it legitimizes the relevance of the emotional and somatic aspects. Active listening, reformulation, non-minimizing and providing early reassurance, reading and using non-verbal communication, and empathic behavior are counseling strategies that can be learnt. Healthcare professionals can facilitate patients' relationships with psychologists when distress becomes a pervasive and persistent cause of suffering and dysfunctional behavior, especially where systematic interventions for managing distress are not implemented.

Recognizing and Managing Psychological Distress in Cancer Patients: Three Case Studies

In this section, three cases of distress, taken from our clinical practice in different departments in an oncological institute, are described, along with the type of professional intervention implemented.

A Case of Unrecognized Distress

Giulia is a 57 year old female patient with non-Hodgkin follicular lymphoma, hospitalized for her first chemotherapy cycle. According to the Hospital Anxiety and Depression Scale, she is a possible case of anxiety and a probable case of depression, with a total indicative score of severe distress. According to the Distress Thermometer, the perceived distress level is moderate and essentially associated with physical problems (Problem List) (nausea, tiredness, trouble sleeping).

In terms of the general psycho-emotional suffering, unrecognized by the patient, the first objective of the intervention is to put the patient into contact with their own emotions, encouraging acknowledgment, expression, reciprocation and awareness. The psychological intervention started by referring Giulia to the outcome of the evaluation, concerning the depressive state and mild anxiety, probably linked to everyday worries. The patient was asked whether she recognized herself in this description and, through open questions, she was stimulated to start expressing her experiences.

The account started with the description of the self as a 'fairly quiet,' 'serene,' 'positive' and 'strong' person, exactly as she had always been and as everybody else described her. She referred to having coped bravely with important losses in her life, family diseases, and caregiving. The description of herself in these terms is linked with the conviction, also expressed verbally, that she will have to confront her disease in the same way: 'I have coped with all this, I will confront my disease bravely, too.'

The psychologist listened actively, without judgment, unconditionally accepting from all points the patient's account and, at the same time, stimulated the reflection and the resignification of the words used, i.e., 'strength' as opposed to 'weakness,' leading the patient into drawing a distinction between weakness and vulnerability and recognizing the latter as a human characteristic which is acceptable under particular circumstances.

During the interview, Giulia succeeded in getting in touch with her emotional suffering (visibly so, on a non-verbal level, as well) and to conceiving it as a condition that can be seen, especially in this phase of the disease, as a reaction and not as weakness or an inability to confront events. With this intervention, Giulia's ability to manage several difficulties in life was stressed to give her faith in her own resources. The goal was reached and the interview ended with restoring to her the possibility of taking care of herself and of her emotions in the same way she was accustomed to take care of others, as she had recognized.

A Case of Mild Distress

Carla is a 30 year old woman who recently underwent surgery for endometrial cancer. In the screening she presented with mild distress, fear and worry. In the light of the problems which had emerged, the aim of our clinical interview was to accompany her in recognizing her own emotions, stimulate her to monitor them over time, and to take care of them.

In a welcoming and active listening climate, the psychological interview started with the worries and fears she had associated with her own psychological suffering, detailing the aspects which generated those worries and fears. In her account, she reported being away from her home on her own for the first time. At this stage of her life, she lives with a partner and she also greatly misses her parents and their protection. At the same time, she referred to not being accustomed to depending on other people, feeling ill at ease when compelled to ask for help from healthcare personnel. Carla's account continues, reporting her fears of the medical procedures (such as taking blood samples) and her feelings of shame for her childish behavior towards healthcare personnel.

Going more in-depth into her self-analysis, in an understanding and non-judgmental environment, Carla recognized that her suffering derived from her feelings of 'weakness' and that this perception contrasted with the image she had had of herself before the disease. Inspired by the idea of 'normality,' as reported by Carla, the psychologist led her to consider other aspects of 'normality,' in which a patient succeeds in individuating that normality, which she recognized as useful for managing the present situation. The results, therefore, allowed Carla to pay attention to her emotional past, contextualize it, standardize it and, above all, recognize it as part of her own personal resources.

A Case of Severe Distress with Referral to a Specialist

Maria is a 51 year old surgeon who had just undergone surgery for breast cancer. She had reluctantly entered the screening program, saying she had never met with a psychologist as she did not believe in the usefulness of this kind of support. The evaluation evidenced severe distress, hence the therapeutic objective was to guide her to recognizing her own emotional state and motivate her onto a psychological path of support.

In a welcoming and understanding atmosphere, the screening results were reported to Maria: severe distress, with anxiety and depression components. Maria was asked to interpret these results and she commented that she was not accustomed to speaking about herself, especially about her own emotions. She started to describe herself, in tears: she could not see and accept herself as an 'oncological patient,' especially because she had always been the professional in charge of taking care of other people's suffering, not a patient. With agitated non-verbal behavior, she reported in detail and, at the same time, rationally, her disease path: self-palpation, subsequent medical tests, the histological report and finally the therapeutic indications. Having allowed her to speak freely about what she felt was urgent and what she found easy to report (medical report), she was asked to talk about her mood at that moment. After a short silence, Maria succeeded in expressing her rage, a sense of impotence and the tiredness caused by exploring how she feels.

The interview proceeded in dealing with the reported emotions to an appropriate degree, but the patient was also invited to look at other aspects of the self: her certainties ('anchor points') and her internal/external resources. Gradually, and in a climate of increasing openness, she spoke about her 'obliged, controlled' strength, of her 'subdued' companion and the uneasiness she felt in asking for support. She also referred to not knowing the causes of this behavior and said she needed to 'understand it, understand myself and I seem not to be able to do it.'

At the end of the interview, the patient expressed success in establishing contact with her emotions and finding the motivation to be helped. It was therefore proposed that she dedicated some time to taking care of herself and of her well-being: she accepted this, and the modalities for starting a structured therapy were defined.

Conclusion

Psychological distress is a natural component of the disease experience. It assumes different manifestations (in the majority of cases it shows with anxiety and/or depression) and is associated with many clinical and socio-demographic factors. Being 'reactive' to the disease, it usually decreases over time, when patients start coping. Nevertheless, professional help may be needed to decrease subjective suffering and to start or accelerate the adjustment.

It is therefore useful for healthcare personnel (especially nurses and physicians, who play an important role) to give patients the possibility of taking care of their psychological aspects, as well as the somatic ones, through their involvement with the emotional part of patients, encouraging them in expressing this part of themselves and taking care of it.

If oncological care is the care of the cancer patient, care must be taken of all components of the patient's wellbeing. In this sense, also the professional intervention of a psychologist represents a piece of a puzzle of the multidisciplinary model of care, and is therefore far from those psycho-pathologizing approaches that, as we said, the same 'distress' terms wants to take the distance from. Moreover, as has emerged from the clinical cases, recognizing and managing distress facilitates the awareness and active participation of patients in the process of the cure, as recommended by the patient-centered approach itself.

Cancer often means pain and suffering (psychological distress). An efficient cancer treatment, that is, a treatment that aims at the best state of health and well-being for each individual is the treatment that takes this aspect into account and is in charge of it along the whole disease path.

Acknowledgments

The Authors wish to thank Ms. Anna Vallerugo, MA, for her editorial assistance.

REFERENCES

Adler, Nancy E. 2008. Cancer care for the whole patient: meeting psychosocial health needs. *Institute of Medicine (IOM). eds.* Washington, DC: The National Academies Press.

Annunziata, Maria A., Giovannini, Lorena, and Muzzatti, Barbara. 2012. "Assessing the body image: relevance, application and instruments for oncological settings." *Supportive Care in Cancer* 20: 901-907.

Annunziata, Maria A., and Muzzatti, Barbara. 2012. "Psychosocial issues in cancer care." *Neuropathological Diseases 1:* 41-56.

Annunziata, Maria A., and Muzzatti, Barbara. 2013. "Improving communication effectiveness in oncology: The role of emotions." In *New Challenges in Communication with Cancer Patients*, edited by Antonella Surbone, Matjaz Zwitter, Mirjana Rajer, and Richard Stiefel, 235-246. New York: Springer.

Annunziata, Maria A., Muzzatti, Barbara, and Bidoli, Ettore. 2011. "Psychological distress and needs of cancer patients: A prospective comparison between the diagnostic and the therapeutic phase." *Supportive Care in Cancer 19:* 291-295.

Annunziata, Maria A., Muzzatti, Barbara, Bidoli, Ettore, and Veronesi, Andrea. 2012. "Emotional distress and needs in Italian cancer patients: prevalence and associations with socio-demographic and clinical factors." Tumori 98: 132-138.

Annunziata, Maria A., Muzzatti, Barbara, Giovannini, Lorena, Mella, Sara, Bomben, Francesca, Flaiban, Cristiana, and Veronesi, Andrea. 2013. "Facilitating the integration of emotional states in patients' personal disease experience with cancer: a new brief intervention for managing psychological distress." *Supportive Care in Cancer 21:* 1815-1819.

Balint, Enid. 1969. "The possibilities of patient-centered medicine." *Journal of the Royal College of General Practice 17*: 269-276.

Ballenger, James C., Davidson, Jonathan R.T., Lecrubier, Yves, Nutt, David J., Jones, Richard D., and Berard, Ray M.F.; International Consensus Group on Depression and Anxiety. 2001. "Consensus statement on depression, anxiety and oncology." *Journal of Clinical Psychiatry 62(Sup*pl. 8): 64-67.

Bringman, Holger, Singer, Susanne, Höckel, Michael, Stolzenburg, Jens U., Krauss, Oliver, and Schwarz, Reinhold. 2008. "Longitudinal analysis of psychiatric morbidity in cancer patients." *Onkologie 31:* 343-344.

Calhoun, Lawrence G., and Tedeschi, Richard G. 2006. *Handbook of post-traumatic growth.* Mahwah, NJ: Erlbaum.

Carlson, Linda E., Angen, Maureen J., Cullum, Jodi, Goodey, Eileen, Koopmans, Jan, Lamont, Lisa, MacRae, Jeanne H., Martin, Monte, Pelletier, Guy, Robinson, Jacqueline, Simpson, Jennifer, Steward, Alexander, Speca, Michael, Tillotson, Lori, and Bultz, Barry D. 2004. "High levels of untreated distress and fatigue in cancer patients." *British Journal of Cancer 14;*90: 2297-2304.

Carlson, Linda E., and Bultz, Barry D. 2003. "Cancer distress screening. Needs, models, and methods." *Journal of Psychosomatic Research 55:* 403-409.

Dolbeault, Sylvie, Bredart, Anne, Mignot, Veronique, Hardy, Patrick, Gauvain-Piquard, Annie, Mandereau, Laurence, Asselain, Bernard, and Medioni, Jacque. 2008. *Palliative Supportive Care 6:* 107-117.

Engel, George L. 1977. "The need for a new medical model: a challenge for biomedicine." *Science 196*: 119-136.

Gil, Francisco, Grassi, Luigi, Travado, Luzia, Tomamichel, Michele, and Gonzalez, Juan R.; Southern European Psycho-Oncology Study Group. 2006. "Use of distress and depression thermometers to measure psychosocial morbidity among southern European cancer patients." *Supportive Care in Cancer 13:* 600–606.

Grassi, Luigi, Johansen, Christoffer, Annunziata, Maria A., Capovilla, Eleonora, Costantini, Anna, Gritti, Paolo, Torta, Riccardo, and Bellani, Marco; on behalf of the Italian Society of Psycho-Oncology Distress Thermometer Study Group. 2013. "Screening for distress in cancer patients A multicenter, nationwide study in Italy." *Cancer 119*: 1714–1721.

Grassi, Luigi, and Riba, Michelle. 2009. "New frontiers and challenges of psychiatry in oncology and palliative care." In, Advances in psychiatry (vol 3), edited by G.N. Christodoulou, M. Jorge, J.E. Mezzich, 105-114. Athens: Beta Medical.

Hamer, Marik, Chida, Yoichi, and Molloy, Gerard J. 2009. "Psychological distress and cancer mortality." *Journal of Psychosomatic Research 66:* 255-258.

Hann, Danette, Baker, Frank, Denniston, Maxine, Gesme, Dean, Reding, Douglas, Flynn, Tom, Kennedy, John,and Kieltyk, Lyn. 2002. "The influence of social support on depressive symptoms in cancer patients. Age and gender differences." *Journal of Psychosomatic Research 52*: 279–283.

Herschbach, Peter, Book, Katrin, Brandl, Tobias, Keller, Monika, Linden, Gabriele, Neuwöhner, Karl, and Marten-Mittag, Birgitt. 2008. "Psychological distress in cancer patients assessed with an expert rating scale." *British Journal of Cancer 8;*99: 37-43.

Herschbach, Peter, Keller, Monika, Knight Lucie, Brandl, Tobias, Huber, Birgit, Henrich, Gerhard, and Marten-Mittag, Birgitt. 2004. "Psychological problems of cancer patients: a cancer distress screening with a cancer-specific questionnaire." *British Journal of Cancer 2*;91: 504-511.

Hill, Jonathan, Holcombe, Christopher, Clark, Louise, Margorit Krespi, Boothby, Hincks, Andreas, Fisher, Jean, Tufail, Sunaina, Salmon, Peter. 2011. "Predictors of onset of depression and anxiety in the year after diagnosis of breast cancer." *Psychological Medicine 41*: 1429–1436.

Hinz, Andreas, Krauss, Oliver, Hauss, Johann P., Heckel, Michael, Kortmann, Rolf D., Stolzenburg, Jens U., and Schwarz Reinhold. 2010. "Anxiety and depression in cancer patients compared with the general population." *European Journal of Cancer Care 19:* 522-529.

Holland, Jimmie C., and Alici, Yesnei. 2010. "Management of distress in cancer patients." *Journal of Supportive Oncology 8:* 4-12.

Holland, Jimmie C., Andersen, Barbara, Breitbart, William S., Compas, Bruce, Dudley, Moreen M., Fleishman, Stewart, Fulcher, Caryl D, Greenberg, Donna B., Greiner, Carl B., Handzo, George F., Hoofring, Laura, Jacobsen, Paul B., Knight, Sara J., Learson, Kate, Levy, Michael M., Loscalzo, Matthew J., Manne, Sharon, McAllister-Black, Randi, Riba, Michelle B., Roper, Kristin, Valentine, Alan D., Wagner, Lynne I., and Zevon, Michael A. 2010. "Distress management." *Journal of the National Comprhensive Cancer Network 8*: 448-485.

Hordern, Amanda. 2008. "Intimacy and sexuality after cancer: A critical review of the literature." *Cancer Nursing 31:* E9–17.

Kadan-Lottick, Nina S., Vanderwerker, Lauren C., Block, Susan D., Zhang, Baohui, and Prigerson, Holly G. 2005. "Psychiatric disorders and mental health service use in patients with advanced cancer: a report from the Coping with Cancer study." Cancer 104: 2872-2881.

Keller, Monika., Sommerfeldt, Sabine, Fischer, Claude, Knight, Lucie, Riesbeck, Mathias, Löwe, Bernd, Herfarth, Christian, and Lehnert, Thomas. 2004. "Recognition of distress and psychiatric morbidity in cancer patients: a multi-method approach." *Annals of Oncology 15:* 1243-1249.

Linden, Wolfgang, MacKenzie, Regina, Rnic, Katerina, Marshall, Caroline, and Vodermaier, Andrea. 2015. "Emotional adjustment over 1 year post-diagnosis in patients with cancer: understanding and predicting adjustment trajectories." *Supportive Care in Cancer 23*: 1391-1399.

Linden, Wolfgang, Vodermaier, Andrea, Mackenzie, Regina, and Greig, Duncan. 2012. "Anxiety and depression after cancer diagnosis: prevalence rates by cancer type, gender, and age." *Journal of Affective Disorders 141:* 343-351.

Luckett, Tim, Butow, Phyllis N., King, Madeleine T., Oguchi, Mayumi, Heading, Gaynor, Hackl, Nadine A., Rankin, Nicole, and Price, Melanie A. 2010. "A review and recommendations for optimal outcome measures of anxiety, depression and general distress in studies evaluating psychosocial interventions for English-speaking adults with heterogeneous cancer diagnoses." *Supportive Care in Cancer 18:* 1241-1262.

Lueboonthavatchai, Peeraphon. 2007. "Prevalence and psychosocial factors of anxiety and depression in breast cancer patients." *Journal of The Medical Association of Thailand, 90:* 2164-2174.

Meggiolaro, Elena, Berardi, Maria A, Andritsch, Elisabeth, Nanni, Maria G., Sirgo, Agustina, Samorì, Elena, Farkas, Clemens, Ruffilli, Federica, Caruso, Rosangela, Bellé, Marta, Juan Linares, Eva, de Padova, Silvia, and Grassi, Luigi. 2015. "Cancer patients' emotional distress, coping styles and perception of doctor-patient interaction in European cancer settings." *Palliative Supportive Care 9*: 1-8.

Mitchell, Alex J. 2010. "Short screening tools for cancer-related distress: a review and diagnostic validity meta-Analysis." *Journal of the National Comprehensive Cancer Network 8.*

Mitchell, Alex J., Chan, Melissa, Bhatti, Henna, Halton, Marie, Grassi, Luigi, Jahansen, Christoffer, and Meader, Nicholas. 2011. "Prevalence of depression, anxiety, and adjustment disorder in oncological, haematological, and palliative-care settings: a meta-analysis of 94 interview-based studies. *Lancet Oncology 12*: 160-174.

Mitchell, Alex J., Ferguson, David W., Gill, Jhon, Paul, James E., and *Symonds, Paul.* 2013. "Depression and anxiety in long-term cancer survivors compared with spouses and healthy controls: a systematic review and meta-analysis." *Lancet Oncology* 12: 160–174.

Mitchell, Alex J., Kaar, Stephen, Oggan, Chris, and Herdman, Joanne. 2008. "Acceptability of common screening methods used to detect distress and related mood disorders: preferences of cancer specialists and non-specialists." *PsychoOncology 17:* 226-236.

Muzzatti, Barbara, and Annunziata, Maria A. 2012. "Psychological distress screening in cancer patients: psychometric properties of tools available in Italy." *Tumori* 98: 501-509.

Muzzatti, Barbara, and Annunziata, Maria A. 2014. "Le dimensioni psicologiche peculiari della lungosopravvivenza oncologica." In, *La qualità di vita dopo il cancro. Aggiornamenti teorici e strumenti di intervento nella lungosopravvivenza oncologica,* edited by Maria A. Annunziata, and Barbara Muzzatti, 93-104. Roma: Il Pensiero Scientifico.

National Comprehensive Cancer Network - NCCN. 1999. "Distress management." *Clinical practice guidelines 1:* 344-374.

National Comprehensive Cancer Network – NCCN. (2014). "Distress management."*Clinical Practice Guidelines in Oncology version 2.* Retrieved from http://www.nccn.org/professionals/physician_gls/pdf/distress.pdf.

Osborne, Richard H., Elsworth, Gerard R., and Hopper, John L. 2003. "Age-specific norms and determinants of anxiety and depression in 731 women with breast cancer recruited through a population-based cancer registry." *European Journal of Cancer 39:* 755-762.

Rogers, Carl. 1951. *Client-Centered Therapy.* Boston: Houghton Mifflin.

Roth, Andrew J., Kornblith, Alice B., Batel-Copel, Laure, Peabody, Elizabeth, Scher, Howard I., Holland, Jimmie C. 1998. "Rapid screening for psychologic distress in men with prostate carcinoma." *Cancer 82:* 1904-1908.

Sawyer, Alexandra, Ayers, Susan, and Field, Andy P. 2010. "Posttraumatic growth and adjustment among individuals with cancer or HIV/AIDS: A meta-analysis." *Clinical Psychology Review 30:* 436–447.

Sellick, Scott M., and Edwardson, Alan D. 2007. "Screening new cancer patients for psychological distress using the Hospital Anxiety and Depression Scale." *Psycho-Oncology 16:* 534-542.

Smith, Hamish R. 2015. "Depression in cancer patients: Pathogenesis, implications and treatment." *Oncology Letters 9:* 1509-1514.

Soussain, Carole, Ricard, Damien, Fike, John R., Mazeron, Jean J., Psimaras, Dimitri, and Delattre, Jean Y. 2009. "CNS complications of radiotherapy and chemotherapy." *Lancet 7;374:* 1639–1651.

Stark, Dan, and Housel, Aallan O. 2000. "Anxiety in cancer patients." *British Journal of Cancer 83:* 1261-1267.

Stark, Dan, Kiely, Maureen, Smith, Adam, Velikova, Galina, House, Allan O., and Selby, Peter. 2002. "Anxiety disorders in cancer patients: their nature, associations, and relation to quality of life." *Journal of Clinical Oncology 20:* 3137-3148.

Stone, Patrick C., and Minton, Oliver. 2008. "Cancer-related fatigue." *European Journal of Cancer 44*: 1097–1104.

Strong, Vanessa, Waters, Rachel, Hibberd, Carina, Rush, Robert, Cargill, Anna, Storey, Dawn, Walker, Jane, Wall, Lucy, Fallon, Marie, Sharpe, Michael. 2007. "Emotional distress in cancer patients: the Edinburgh Cancer Centre symptom study." *British Journal of Cancer 26;*96: 868-874.

Tuinman, Marrit A., Van Nuenen, Floor M., Hagedoorn, Mariët, and Hoekstra-Weebers, Josette E. 2015. "Distress, problems and referral wish of cancer patients: differences according to relationship status and life phase." *Psychooncology 24*: 699-704.

VanHoose, Lia, Black, Lora l., Doty, Kimberly, Sabata, Dory, Twumasi-Ankrah, Philip, Taylor, Sarah, and Johnson, Rhonda. 2015. "An analysis of the distress thermometer problem list and distress in patients with cancer." *Supportive Care in Cancer 23*: 1225-1232.

van't Spijker, Adriaan, Trijsburg, Rudger W., and Duivenvoorden, Hugo J. 1997. "Psychological sequelae of cancer diagnosis: a meta-analytical review of 58 studies after 1980." *Psychosomatic Medicine 59:* 280-293.

Vardy, Janette, Wefel, Jeffrey, Ahles, Tim, and Schagen, Sanne. 2008. "Cancer and cancer-therapy related cognitive dysfunction: An international perspective from the Venice Cognitive Workshop." *Annals of Oncology 19:* 623–629.

Vodermaier, Andrea, Linden, Wolfgang, and Siu, Christopher. 2009. "Screening for emotional distress in cancer patients: a systematic review of assessment instruments." *Journal of National Cancer Institute 101:* 1464-1488.

World Health Organization. 1948. *Constitution of the World Health Organization.* April 7th, Geneva.

World Health Organization, QOL GROUP. 1993. "Study protocol for the World Health Organization project to develop a Quality of Life assessment instrument (WHOQOL)." *Quality of Life Research 2:* 153-159.

Zabora, James, Binzzenhofeszoc, Karlinn, Burbow, Barbara, Hooker, Craig, and Piantadosi, Steven. 2001. "The prevalence of psychological distress by cancer site." *Psycho-Oncology 10:* 19-28.

Zigmond, Anthony S., and Snaith, R. Philip. 1983. "The Hospital Anxiety and Depression Scale." *Acta Psychiatrica Scandinavica 67:* 361–370.

In: Psychological Distress
Editors: A. Compare, C. Elia, A. G. Simonelli et al.

ISBN: 978-1-63485-405-4

Chapter 4

DOES COPING STYLE ADD TO THE EFFECTS OF SEX AND TRAUMA TYPE ON PTSD AND MENTAL HEALTH OUTCOMES?

Melanie D. Hetzel-Riggin**, PhD
School of Humanities and Social Sciences,
Penn State Behrend, Erie, PA, US

ABSTRACT

While a large percentage of the population experiences trauma, only 8-10% of those individuals develop posttraumatic stress disorder (PTSD) and other trauma-related mental health problems. Previous research has shown that female sex is associated with higher rates of negative mental health outcomes. Survivors of interpersonal violence (physical and sexual abuse or assault) report higher rates of PTSD than survivors of most other forms of trauma, such as death of a loved one or natural disasters. Among the possible explanations for these differences (including biological, social, cognitive, and behavioral factors), coping style has been suggested as an additional reason for increased mental health problems after trauma. Research has shown that avoidant coping is associated with increases in PTSD symptoms and other mental health outcomes. Yet there is a paucity of research examining the interplay among participant sex, trauma type, and coping style on PTSD symptoms and other trauma-related outcomes. A large sample of college student participants completed a survey study examining demographic information (including participant sex), trauma history, coping style, PTSD outcomes, and other mental health issues. We conducted a series of hierarchical linear regressions; the results indicated that female sex, interpersonal violence exposure, and avoidant coping styles were associated increases in PTSD symptoms and other negative mental health outcomes. Male sex and problem-focused coping seemed to buffer the effects of trauma on PTSD and negative mental health outcomes. The results confirm that being female and interpersonal violence exposure are both independently and in concert strongly related to PTSD while the influence of experiencing the death of a loved one seems to be important but mild. These

* Correspondence regarding this manuscript should be directed to Melanie D. Hetzel-Riggin, PhD, School of Humanities and Social Sciences, Penn State Erie, The Behrend College, Erie, PA, 16563. Telephone: 814-898-6949. Email: mdh33@psu.edu.

findings support the assertion that problem-focused coping leads to desirable outcomes and avoidant coping leads to poor outcomes. Clinicians and first responders working with survivors of trauma should carefully assess for this constellation of risk factors (female sex, interpersonal violence, and avoidant coping), as individuals with these risk factors seem to be at a significantly high risk for negative outcomes. In addition, interventions that decrease avoidance coping and improve problem-focused coping will likely be useful for survivors of trauma.

INTRODUCTION

A traumatic event is an unpleasant or difficult experience that leads to physical injury, emotional upset, or disordered mental health. According to the DSM-5 (American Psychiatric Association, 2013), traumatic events can include exposure to war, physical abuse or assault, sexual assault, being kidnapped or taken hostage, torture, imprisonment, natural or man-made disasters, motor vehicle accidents, serious illness or injury, and unexpected death of a loved one. While specific prevalence rates vary concerning exposure to trauma, trauma exposure is a common reality for a significant proportion of the population. A longitudinal study tracking children from puberty into adulthood examined the prevalence of trauma exposure (Costello, Erkanli, Fairbank, and Angold, 2002). Twenty-five percent of participants reported experiencing a high magnitude traumatic experience in his or her lifetime and more than one fourth had experienced a low magnitude event in the three months prior to the interview. Furthermore, Hanson et al. (2002) reported that over 50% of clients presenting to mental health clinics in their sample had experienced a severe traumatic event during their lifetime. Elhai and Simons (2007) found that 74.5% of their participants were exposed to at least one traumatic event; Elliott (1997) found a similar prevalence rate of trauma exposure of 72%.

Furthermore, an overwhelming array of literature suggests that exposure to trauma can precede a variety of negative psychological outcomes. In mental health agency surveys, Hanson et al., (2002) discovered that a majority of clients had not only experienced trauma, but 56% of clients had a trauma-related diagnosis. Kolassa and colleagues (2010) reported that individuals exposed to a greater number of traumatic events developed high rates of lifetime and current PTSD. Further, traumatic exposure has an impact on other areas of mental health. In a survey of adolescents, Macdonald, Danielson, Resnick, Saunders, and Kilpatrick (2010) found that approximately 55% of girls and 57% of boys reported experiencing more than one potentially traumatic event. Of those adolescents that demonstrated PTSD, only 12% of girls and 20% of boys reported non-comorbid PTSD. Other prevalent mental health problems displayed were mood disorder and substance abuse (Macdonald et al., 2010).

The variation in the results of previous studies shows that the path from traumatic event to mental health outcomes is a variable one. Women report higher rates of PTSD, depression, and anxiety (Tolin and Foa, 2006). Different types of traumatic events seem to have a different conditional risk for the development of posttraumatic stress disorder (PTSD) and other psychopathology (Norris, 1992). Survivors of interpersonal violence (physical and sexual abuse or assault) report higher rates of PTSD than survivors of most other forms of trauma, such as motor vehicle accidents or natural disasters (Breslau, Chilcoat, Kessler, and Davis, 1999). Research has also shown that coping style may be associated with increases in

PTSD symptoms and other mental health concerns (Bryant and Harvey, 1995). Yet little research has examined the interplay among sex, trauma type, and coping style on PTSD symptoms and other mental health outcomes. Given the strong linkage among these variables, a thorough examination of how sex, trauma type, and coping style interact to predict PTSD and other mental health outcomes is called for. In this chapter, we will first review the literature on the effects of participant sex, trauma type, and coping style on PTSD development and other mental health outcomes. We then examine how these variables add to each other to predict PTSD and mental health outcomes in college students.

Sex

A person's sex seems to have a significant influence on the experience of trauma and its related outcomes. There are a number of possible explanations as to why women consistently report higher rates of PTSD (and to some extent other psychopathology) than men (Maguen, Ren and Bosch, 2010). Sex is a biological determinant of psychosocial stress vulnerability (Wang et al., 2007); men and women show age-related differences in brain development, which could influence how trauma exposure is perceived (Bloom, Nelson, and Lazerson, 2001). When viewing unpleasant images, women exhibit greater fear-related heart slowing compared to men (Bradley, Codispoti, Sabatinelle, and Lang, 2001; McManis, Bradley, Berg, Cuthbert, and Lang, 2001). Rasmusson, Vythilingham, and Morgan (2003) found that in males and postmenopausal women, low levels of cortisol were associated with PTSD, whereas in premenopausal women, high levels of cortisol were associated with PTSD. These biological differences between the sexes may be linked to evolutionary differences in stress responses (Taylor, Klein, Lewis, Gruenewald, Gurung, and Underfraff, 2000).

Some researchers have suggested that the increased risk of PTSD and other psychopathology in women is due to an increased likelihood for women to experience interpersonal trauma (Kessler, 2000). Breslau (2009) reported that the two-fold increase in conditional probability of PTSD in females was partially due to assaultive violence exposure (35.7% vs. 6.0%); however, when assaultive violence risk was controlled, the risk for PTSD was still higher in women compared to men (11.5% vs. 6.2%). Galovski, Mott, and Young-Xu (2011) compared male and female victims of physical and sexual assault and found no differences in PTSD symptoms, guilt, or trait anger. Men reported higher state anger, whereas women reported more health concerns. Lilly and Valdez (2011) found that while women were overrepresented in the interpersonal violence group, when both sex and interpersonal violence exposure were used to predict PTSD, only interpersonal violence exposure (not sex) predicted PTSD symptoms.

Men and women may also have different factors that increase the risk of developing psychopathology. King, King, Foy, and Gudanoski (1996) assessed 1,632 male and female participants from the National Vietnam Veterans' Readjustment Study and found that while family instability was the only predictor of PTSD for women, men had a number of additional risk factors (previous trauma history, combat exposure distress, younger age, and childhood antisocial behavior). In a follow-up study on the same sample, King, King, Foy, Keane, and Fairbank (1999) showed that war zone stressors were the best predictors of PTSD in men while posttrauma resilience and recovery factors were better predictors of PTSD in women. Luxton, Skopp, and Maguen (2010) assessed a large, mixed-sex sample of active duty soldiers and found that female gender increased the association between combat exposure and both depression and PTSD. Pereira (2002) assessed the effects of combat exposure on 110 veterans. While men reported greater levels of combat stress, and stress exposure was associated with increased PTSD symptoms, men and women who were exposed to similar levels of stress were equally likely to report PTSD. While women may experience many of the same traumatic stressors as men in combat, they are also more likely to be subjected to additional traumas, like military sexual trauma and providing health care in battle (Pereira, 2002).

Autobiographical memories of past experiences are socially constructed, and there are sex differences in how autobiographical memories are processed and stored (Davis, 1999; Nelson and Fivush, 2004). Women may be better able to develop complex representations of past experiences and have more accessible emotional memories (Bloise and Johnson, 2007; Davis, 1999; Fivush, 1989). Women may be more prone than men to constructing emotional events as central to one's identity because these memories are more emotional and easily accessible (Boals, 2010; Niedźwieńska, 2003). Women also report higher levels of subjective distress and perceive traumatic events as more threatening than men (Frans, Rinno, and Aberg, 2005; Yehuda, 2002). Irish, Fischer, Fallon, Spoonster, Sledjeski, and Delahanty (2011) found that in a sample of motor vehicle accident victims, women reported higher levels of initial posttraumatic stress, dissociation, and perceived life threat, which partially accounted for the increased levels of PTSD symptoms at both six weeks and six months as compared to men.

While a few studies have reported no differences in sex on the number of traumatic events men and women experience (Breslau, Davis, Andreski, 1997; Creamer, Burgess, McFarlane, 2001), most research does show differences between sexes in both the experience of trauma and its long-term effects. Using data from the National Comorbidity Survey, Kessler, Sonnega, Bromet, Hughes, and Nelson (1995) reported that 60% of men and 50% of women are exposed to trauma over their lifetime. Men were exposed to all forms of trauma more frequently than women except for sexual violence trauma. Other forms of assaultive violence besides sexual violence have been found to be more common in men than in women (Breslau et al., 1998) in both adults (Gavranidou and Rosner, 2003; Stein, Walker, and Forde, 2000) and adolescents (Muldoon and Trew, 2000).Yet other researchers have reported that women are more likely to experience trauma (Breslau and Kessler, 2001, Norris, Foster, Weisshaar, 2002). Read, Ouimette, While, Colder, and Farrow (2011) examined the rate of trauma exposure and PTSD among 3,014 incoming college students. Women reported more trauma exposure than men and experienced more traumatic events than men (except combat exposure). These differences do not seem to be related to sex-bias in reporting rates (Chung and Breslau, 2008).

Most research consistently shows that women experience a lifetime prevalence rate of PTSD two times that of men (Breslau, Chilcoat, Kessler, and Davis, 1999; Breslau, Chilcoat, Kessler, Peterson, and Lucia, 1999; Brewin, Andrews, and Valentine, 2000; Christiansen and Elkit, 2008; Chung and Breslau, 2008; Kessler et al., 1995; Tolin and Foa, 2006). Once a trauma has occurred, no matter what kind of trauma, women seem to develop PTSD at higher rates than men. This pattern is true from childhood (Doron-LaMarca, Vogt, King, King, and Saxe, 2010) to middle age (Ditlevsen and Elkit, 2010). PTSD is also more chronic in women than in men (Norris, Foster, and Weisshass, 2002). Hetzel-Riggin and Roby (2013) reported that women experienced higher symptom rates of both PTSD and other psychopathology in a large sample of college students, regardless of the type of trauma.

Trauma Type

Different traumatic events may lead to different outcomes for a number of reasons. Constant reminders of the trauma in the environment, such as news and media coverage, as well as a direct threat on one's life and continued stressors and adversity due to the trauma (such as economic and physical costs) are associated with increased PTSD and depressive symptoms (Goenjian et al., 2000). It is possible that the role of the traumatized individual, such as aggressor (combat veteran), victim (sexual or physical assault), or bystander (witnessing trauma to others), may influence the development of pathological outcome (Figley and Leventman, 1980). Trauma with agency, or a belief that one could have changed the outcome, seems to lead to worse outcomes, such as self-blame (Webb and Widseth, 2009). Events that are intentionally inflicted by others are associated with more difficulty coping (Janoff-Bulman, 1992). Interpersonal trauma may lead to more severe symptoms because it is a betrayal trauma (Freyd, 1994).

Breslau, Chilcoat, Kessler, and Davis (1999) reported that assaultive violence conferred the highest risk of PTSD in an epidemiological study – ten times that of learning about a trauma happening to a loved one. In a sample of 157 help-seeking children, Luthra and colleagues (2009) found that confrontation with traumatic news, witnessing traumatic violence, physical abuse and sexual abuse were associated with PTSD, whereas witnessing a crime, being a victim of crime, exposure to accidents, fire, and natural disasters were not associated with PTSD. Green, Krupnick, Stockton, Goodman, and Corcoran (2001) compared the severity of PTSD in female undergraduates who experienced either physical assault or traumatic loss. Green and colleagues found that the while the traumatic loss group reported significantly high levels of reexperiencing symptoms, only the physical assault group sensitized participants to the effects of further trauma. In addition, each trauma type led to a unique symptom cluster profile. Chung and Breslau (2008) found measurement variability due to trauma type, with survivors of assaultive violence more likely to report PTSD symptoms, especially emotional numbing and startle.

Sexual violence is typically associated with a high prevalence rate of PTSD (Kilpatrick, Acierno, Resnick, Saunders, and Best, 1997). Krupnick et al., (2004) compared six groups (no trauma, traumatic loss, single physical assault, single sexual assault, ongoing abuse, and multiple single traumas) in a large sample of women. The multiple trauma groups and the single abuse groups reported higher rates of PTSD, depression, substance use disorders, anxiety disorder, eating disorders, and borderline personality disorder symptoms than the no trauma and traumatic loss groups. In addition, the single sexual assault group reported more PTSD and other psychopathology than the single physical assault group. The single sexual assault group and the multiple abuse groups reported the highest rates of risky sexual behavior, self-harm, and violence perpetration (Green et al., 2005). Results from the Australian National Survey of Mental Health and Well-being showed that victims of sexual assault and rape reported the highest prevalence of PTSD, whereas survivors of natural disasters and witnessing injury to others had the lowest (Creamer, Burgess, and McFarlane, 2001).

Elhai, Frueh, Gold, Gold, and Hamner (2000) compared MMPI-2 profiles of survivors of childhood sexual abuse to those of combat veterans, another trauma-exposed group that has consistently reported high rates of PTSD (Amir, Kaplan, Kotler, 1996; Rosenheck and Fontana, 1994). The trauma groups initially differed on anxiety, anger, hostility, fears, health concerns, problems thinking and concentrating, elevated mood, and social discomfort and introversion. The childhood sexual abuse group scored higher on four scales, but the combat veteran group scored higher on five; this effect disappeared when age was considered. Kirz, Drescher, Klein, Gusman, and Schwartz (2001) found that sexual trauma survivors scored higher on the infrequent response and defensiveness scales, hypochondriasis, depression, hysteria, psychopathic deviate, and family problems scales of the MMPI-2, whereas combat veterans scored higher on social introversion, antisocial practices, anger, cynicism, and social discomfort. In addition, different PTSD scales on the MMPI-2 were better predictors of PTSD presence for sexual abuse and combat trauma. Kirz and colleagues reported that threat to life more consistent with combat trauma, whereas threat to physical integrity was more common in sexual trauma.

Kelley, Weathers, McDevitt-Murphy, Eakin, and Flood (2009) conducted a profile analysis on the PTSD symptoms of 1,420 female undergraduates who experienced either a motor vehicle accident, the sudden and unexpected death of a loved one, or sexual violence. The sexual violence group was higher than the other two trauma groups on most PTSD symptoms; the sudden and unexpected death of a loved one group reported more avoidance, detachment, sleep problems, and restricted range of affect than the motor vehicle accident victims. The motor vehicle accident group reported a higher degree of amnesia and hypervigilance. Shakespeare-Finch and Armstrong (2010) looked at PTSD symptoms and posttraumatic growth in 94 survivors of trauma in three groups (sexual abuse, motor vehicle accident, and bereavement). The sexual abuse group had the highest rates of PTSD, whereas the motor vehicle accident group had the lowest PTSD scores overall and lowest level of intrusive symptoms. The bereavement group reported the lowest levels of avoidance but reported the highest levels of posttraumatic growth. Hetzel-Riggin and Roby (2013) examined a large sample of college students and found that survivors of interpersonal violence, as compared to students who experienced death of a loved one or a natural disaster, had higher rates of PTSD symptoms, PTSD diagnosis, and other mental health symptoms. These studies suggest that different trauma types may give rise to different levels of general psychopathology and PTSD symptoms.

Coping Style

Another possible reason for differences in psychological outcomes after trauma is the coping styles used in response to the traumatic experience. According to Monet and Lazarus (1985), coping can be defined as attempt to adapt to difficult or stressful situations. Stated differently, coping includes any conscious attempt to solve problems or minimize stress in the environment. Lazarus and Folkman (1984) described two types of coping styles used by people when faced with stress. Problem-focused coping occurs when a person attempts to change something about the stressor or problem so that it is more manageable. Examples of problem-focused coping include seeking out emotional or instrumental support or developing a plan to change the situation. In contrast, emotion-focused coping is an effort to alter one's emotional reactions to a stressor rather than change the stressor itself. Examples of emotion-focused coping include wishful thinking and focusing on the positive. Folkman and Moskowitz (2004) suggested that while neither problem-focused nor emotion-focused coping is superior to the other, coping flexibility, or the ability to use different types of coping depending on the context of the situation, is more adaptive than using one type of coping exclusively (Cheng, 2003; Cheng, Kogan, and Chio, 2012). Other research has supported the superiority of problem-focused coping, especially after trauma. Karsoft, Armour, Elklit, and Solomon (2015) examined the PTSD trajectories (resilient, recovering, delayed, and chronic PTSD) in Israeli soldiers and found that increased use of problem-focused coping and decreased use of emotion-focused coping were associated with more resilient outcomes. Combat-exposed Israeli soldiers who engaged in a greater degree of emotion-focused coping and did not engage in problem-focused coping were more likely to have delayed or chronic PTSD trajectories.

Both problem-focused and emotion-focused coping can be considered approach-coping styles. Approach-coping strategies are those in which the focus is on the trauma or the person's response to the trauma. In contrast, research has identified avoidant coping as an alternative way to react to stressful situations (Zeidner and Endler, 1996). Avoidant coping is characterized by efforts to escape from stressors or problems. Examples of avoidant coping include detachment and keeping to oneself. Avoidance coping tends to reduce distress in the immediate aftermath of the trauma and is frequently used after severe traumatic events in order to help trauma victims meet their basic survival needs. Freh, Dallos, and Chung (2012) conducted qualitative interviews with nine survivors of bombing attacks who reported that avoidance coping (such as avoiding places, memories, and other trauma-related things), was frequently used by survivors and believed by the survivors to be necessary to prevent negative long-term outcomes. Indeed, Parker and McNally (2008) found that in their sample of participants who lost a loved one to suicide, avoidance coping was associated with decreased levels of depressive symptoms and somatic symptoms of grief.

However, avoidant types of coping in response to trauma have generally been seen as maladaptive (Folkman and Moskowitz, 2004). Research provides evidence that utilization of these strategies over time is related to negative mental health outcomes and PTSD symptoms (An, Fu, Wu, Lin, and Zhang, 2013; Folkman and Moskowitz, 2004; Orcutt, Pickett, and Pope, 2005). Avoidant coping has been linked to quicker disease progression in cancer patients (Epping-Jordan, Compas, and Howell, 1994) and increases in PTSD and depression symptoms in combat veterans (Holahan, Moos, Holahan, Brennan, and Schutte, 2005).

Kira, Omidy, and Ashby (2014) examined coping and mental health outcomes in samples of Native Americans and Palestinians in Gaza who had experienced multiple traumatic events. They found that problem-solving coping was associated with better mental and physical health in both samples. Consistent with the results of Karsoft and colleagues (2015), emotion-focused-coping was associated with poorer mental and physical health. In addition, avoidance coping was also associated with poorer mental and physical health but also seemed to lead to less comorbid mental health problems, suggesting avoidance may serve to protect against the development of additional problems in this sample. In another study, Dardas and Ahmad (2015) assessed parents of children with autistic disorder to see if coping style mediated or moderated the relationship between parenting stress and mental health outcomes. Dardas and Ahmad found that the emotion-focused technique of accepting responsibility mediated the relationship between parenting stress and mental health outcomes. In addition, seeking social support and escape-avoidance strategies buffered the effects of parenting stress on the development of negative mental health outcomes.

Dickstein et al. (2012) used a telephone interview to assess Israeli citizens who were under constant threat of terrorism. Dickstein and colleagues reported that social support seeking, denial/disengagement, and the use of substances led to increases in negative mental health outcomes (including depression, anxiety, and PTSD symptoms) after trauma while acceptance and positive reframing led to decreases in mental health outcomes. In contrast, Hassija, Luterek, Naragon-Gainey, Moore, and Simpson (2012) reported that poor emotional expression and greater levels of emotional avoidance were significantly associated with higher rates of PTSD and depressive symptoms in trauma-exposed veterans. Held, Owens, Schumm, Chard, and Hansel (2011) also examined trauma-exposed veterans and showed that disengagement coping and guilt were positively related to PTSD severity.

Blame, especially self-blame, has also been found to be associated with negative outcomes (Campbell, Dworkin, and Cabral, 2009). In a sample of emergency workers, Prati, Pietrantoni, and Cicognani (2011) found that use of avoidant coping strategies, especially self-blame and distraction, were associated with increased burnout and compassion fatigue. Problem-focused coping was associated with more compassion satisfaction and overall better outcomes for their sample. In contrast, Ullman, Peter-Hagene, and Relyea (2014) found that while some emotion-focused and avoidant coping strategies mediated the relationship between trauma exposure and PTSD and depression in large sample of interpersonal violence survivors, self-blame was not associated with more severe symptoms in this sample.

Grasso and colleagues (2012) compared college students who did and did not meet criteria for PTSD after exposure to potentially traumatic events. They reported that those college students exposed to trauma that did not meet criteria for PTSD reported higher rates of perceived social support and lower rates of avoidant coping strategies. In contrast, those trauma-exposed college students who met criteria for PTSD reported greater use of avoidance coping strategies and less use of problem-focused and emotion-focused coping strategies. In a sample of Chilean earthquake survivors, increased PTSD symptoms were explained by higher rates of avoidance coping and lower use of problem-focused coping (Leiva-Bianchi, Baher, and Poblete, 2012). Littleton, Horsley, John, and Nelson (2007) conducted a meta-analysis of the relationship between coping style and later psychological outcomes (including PTSD, depression, and general psychopathology). Littleton and colleagues found that avoidance coping strategies were associated with more negative mental health outcomes and PTSD symptoms while approach coping styles showed no relationship with mental health outcomes. In another study, Elzy, Clark, Dollard, and Hummer (2013) reported that the use of avoidant coping strategies by adolescents after high levels of exposure to child maltreatment led to better mental health outcomes; that is, avoidant coping buffered the effects of complex child abuse trauma. Approach coping, such as problem solving, seeking social support, and positive reappraisal, did not lead to better outcomes for this sample of adolescent girls.

Yet some studies have found that all forms of coping are associated with more problematic outcomes. Nuttman-Shwartz and Dekel (2009) assessed Israeli college students exposed to terrorism for coping style and PTSD. They reported that acceptance and decreased detachment were associated with lower levels of PTSD symptoms. In addition, alcohol use and seeking social support were associated with higher levels of PTSD symptoms. Chung, Walsh, and Dennis (2011) examined the relationship among PTSD and other mental health outcomes, coping strategies, and the experience of trauma associated with anaphylactic shock.

The results indicated that for survivors of a severe anaphylactic shock, those participants with higher rates of both PTSD symptoms and other mental health symptoms reported greater use of all forms of coping (problem-focused, emotion-focused, and avoidance). Somer, Ruvio, Sever, and Soref (2007) found similar results in a sample of people who survived continuous terrorist attacks. In another study on caregivers of people with cancer, Han and colleagues (2014) reported that all forms of coping (problem-focused, emotion-focused, and both cognitive and behavioral avoidance strategies) were associated with increased levels of depression. Only social support was linked with better outcomes in this sample.

Chang, Lee, Connor, Davidson, and Lai (2008) examined how coping strategies could affect the relationship between trauma exposure and behavioral and emotional outcomes in male firefighters who responded to a large earthquake. Chang et al., reported that while problem-focused, emotion-focused, and avoidance strategies were all significantly and positively related to both PTSD symptoms and other mental health outcomes, none of the coping styles moderated the relationship between trauma exposure and PTSD outcomes. Only problem-focused coping, distancing, and confrontive coping moderated the relationship between trauma exposure and mental health outcomes in this sample.

Women tend to focus on the feelings and worry that traumatic events evoke, whereas men tend to minimize the threat of the event (Bar-Tal, Lurie, and Glick, 1994). Laufer and Solomon (2009) assessed 2,999 Israeli adolescents and found that girls reported more PTSD and intense fear than boys at all exposure levels except the most severe. Boals (2010) found that women are more likely than men to report negative emotions, increased emotional intensity, avoidance, intrusion, depression, and physical health problems. Peritraumatic emotions and reactions are strong predictors of PTSD (Ozer, Best, Lipsey, and Weiss, 2003) and seem to differ based on sex.

The results of research with caregivers of cancer patients (Han et al., 2012), survivors of anaphylactic shock (Chung et al., 2011) and terrorist threat (Somer et al., 2007) suggest that the type of trauma played a role in the increased use of all forms of coping, suggesting that trauma type may influence coping strategies used and the development of later mental health issues. Littleton et al., (2007) examined potential moderators in their meta-analysis of coping style and psychological distress after trauma. They showed that length of trauma was associated with a greater degree of negative outcomes; however, when they examined trauma type (interpersonal violence vs. severe injury) they found no effect of trauma type on the relationship between coping style and psychological outcomes.

Present Study

As reviewed above, a wealth of research has shown that sex, trauma type, and coping style are all independently associated with increased PTSD and mental health outcomes. However, little research has examined the added effects of participant sex, trauma type, and coping style on PTSD symptoms and other mental health outcomes. Therefore, the purpose of the present paper is to examine how sex, trauma type, and coping style together predict PTSD symptoms and other mental health problems in a large sample of college students. Specifically, we hypothesize that:

1) Participant sex would significantly predict PTSD and mental health symptoms; that is, female sex would be associated with more negative mental health outcomes than male sex.
2) Interpersonal violence would be a strong predictor of PTSD and other mental health outcomes and be more likely to predict negative mental health outcomes than other trauma types (in this sample, sudden loss of a loved one and natural disaster).
3) Problem-focused coping strategies would be associated with better mental health outcomes, while avoidant coping strategies would be associated with poorer mental health outcomes.
4) Participant sex, trauma type, and coping strategies would both individually and collectively predict the presence of PTSD and other mental health problems; however, the combination of the three factors would significantly predict negative mental health outcomes.

METHOD

Participants

A total of 1,677 college student participants were recruited for this study. The average age of the participants was 19.3 (SD = 2.70) and 57.8% of the participants were women. The majority of the participants were single (94.6%) while a few of the participants were married (4.8%) or divorced (0.6%). Most of the participants were in their freshman year of college (63.3%); however, we did have participants who were in their sophomore (18.7%), junior (11.3%), and senior (6.7%) years in college. Consistent with the population of students at the university where the study took place, the majority of participants were white (83.9%). The remainder of the participants reported a variety of ethnic identities: 8.0% Black/African American, 4.2% Hispanic/Latino, 1.9% Biracial/Other, 1.3% Asian or Asian American, 0.4% Native American, and 0.4% Pacific Islander. Most of the participants also reported that they were heterosexual (94.8%), 1.6% reported that they were homosexual, 1.3% reported they were bisexual, and 2.3% stated they preferred not to disclose their sexual orientation.

In terms of community of origin, 2.5% of participants reported that they grew up in an area that was unincorporated, 23.4% grew up in a town of less than 10,000 people, 40.0% grew up in a town with between 10,000 and 50,000 people, 11.7% grew up in a town with between 50,000 and 100,000 people, and the remaining 22.4% reported they lived in a town of more than 100,000 people. We also asked participants to describe their parents' level of education as a proxy for socioeconomic status. Only 2.7% of participants reported their mother had no high school degree. Twenty-seven percent reported their mother had a high school degree, 29.1% reported she had some college education, 29.1% reported she had a college degree, and 10.4% reported she had a graduate degree (1.7% did not know their mother's level of education). For fathers, 4.6% of participants reported that their father had no high school degree, 29.9% said he had a high school degree, 23.6% said he had some college education, and 27.0% reported he had a college degree. Just over ten percent (10.1%) of participants reported their fathers had a graduate degree, while 4.9% of participants did not know their fathers' level of education. The majority of participants had never been in counseling (77.2%).

Measures

Demographics. Participants were asked to provide information about their sex, age, year in school, ethnicity, sexual orientation, relationship status, home community population, and therapy history.

Trauma history. We used a revised version of the Traumatic Life Events Questionnaire (TLEQ; Kubany et al., 2000) to assess for participants' history of traumatic events. The TLEQ is a self-report measure that asks participants to mark if they have experienced 21 potentially traumatic events. Examples include natural disasters, childhood abuse, sexual assault, or death of a loved one. Participants can also provide a description of other life-threatening or frightening events if they have not experienced any of the listed events. Participants checked all of the traumatic events they may have experienced during their life, and then provided more details about the outcome of the traumatic events (fear reactions, injury sustained, etc.). Test-retest reliability coefficients for the original TLEQ range from .86 to .89. The TLEQ has also exhibited adequate convergent and discriminant validity in samples of undergraduate students, Vietnam veterans, and battered women (Kubany et al., 2000). For this sample, we coded participants based on if they had experienced one of three overarching types of trauma: interpersonal violence (including sexual assault, physical assault, stalking, child abuse, or domestic violence; 39.7%), sudden and unexpected loss of a loved one (75.7%), and natural disaster (54.7%).

Coping. The Ways of Coping Scale (WOCS; Folkman and Lazarus, 1985) was used to assess a wide range of thoughts and acts that participants may have used to cope with the internal or external demands of traumatic events. The WOCS is a 66-item, self-report measure in which participants used a 4-point, Likert scale ranging from 0 (*not used*) to 3 (*used a great deal*) to indicate how often each coping style was utilized following the identified traumatic event. It has previously exhibited acceptable levels of reliability and validity (Folkman and Lazarus, 1985). The WOC contains eight factors: Problem-Focused Coping (11 items, $M = 9.18$, $SD = 7.20$), Wishful Thinking (5 items, $M = 5.75$, $SD = 4.15$), Detachment (6 items, $M = 5.66$, $SD = 3.61$), Seeking Social Support (7 items, $M = 7.55$, $SD = 4.79$), Focusing on the Positive (4 items, $M = 4.36$, $SD = 2.96$), Self-Blame (3 items, $M = 2.30$, $SD = 2.28$), Tension Reduction (3 items, $M = 2.15$, $SD = 1.99$), and Keep To Oneself (3 items, $M = 2.72$, $SD = 2.30$).

Posttraumatic stress symptoms. To assess for posttraumatic stress symptoms, we used the Posttraumatic Stress Disorder Questionnaire (PTSD-Q; Cross and McCanne, 2001). The PTSD Questionnaire is based on the Posttraumatic Stress Disorder Interview (PTSD-I; Watson, Juba, Manifold, Kucala, and Anderson, 1991) and was revised into a survey measure. The PTSD-Q assesses PTSD symptom severity during the past month and was developed specifically to screen college students for trauma and PTSD. Participants identified traumatic experiences from the modified TLEQ and rated how often they experienced symptoms of re-experiencing, avoidance, numbing, and arousal on a seven-point Likert scale from 1 (*no or never*) to 7 (*extremely or always*) in regards to that experience. Scores at or above 60 are consistent with a diagnosis of PTSD and scores at or above 35 consistent with sub-clinical levels of PTSD (Cross and McCanne, 2001). Cross and McCanne concluded that the PTSD-Q was a useful measure for screening college students who are not seeking treatment. One hundred and forty-nine participants (8.9%) met criteria for PTSD based on a cutoff score of 60, while 381 participants (22.8%) of participants reported elevated levels of symptoms consistent with sub-clinical levels of PTSD. In addition, we calculated subscale scores for the four symptom clusters of PTSD: Reexperiencing (5 items, M = 10.22, SD = 5.75), Avoidance (2 items, M = 4.75, SD = 3.06), Dysphoria/Numbing (5 items, M = 8.78, SD = 5.23), and Arousal (5 items, M = 8.85, SD = 5.41).

Other Mental Health Outcomes. We used the Symptom Checklist-Revised (SCL-90-R) to assess for other forms of mental health concerns. This 90-item self-report measure was used to measure general mental health outcomes across a number of diagnostic categories (Derogatis, 1983). Participants responded to the questions using a five-point, Likert-type scale from 0 (*not at all*) to 4 (*extremely*). Average scores for total and subscale scores were calculated and then transformed into T scores using standardized norms. The SCL-90-R measures nine symptom dimensions of psychological distress; for the purposes of this study we focused only on four of the subscales: Somatization (12 items, M = 51.23, SD = 10.78), Interpersonal Sensitivity (9 items, M = 61.83, SD = 17.32), Depression (13 items, M = 57.74, SD = 13.34), and Anxiety (10 items, M = 53.96, SD = 13.69).

Derogatis, Rickels, and Rock (1976) found the SCL-90-R to have adequate levels of reliability. Derogatis, Rickels, and Rock reported internal consistency coefficients from .77 for psychoticism to .90 for depression. Derogatis and Savitz (1999) reported good test-retest reliabilities over a week, with coefficients ranging from .78 to .90. When contrasted with the MMPI, the SCL-90-R was found to have good convergent and good discriminant validity (Derogatis et al., 1976). The global indices and the individual dimensions of the SCL-90-R have also been reported to have sufficient construct, criterion, and concurrent validity (Peveler and Fairburn, 1990).

Procedure

As part of a larger study on coping, stress, and trauma, participants were assessed in groups of no more than 25 in a large classroom by trained undergraduate researchers. Participants were seated so as to insure privacy. Participants read and signed an informed consent document before beginning the hour-long study. Participants then completed the survey measures, which included measures assessing demographic information, trauma history, coping style, posttraumatic stress symptoms, and other mental health outcomes. Participants were able to ask questions before and during the survey. All participants were verbally debriefed and given a handout with information about local counseling resources and the author. Participants also received credit toward their research participation requirement for their psychology course. This study received IRB approval prior to data collection.

RESULTS

Data Analysis Plan

Table 1 presents the correlations among the variables of interest. Missing data was minimal and was accounted for using listwise deletion. We ran a series of hierarchical, stepwise regressions for our outcome variables of PTSD diagnostic category, the four subscales of the PTSD-Q (Reexperiencing, Avoidance, Numbing, and Arousal), and the four subscales of the SCL-90-R (Somatization, Interpersonal Sensitivity, Depression, and Anxiety). Participant sex (1 = male; 2 = female) was entered in the first step to account for variance related to sex of the participant. In the second step, the three trauma types (interpersonal violence, sudden loss of a loved one, and natural disaster) were allowed to enter into the equation. In the third step, the eight coping styles measured by the Ways of Coping Scale (Problem-Focused Coping, Wishful Thinking, Detachment, Seeking Social Support, Focusing on the Positive, Self-Blame, Tension Reduction, and Keep to Oneself) were allowed to enter the equation.

Posttraumatic Stress Disorder

Table 2 presents the final regression model summary for posttraumatic stress disorder diagnosis and symptoms. We first ran the stepwise hierarchical regressions to predict PTSD diagnostic category. When sex was added to the equation the regression was significant, $R^2 = .02$, $F(1, 1659) = 32.34$, $p < .001$. The significant regression shows that female sex was positively associated with PTSD diagnosis. All three types of traumatic events (interpersonal violence, death of a loved one, and natural disaster) entered the equation in the second step. The regression equation was still significant, $R^2 = .11$, $F(4, 1656) = 51.51$, $p < .001$. The change in R^2 was also significant, $\Delta R^2 = .09$, $F(3, 1659) = 56.68$, $p < .001$. In the third step, five of the coping style subscales entered the equation (Keep to Oneself, Wishful Thinking, Focus on the Positive, Self-Blame, and Problem-Focused Coping). The overall regression equation was significant, $R^2 = .33$, $F(9, 1651) = 88.66$, $p < .001$. The change in R^2 was also significant, $\Delta R^2 = .22$, $F(5, 1654) = 105.81$, $p <.001$.

We then ran the stepwise hierarchical regressions to predict each of the four subscales of the PTSD-Q. For Reexperiencing symptoms, adding sex resulted in a significant regression equation, $R^2 = .03$, $F(1, 1664) = 53.92$, $p < .001$. Only interpersonal violence and death of a loved one entered the equation in the second step. The regression equation was still significant, $R^2 = .11$, $F(3, 1662) = 68.25$, $p < .001$.There was also a significant increase in the regression coefficient, $\Delta R^2 = .08$, $F(2, 1667) = 73.48$, $p < .001$. In the third step, four of the coping style subscales entered the equation (Keep to Oneself, Wishful Thinking, Self-Blame, and Problem-Focused Coping). The overall regression equation was still significant, $R^2 = .30$, $F(7, 1658) = 101.09$, $p < .001$. The change in R^2 was also significant, $\Delta R^2 = .19$, $F(4, 1663) = 112.07$, $p < .001$.

Table 1. Correlations among Predictor and Dependent Variables

	1	2	3	4	5	6	7	8	9	10	11	12	13
1. Sex[a]	1												
2. Interpersonal violence[a]	.04	1											
3. Death of a loved one[a]	.03	.10**	1										
4. Natural disaster[a]	-.10**	.11**	.14**	1									
5. WOC Problem-Focused Coping	-.02	.17**	.10**	.09**	1								
6. WOC Wishful Thinking	.13**	.22**	.17**	.02	.56**	1							
7. WOC Detachment	.03	.22**	.12**	.03	.56**	.54**	1						
8. WOC Social Support Seeking	.14**	.09**	.12**	.02	.64**	.57**	.40**	1					
9. WOC Focus on the Positive	.05**	.07**	.14**	.04	.64**	.45**	.48**	.62**	1				
10. WOC Self-Blame	.01	.20**	.08**	.03	.65**	.54**	.53**	.41**	.41**	1			
11. WOC Tension Reduction	-.04	.19**	.14**	.08**	.61**	.50**	.47**	.48**	.45**	.52**	1		
12. WOC Keep to Oneself	.02	.29**	.16**	.07**	.45**	.57**	.56**	.25**	.59**	.49**	.45**	1	
13. PTSD Category[a]	.13**	.29**	.15**	.09**	.28**	.46**	.30**	.20**	.17**	.34**	.30**	.46**	1
14. PTSD Reexperiencing	.17**	.28**	.20**	.09**	.23**	.47**	.28**	.24**	.17**	.29**	.27**	.43**	.75**
15. PTSD Avoidance	.20**	.28**	.15**	.05*	.20**	.45**	.31**	.19**	.16**	.30**	.24**	.43**	.69**
16. PTSD Numbing	.11**	.33**	.16**	.09**	.25**	.46**	.34**	.17**	.15**	.34**	.31**	.50**	.79**
17. PTSD Arousal	.09**	.29**	.15**	.13**	.27**	.42**	.31**	.20**	.16**	.32**	.29**	.44**	.75**
18. SCL Somatization	.17**	.24**	.10**	.06*	.19**	.28**	.24**	.15**	.08**	.24**	.26**	.28**	.30**
19. SCL Interpersonal Sensitivity	.16**	.23**	.05*	.04	.16**	.32**	.28**	.14**	.03	.30**	.22**	.33**	.37**
20. SCL Depression	.22**	.26**	.09**	.01	.16**	.37**	.29**	.15**	.03	.32**	.25**	.37**	.39**
21. SCL Anxiety	.09**	.25**	.07**	.05*	.18**	.32**	.27**	.15**	.07**	.29**	.27**	.34**	.38**
1. Sex[a]	14	15	16	17	18	19	20	21					
2. Interpersonal violence[a]													
3. Death of a loved one[a]													
4. Natural disaster[a]													
5. WOC Problem-Focused Coping													
6. WOC Wishful Thinking													
7. WOC Detachment													
8. WOC Social Support Seeking													

	14	15	16	17	18	19	20	21
9. WOC Focus on the Positive								
10. WOC Self-Blame								
11. WOC Tension Reduction								
12. WOC Keep to Oneself								
13. PTSD Category[a]								
14. PTSD Reexperiencing	1							
15. PTSD Avoidance	.74**	1						
16. PTSD Numbing	.69**	.64**	1					
17. PTSD Arousal	.73**	.62**	.73**	1				
18. SCL Somatization	.31**	.29**	.34**	.33**	1			
19. SCL Interpersonal Sensitivity	.34**	.31**	.39**	.35**	.58**	1		
20. SCL Depression	.38**	.36**	.45**	.39**	.66**	.82**	1	
21. SCL Anxiety	.38**	.33**	.42**	.42**	.73**	.74**	.80**	1

Note. *$p < .05$; **$p < .01$; [a]denotes Spearman correlations due to dichotomous variable (all other values are Pearson correlations).

WOC = Ways of Coping Scale (Folkman and Lazarus, 1985); PTSD = Posttraumatic Stress Disorder Checklist (Cross and McCanne, 2001); SCL = Symptom Checklist 90—Revised (Derogatis, 1983).

Table 2. Final Regression Model Summary for Posttraumatic Stress Disorder Symptoms

Step	Predictor Variable	*B*	SE_B	β	*t*	R^2	ΔR^2	ΔF
Posttraumatic Stress Disorder Category								
1	Sex	.13	.03	.10	4.65***	.02	.02	32.34***
2	IPV	.04	.01	.13	5.98***	.10	.08	140.18***
3	Death of a loved one	.02	.01	.05	2.27*	.11	.01	23.27***
4	Natural disaster	.07	.03	.06	2.75**	.11	.003	4.75*
5	WOC Keep to Oneself	.07	.01	.26	10.05***	.27	.16	357.88***
6	WOC Wishful Thinking	.05	.004	.29	10.15***	.31	.05	107.94***
7	WOC Focus on the Positive	-.02	.01	-.08	-2.86**	.32	.01	15.74***
8	WOC Self-Blame	.03	.01	.10	3.67***	.32	.004	8.80**
9	WOC Problem-Focused Coping	-.01	.003	-.08	-2.30*	.33	.002	5.29*
Reexperiencing Symptoms								
1	Sex	1.42	.24	.12	5.82***	.03	.03	53.92***
2	IPV	.34	.06	.11	5.28***	.09	.06	111.49***
3	Death of a loved one	.32	.09	.07	3.38***	.11	.02	32.56***
4	WOC Wishful Thinking	.45	.04	.32	11.25***	.26	.15	346.84***
5	WOC Keep to Oneself	.55	.07	.22	8.23***	.29	.03	69.15***
6	WOC Problem-Focused Coping	-.09	.02	-.11	-3.82***	.30	.004	10.43***
7	WOC Self-Blame	.15	.07	.06	2.05*	.30	.002	4.21*
Avoidance Symptoms								
1	Sex	.89	.13	.14	6.92***	.04	.04	67.90***
2	IPV	.22	.03	.14	6.39***	.11	.07	131.29***
3	Death of a loved one	.10	.05	.04	2.06*	.12	.01	19.16***
4	WOC Wishful Thinking	.22	.02	.30	10.32***	.26	.14	302.33***
5	WOC Keep to Oneself	.31	.04	.23	8.72***	.29	.03	78.56***
6	WOC Problem-Focused Coping	-.07	.01	-.16	-5.39***	.30	.01	18.26***
7	WOC Self-Blame	.13	.04	.10	3.42***	.30	.01	11.71***

Step	Predictor Variable	B	SE_B	β	t	R^2	ΔR^2	ΔF
Numbing Symptoms								
1	Sex	.90	.22	.09	4.17***	.01	.01	22.99***
2	IPV	.44	.06	.16	7.78***	.11	.10	180.08***
3	Death of a loved one	.15	.08	.04	1.86	.12	.01	18.28***
4	WOC Keep to Oneself	.67	.06	.29	11.28***	.30	.18	417.21***
5	WOC Wishful Thinking	.36	.04	.29	9.76***	.33	.03	83.97***
6	WOC Social Support Seeking	-.11	.03	-.10	-3.33***	.34	.01	17.70***
7	WOC Tension Reduction	.18	.07	.07	2.71**	.34	.002	5.88*
8	WOC Focus on the Positive	-.10	.05	-.06	-2.08*	.34	.002	4.32*
Arousal Symptoms								
1	Sex	.70	.23	.06	2.98**	.01	.01	14.89***
2	IPV	.36	.06	.13	5.82***	.08	.07	128.36***
3	Death of a loved one	.10	.09	.02	1.08	.09	.01	13.45***
4	Natural disaster	.75	.23	.07	3.21***	.09	.01	8.34***
5	WOC Keep to Oneself	.59	.06	.25	9.22***	.23	.14	295.75***
6	WOC Wishful Thinking	.30	04	.23	7.92***	.26	.03	75.42***
7	WOC Focus on the Positive	-.13	.04	-.07	-2.96**	.27	.003	6.03*
8	WOC Self-Blame	.16	.06	.07	2.53*	.27	.003	6.04*

Note. IPV = Interpersonal Violence. WOC = Ways of Coping Scale.
*$p < .05$; **$p < .01$; ***$p < .001$.

For Avoidance symptoms, the addition of sex to the equation led to a significant regression equation, R^2 = .04, F(1, 1662) = 67.90, p < .001. Similar to the regression for Reexperiencing symptoms, only interpersonal violence and death of a loved one entered the equation in the second step. The regression equation was still significant, R^2 = .12, F(3, 1660) = 75.30, p < .001, and change in R^2 was also significant, ΔR^2 = .08, F(2, 1665) = 76.12, p < .001. In the third step, four of the coping style subscales entered the equation (Keep to Oneself, Wishful Thinking, Self-Blame, and Problem-Focused Coping). The overall regression equation remained significant, R^2 = .30, F(7, 1656) = 102.28, p < .001. The change in the regression coefficient was significant, ΔR^2 = .18, F(4, 1661) = 108.35, p < .001.

We ran the same stepwise hierarchical regression equation for the Numbing symptoms of PTSD. The addition of sex to the equation produced a significant regression equation, R^2 = .02, F(1, 1661) = 22.99, p < .001. The addition of interpersonal violence and death of a loved one led to a significant change in R^2, ΔR^2 = .11, F(2, 1663) = 101.64, p < .001, as well as a significant overall regression equation, R^2 = .12, F(3, 1659) = 75.32, p < .001. For the third step, five of the coping subscales (Keep to Oneself, Wishful Thinking, Social Support Seeking, Tension Reduction, and Focus on the Positive) entered the equation. The change in R^2 was significant, ΔR^2 = .22, F(5, 1658) = 111.15, p < .001, as was the overall regression equation, R^2 = .34, F(8, 1654) = 107.40, p < .001.

Lastly, the regression was run for the Arousal symptoms of PTSD. The first step (addition of sex) was significant, R^2 = .01, F(1, 1662) = 14.87, p < .001. All three of the trauma types entered the equation in the second step, leading to a significant change in R^2, ΔR^2 = .08, F(3, 1662) = 50.60, p < .001. The regression equation also remained significant, R2 = .09, F(4, 1659) = 41.98, p < .001. For the final step, four of the coping styles (Keep to Oneself, Wishful Thinking, Focus on the Positive, and Self-Blame) entered the equation. The regression equation was significant, R^2 = .27, F(8, 1655) = 75.91, p < .001. The change in the regression equation was also significant, ΔR^2 = .18, F(4, 1658) = 100.22, p < .001.

Other Mental Health Outcomes

Table 3 presents the final regression model summary for four subscales of the SCL-90-R: Somatization, Interpersonal Sensitivity, Depression, and Anxiety. We first ran the stepwise hierarchical regressions to predict Somatization scores. When sex was added to the equation the regression was significant, R^2 = .03, F(1, 1664) = 48.75, p < .001. Only interpersonal violence and death of a loved one entered the equation in the second step. The regression equation was still significant, R^2 = .08, F(3, 1662) = 50.36, p < .001. The change in R^2 was also significant, ΔR^2 = .05, F(2, 1663) = 49.37, p < .001. In the third step, five of the coping style subscales entered the equation (Keep to Oneself, Tension Reduction, Wishful Thinking, Focus on the Positive, and Self-Blame). The overall regression equation was significant, R^2 = .16, F(8, 1657) = 40.00, p < .001. The change in R^2 was also significant, ΔR^2 = .08, F(5, 1658) = 31.17, p <.001.

Table 3. Final Regression Model Summary for the Symptom Checklist Subscales

Step	Predictor Variable	*B*	SE_B	β	*t*	R^2	ΔR^2	ΔF
Somatization								
1	Sex	3.40	.50	.16	6.85***	.03	.03	48.75***
2	IPV	.75	.13	.14	5.81***	.08	.05	90.39***
3	Death of a loved one	.34	19	.04	1.78	.08	.01	8.67**
4	WOC Keep to Oneself	.48	.14	.10	3.51***	.13	.05	85.03***
5	WOC Tension Reduction	.73	.16	.14	4.64***	.15	.02	34.17***
6	WOC Wishful Thinking	.27	.08	.11	3.34***	.15	.01	9.33**
7	WOC Focus on the Positive	-.42	.10	-.12	-4.34***	.16	.01	16.04***
8	WOC Self-Blame	.36	.14	.08	2.58**	.16	.003	6.66**
Interpersonal Sensitivity								
1	Sex	4.83	.78	.14	6.24***	.03	.03	45.06***
2	IPV	1.06	.20	.12	5.26***	.08	.05	96.53***
3	WOC Keep to Oneself	.94	.22	.13	4.26***	.16	.08	150.45***
4	WOC Self-Blame	1.34	.24	.18	5.72***	.18	.02	43.44***
5	WOC Focus on the Positive	-1.07	.17	-.18	-6.26***	.20	.02	35.31***
6	WOC Wishful Thinking	.68	.13	.16	5.25***	.21	.02	32.34***
7	WOC Detachment	.55	.15	.12	3.80***	.22	.01	12.88***
8	WOC Problem-Focused Coping	-.28	-.09	-.12	-3.20***	.22	.003	7.18**
9	WOC Tension Reduction	.61	.25	.07	2.40*	.22	.003	5.78*
Depression								
1	Sex	4.90	.57	18	8.55***	.05	.05	77.62***
2	IPV	.92	.15	.13	6.14***	.11	.07	123.55***
3	Death of a loved one	.21	.22	.02	.96	.11	.003	5.30*
4	WOC Keep to Oneself	.82	.16	.14	4.97***	.20	.09	184.77***
5	WOC Self-Blame	1.16	.17	.20	6.66***	.23	.02	52.55***
6	WOC Focus on the Positive	-.87	.13	-.19	-6.90***	.25	.02	48.27***
7	WOC Wishful Thinking	.65	.10	.20	6.76***	.27	.02	49.69***
8	WOC Problem-Focused Coping	-.28	.07	-.15	-4.26***	.28	.004	9.91**
9	WOC Tension Reduction	.61	.19	.09	3.28***	.28	.01	11.69***
10	WOC Detachment	.33	.11	.09	3.06**	.28	.004	9.33**

Table 3. (Continued)

Step	Predictor Variable	*B*	SE_B	β	*t*	R^2	ΔR^2	ΔF
Anxiety								
1	Sex	2.24	.62	.08	3.63***	.01	.01	18.11***
2	IPV	.84	.16	.12	5.24***	.07	.05	96.22***
3	WOC Keep to Oneself	.83	.18	.14	4.66***	.15	.08	157.29***
4	WOC Wishful Thinking	.52	.10	.16	5.10***	.17	.02	37.52***
5	WOC Focus on the Positive	-.66	.14	-.14	-4.85***	.17	.01	19.80***
6	WOC Self-Blame	.78	.19	.13	4.18***	.19	.01	24.91***
7	WOC Tension Reduction	.84	.20	12	4.19***	.19	.01	14.26***
8	WOC Problem-Focused Coping	-.19	.07	-.10	-2.76**	.20	.003	6.31*
9	WOC Detachment	.27	.12	.07	2.35*	.20	.003	5.51*

Note. IPV = Interpersonal Violence. WOC = Ways of Coping Scale.
*$p < .05$; **$p < .01$; ***$p < .001$.

We then ran the stepwise hierarchical regressions to predict Interpersonal Sensitivity scores. The addition of sex resulted in a significant regression equation, $R^2 = .03$, $F(1, 1664) = 45.06$, $p < .001$. Only interpersonal violence entered the equation in the second step. The regression equation was still significant, $R^2 = .08$, $F(2, 1663) = 72.08$, $p < .001$. There was also a significant increase in the regression coefficient, $\Delta R^2 = .05$, $F(1, 1664) = 95.69$, $p < .001$. In the third step, all of the coping style subscales except for Seeking Social Support entered the equation. The overall regression equation was still significant, $R^2 = .22$, $F(9, 1656) = 52.62$, $p < .001$. The change in R^2 was also significant, $\Delta R^2 = .14$, $F(7, 1657) = 43.44$, $p < .001$.

For Depression scores, the addition of sex to the equation led to a significant regression equation, $R^2 = .05$, $F(1, 1664) = 77.62$, $p < .001$. For the second step, both interpersonal violence and death of a loved one entered the equation. The regression equation was still significant, $R^2 = .11$, $F(3, 1662) = 70.91$, $p < .001$, and change in R^2 was also significant, $\Delta R^2 = .07$, $F(2, 1663) = 64.28$, $p < .001$. Similar to the results for Interpersonal Sensitivity, all of the coping styles except for Seeking Social Support entered the equation in the third step. The overall regression equation remained significant, $R^2 = .28$, $F(10, 1655) = 65.61$, $p < .001$. The change in the regression coefficient was significant, $\Delta R^2 = .17$, $F(7, 1656) = 56.35$, $p < .001$.

We ran the same stepwise hierarchical regression equation for the Anxiety scores of the SCL-90-R. The addition of sex to the equation produced a significant regression equation, $R^2 = .01$, $F(1, 1664) = 18.11$, $p < .001$. The addition of interpersonal violence led to a significant change in R^2, $\Delta R^2 = .05$, $F(1, 1664) = 95.87$, $p < .001$, as well as a significant overall regression equation, $R^2 = .07$, $F(2, 1663) = 57.69$, $p < .001$. Once again, all of the coping styles except for Seeking Social Support entered the equation for the third step, leading to a significant change in R^2, $\Delta R^2 = .14$, $F(7, 1657) = 39.79$, $p < .001$. The overall regression equation was also significant, $R^2 = .20$, $F(9, 1656) = 45.80$, $p < .001$.

CONCLUSION

This chapter examined how participant sex, trauma type, and coping style predicted PTSD symptoms and other mental health problems in a large sample of college students. We hypothesized that female sex, interpersonal violence, and avoidant coping would be predictive of higher levels of PTSD and other mental health problems, while problem-focused coping would be associated with decreased mental health problems. We also hypothesized that sex, trauma type, and coping style would each add significantly to the prediction equations but that together would account for significant proportion of the variance in symptom outcomes. We assessed a large sample of college students for their trauma history, demographic information, coping styles, and mental health outcomes.

The results confirm our hypothesis that female sex would be associated with greater PTSD and other negative mental health outcomes. Female sex was predictive higher rates of PTSD diagnosis, all four PTSD symptom clusters, and other mental health problems. These results are consistent with previous research that suggests that being a woman leads to an increased risk for negative mental health outcomes after trauma (Breslau, Chilcoat, Kessler, and Davis, 1999; Breslau, Chilcoat, Kessler, Peterson, and Lucia, 1999; Brewin et al., 2000; Christiansen and Elkit, 2008; Chung and Breslau, 2008; Hetzel-Riggin and Roby, 2013;

Kessler et al., 1995; Tolin and Foa, 2006). Unlike previous studies that showed that women experienced more interpersonal trauma than men (Kessler, 2000), the current study showed that there were no differences between men and women on interpersonal violence exposure, $\chi^2(1, N = 1677) = 2.23, p > .10$, or reported sudden death of a loved one, $\chi^2(1, N = 1677) = 1.605, p > .10$. Men did experience natural disasters at a higher rate than women, $\chi^2(1, N = 1677) = 16.58, p < .001$, which is consistent with the extant literature (Foa and Tolin, 2006). The present results also support the theory that there may be evolutionary-based biological differences in how men and women respond to stress (Bloom et al., 2001; Bradley et al., 2001; McManis et al., 2001; Taylor et al., 2000; Wang et al., 2007). It could also mean that women, as compared to men, may be experiencing other risk factors in their life at a greater rate in this sample (King et al., 1996; Luxton et al., 2010).

Our results also support our second hypothesis that interpersonal violence would be a strong predictor of negative mental health outcomes. Reports of interpersonal violence exposure were positively and significantly associated with a PTSD diagnosis, PTSD symptom clusters, and other mental health outcomes. The results are similar to findings in epidemiological studies (Breslau et al., 1999), children (Luthra et al., 2009), and college students (Green et al., 2001). The results also expand the literature supporting the strong link between interpersonal violence and negative mental health outcomes (Creamer et al., 2001; Elhai et al., 2000; Hetzel-Riggin and Roby, 2013) by showing that this link applies not only to PTSD outcomes but a wide variety of other mental health outcomes including interpersonal sensitivity, somatic symptoms, depression, and anxiety. While not as strong a predictor of negative outcomes, sudden and unexpected death of a loved one was also a significant predictor of some of our outcome measures; specifically, death of a loved one was associated with increased rates of PTSD diagnosis, all PTSD symptom clusters, somatization, and depression outcomes. These results suggest that sudden death of a loved one is associated with increased negative mental health outcomes, specifically those that may be similar to grief and mourning. Kelley et al. (2009) reported similar findings in another sample of undergraduate participants when they found a relationship between death of a loved one, affect, and sleep related issues. The present findings are also consistent with research supporting the presence of unique symptom profiles after different traumatic events (Chung and Breslau, 2008).

We also confirm that use of avoidant coping strategies was associated with increased negative mental health outcomes (Folkman and Moskowitz, 2004). In this study, the subscales of Keeping to Oneself and Wishful Thinking were positively and significantly associated with increases in all negative mental health outcomes. These subscales represent actions such as keeping thoughts and feelings about the trauma private, avoiding cues that may remind one of the traumatic event(s), wishing for better outcomes, daydreaming about how things used to be, and other cognitive avoidance strategies. The strong positive relationship between these two subscales and all forms of negative mental health outcomes support the general wisdom that avoidant coping is maladaptive after trauma (An et al., 2013; Epping-Jordan et al., 1994; Holahan et al., 2005; Littleton et al., 2007; Orcutt et al., 2005). However, the strong and positive relationship between avoidant coping and negative mental health outcomes is in contrast with previous research that suggests that avoidance can lead to beneficial outcomes. For example, Parker and McNally (2008) showed that avoidance coping led to beneficial outcomes after participants lost loved ones to suicide. Freh and colleagues (2012) reported that their participants found avoidance coping to be necessary and helpful after bombing attacks. Neither of these studies specifically examined PTSD or examined multiple traumatic event types, which could explain the differences in the results among the studies.

Self-blame was also a significant predictor of most negative mental health outcomes (all but Numbing). These findings are not surprising given the wealth of research that links self-blame to increased negative mental health (Campbell et al., 2009; Prati et al., 2011). The results also support the theory that trauma often will challenge personal beliefs about how one could have changed the outcome (Webb and Widseth, 2009), leading to increased self-blame. Also consistent with our hypotheses, problem-focused coping was associated with better mental health outcomes. Specifically, problem-focused coping was associated with decreased PTSD diagnosis, symptoms of Reexperiencing, Avoidance, Interpersonal Sensitivity, Depression, and Anxiety. These results lend support to the larger body of literature that shows that problem-focused coping is a buffer against more severe psychopathology (Elzy et al., 2013; Grasso et al., 2012; Leiva et al., 2012).

In addition, focusing on the positive (otherwise understood as positive reappraisal) was associated with better mental health outcomes. While this is an emotion-focused coping strategy, previous models of coping and emotion regulation have suggested that positive reappraisal can be a very helpful coping strategy when one is faced with a situation that is uncontrollable and unpredictable (Gross and John, 2003). In this sample, focusing on the positive was specifically associated with decreased Numbing, Somatization, and Anxiety symptoms, suggesting that positive reappraisal may be uniquely associated with reducing anxiety-related symptoms (Beltzer, Nock, Peters, and Jamieson, 2014; Dickstein et al., 2012; Foa and Kozak, 1986).

Surprisingly, seeking social support was a significant predictor of increases in most negative mental health outcomes and was only negatively related to Numbing symptoms. These results are in direct contrast to Grasso and colleagues that found that social support was associated with lower rates of PTSD. In fact, most of the extant literature has supported the strong buffering effect of social support on negative mental health outcomes after trauma (Dardas and Ahmed, 2015; Han et al., 2014). Perhaps the difference between previous research and the current study is that we measured social support seeking, not social support available to participants. In this context, our results are similar to research with survivors of terrorist threat (Dickstein et al., 2012; Nuttman-Schwartz and Dekel, 2009) that reported that social support seeking led to increases in negative mental health outcomes. Future research should examine in more detail the positive and negative effects on mental health of actual social support available to trauma survivors and the social support seeking behavior on the part of the survivor to tease out this issue further.

Lastly, the results of all of our regression analyses support the hypothesis that participant sex, trauma type, and coping style each uniquely predicted negative mental health outcomes. Each factor was a significant predictor of mental health outcomes in its own right in all of the regression analyses as the addition of each factor led to significant improvements in the regression equations. However, in combination the factors provided a much stronger prediction of negative mental health outcomes for all of our outcome variables. The final regression equations accounted for between 16% and 34% of the outcome variables. The results of this chapter add to the literature showing that the recovery from trauma is complex and that both researchers and clinicians working with trauma survivors should examine the myriad of factors that could lead to negative outcomes in this population (Littleton et al., 2007; Hetzel-Riggin and Roby, 2013; Ozer et al., 2003; Somer et al., 2007).

Limitations

One limitation of the study is the use of college students. College students represent a specific subset of the general population and their experiences may not generalize to members of the general community. While this is a limitation, recent studies have shown that between 67% and 85% of college students encounter events that would meet criteria as a trauma. Ten percent of college students report symptoms consistent with a diagnosis of PTSD (Moser, Hajcak, Simons, and Foa, 2007; Schnider, Elhai, and Gray, 2007; Smyth, Hockemeyer, Heron, Wonderlich, and Pennebaker, 2008). While caution should be taken in generalizing the results of this study to people of different educational, ethnic, and age groups from this sample, the results still may provide initial support for the importance of examining the complex relationship among sex, trauma type, and coping style in trauma survivors.

We also measured only negative outcomes, such as PTSD diagnosis, PTSD symptoms, and other mental health outcomes. Due to the scope of the study, we did not measure other outcomes such as posttraumatic growth, interpersonal functioning, substance use, or trauma revictimization. Future research should replicate and extend the study to see if participant sex, trauma type, and coping style may impact these outcomes differently as compared to negative mental health. In addition, we did not measure all forms of trauma. Previous research has shown that combat exposure (Amir et al., 1996; Rosenheck and Fontana, 1994) and terrorist threat (Dickstein et al., 2012; Somer et al., 2007) also lead to increase negative mental health outcomes, so it will be important to see if the results of the present study can be replicated in these populations.

Littleton and colleagues (2007) identified coping measure as a significant moderator of the relationship between coping style and negative outcomes after a traumatic event. Specifically, they identified the measure we used for this study, the Ways of Coping Scale, as being associated with bigger effect sizes than other coping measures. One possible explanation for the large percentage of the variance explained by coping could be due to the use of this measure. Therefore, the study should be replicated using alternative or multiple measures of coping. We also used self-reported measures; the gold standard in PTSD assessment is the use of a standardized interview and future research should use alternative methods for data collection in order to confirm our findings.

Limitations notwithstanding, the results of the present study show solid support for the strong predictive value of female sex, interpersonal violence exposure, and avoidant coping on the development of negative mental health outcomes in college students. Clinicians working with this population should be aware of these relationships and take note of these risk factors in their assessment, conceptualization, and treatment of trauma survivors. It may also be helpful for colleges and universities, as well as other agencies and organizations that work closely with women and trauma survivors, to educate their students and clients about these relationships in an attempt to minimize their effects. Colleges and universities may even want to begin teaching students in first-year seminar classes about healthy coping styles as a way to protect students from negative outcomes (Hetzel-Riggin and Lindemann, 2012). The results also provide first responders a picture of the most at-risk trauma survivors; it is our hope that future research will show that psychological first aid provided to these at-risk survivors will decrease their negative mental health outcomes.

The authors have no personal, financial, or institutional conflicts of interest to disclose.

ACKNOWLEDGMENTS

The author would like to thank the members of the Coping, Stress, and Trauma Research Lab for their assistance in data collection.

REFERENCES

American Psychiatric Association. (2013). *Diagnostic and statistical manual of mental disorders: DSM-5.* Washington, D.C: American Psychiatric Association.

Amir, M., Kaplan, Z. and Kotler, M. (1996). Type of trauma, severity of posttraumatic stress disorder core symptoms, and associated features. *The Journal of General Psychology, 123*(4), 341-351.

An, Y., Fu, F., Wu, X., Lin, C. and Zhang, Y. (2013). Longitudinal relationships between neuroticism, avoidant coping, and posttraumatic stress disorder symptoms in adolescents following the 2008 Wenchuan earthquake in China. *Journal of Loss and Trauma, 18*(6), 556-571.

Bar-Tal, Y., Lurie, O. and Glick, D. (1994). The effect of gender on the stress process of Israeli soldiers during the Gulf War. *Anxiety, Stress, and Coping, 7*(3), 263-276.

Beltzer, M. L., Nock, M. K., Peters, B. J. and Jamieson, J. P. (2014). Rethinking butterflies: The affective, physiological, and performance effects of reappraising arousal during social evaluation. *Emotion, 14*(4), 761-768.

Bloise, S.M. and Johnson, M.K. (2007). Memory for emotional and neutral information: Gender and individual differences in emotional sensitivity. *Memory, 15*(2), 192-204.

Bloom, F.E., Nelson, C.A. and Lazerson, A. (2001). *Brain, mind, and behavior* (3rd ed.). New York, NY US: Worth Publishers.

Boals, A. (2010). Events that have become central to identity: Gender differences in the centrality of events scale for positive and negative events. *Applied Cognitive Psychology, 24*(1), 107-121.

Bradley, M.M., Codispoti, M., Sabatinelli, D. and Lang, P.J. (2001). Emotion and motivation II: Sex differences in picture processing. *Emotion, 1*(3), 300-319.

Breslau, N. (2009). The epidemiology of trauma, PTSD, and other posttrauma disorders. *Trauma, Violence, and Abuse, 10*(3), 198-210.

Breslau, N., Chilcoat, H. D., Kessler, R. C. and Davis, G. C. (1999). Previous exposure to trauma and PTSD effects of subsequent trauma: Results from the Detroit Area Survey of trauma. *American Journal of Psychiatry, 156*(6), 902-907.

Breslau, N., Chilcoat, H. D., Kessler, R. C., Peterson, E. L. and Lucia, V. C. (1999). Vulnerability to assaultive violence: further specification of the sex difference in post-traumatic stress disorder. *Psychological Medicine, 29*(04), 813-821.

Breslau, N., Davis, G. C., Andreski, P., Peterson, E. L. and Schultz, L. R. (1997). Sex differences in posttraumatic stress disorder. *Archives of General Psychiatry, 54*(11), 1044-1048.

Breslau, N. and Kessler, R. C. (2001). The stressor criterion in DSM-IV posttraumatic stress disorder: an empirical investigation. *Biological Psychiatry, 50*(9), 699-704.

Breslau, N., Kessler, R. C., Chilcoat, H. D., Schultz, L. R., Davis, G. C. and Andreski, P. (1998). Trauma and posttraumatic stress disorder in the community: the 1996 Detroit Area Survey of Trauma. *Archives of General Psychiatry, 55*(7), 626-632.

Brewin, C. R., Andrews, B. and Valentine, J. D. (2000). Meta-analysis of risk factors for posttraumatic stress disorder in trauma-exposed adults. *Journal of Consulting and Clinical Psychology, 68*(5), 748.

Campbell, R., Dworkin, E. and Cabral, G. (2009). Ecological model of the impact of sexual assault on women's mental health. *Trauma, Violence, and Abuse, 10*(3), 225-246.

Chang, C., Lee, L., Connor, K.M., Davidson, J.R.T. and Lai, T. (2008). Modification effects of coping on post-traumatic morbidity among earthquake rescuers. *Psychiatry Research, 158*, 164-171.

Cheng, C. (2003). Cognitive and motivational processes underlying coping flexibility: A dual-process model. *Journal of Personality and Social Psychology, 84*, 425-438.

Cheng, C., Kogan, A. and Chio, J.H.M. (2012). The effectiveness of a new, coping flexibility intervention as compared with a cognitive behavioural intervention in managing work stress. *Work and Stress, 26*, 272-288.

Christiansen, D. M. and Elklit, A. (2008). Risk factors predict post-traumatic stress disorder differently in men and women. *Annals of General Psychiatry, 7*(1), 24.

Chung, H. and Breslau, N. (2008). The latent structure of post-traumatic stress disorder: tests of invariance by gender and trauma type. *Psychological Medicine, 38*(04), 563-573.

Chung, M.C., Walsh, A. and Dennis, I. (2011). Trauma exposure characteristics, past traumatic life events, coping strategies, posttraumatic stress disorder, and psychiatric cormobidity among people with anaphylactic shock experience. *Comprehensive Psychiatry, 52*, 394-404.

Costello, E. J., Erkanli, A., Fairbank, J. A. and Angold, A. (2002). The prevalence of potentially traumatic events in childhood and adolescence. *Journal of Traumatic Stress, 15*(2), 99-112.

Creamer, M., Burgess, P. and McFarlane, A. C. (2001). Post-traumatic stress disorder: findings from the Australian National Survey of Mental Health and Well-being. *Psychological Medicine, 31*(7), 1237-1247.

Cross, M. R. and McCanne, T. R. (2001). Validation of a self-report measure of posttraumatic stress disorder in a sample of college-age women. *Journal of Traumatic Stress, 14*(1), 135-147.

Dardas, L.A. and Ahmad, M.M. (2015). Coping strategies as mediators and moderators between stress and quality of life among parents of children autistic disorder. *Stress Health, 31*, 5-12.

Davis, J. (1999). Effects of trauma on children: Occupational therapy to support recovery. *Occupational Therapy International, 6*(2), 126-142.

Derogatis, L. R. (1983). *SCL-90-R revised manual.* Baltimore: John Hopkins School of Medicine.

Derogatis, L. R., Rickels, K. and Rock, A. F. (1976). The SCL-90 and the MMPI: a step in the validation of a new self-report scale. *The British Journal of Psychiatry, 128*(3), 280-289.

Derogatis, L. R. and Savitz, K. L. (1999). *The SCL-90-R, Brief Symptom Inventory, and Matching Clinical Rating Scales.* Baltimore: John Hopkins School of Medicine.

Dickstein, B.D., Schorr, Y., Stein, N., Krantz, L., Solomon, Z. and Litz, B.T. (2012). Coping and mental health outcomes among Israelis living with the chronic threat of terrorism. *Psychological Trauma: Theory, Research, Practice, and Policy, 4*(4), 392-399.

Ditlevsen, D. N. and Elklit, A. (2010). The combined effect of gender and age on post-traumatic stress disorder: do men and women show differences in the lifespan distribution of the disorder? *Annals of General Psychiatry, 9*(1), 1-12.

Doron-LaMarca, S., Vogt, D. S., King, D. W., King, L. A. and Saxe, G. N. (2010). TI: Title Pretrauma problems, prior stressor exposure, and gender as predictors of change in posttraumatic stress symptoms among physically injured children and adolescents. *Journal of Consulting and Clinical Psychology, 78*(6), 781-793.

Elhai, J.D., Frueh, B., Gold, P.B., Gold, S.N. and Hamner, M.B. (2000). Clinical presentations of posttraumatic stress disorder across trauma populations: A comparison of MMPI-2 profiles of combat veterans and adult survivors of child sexual abuse. *Journal of Nervous and Mental Disease, 188*(10), 708-713.

Elhai, J. D. and Simons, J. S. (2007). Trauma exposure and posttraumatic stress disorder predictors of mental health treatment use in college students. *Psychological Services, 4*(1), 38-45.

Elliott, D. M. (1997). Traumatic events: prevalence and delayed recall in the general population. *Journal of Consulting and Clinical Psychology, 65*(5), 811-820.

Elzy, M., Clark, C., Dollard, N. and Hummer, V. (2013). Adolescent girls' use of avoidant and approach coping as moderators between trauma exposure and trauma symptoms. *Journal of Family Violence, 28,* 763-770.

Epping-Jordan, J. E., Compas, B. E. and Howell, D. C. (1994). Predictors of cancer progression in young adult men and women: avoidance, intrusive thoughts, and psychological symptoms. *Health Psychology, 13*(6), 539-547.

Figley, C. (Ed.), and Leventman, S. (Ed.). (1980). *Strangers at home: Vietnam veterans since the war.* Philadelphia, PA US: Brunner/Mazel.

Fivush, R. (1989). Exploring sex differences in the emotional content of mother-child conversations about the past. *Sex Roles, 20*(11-12), 675-691.

Folkman, S. and Lazarus, R. S. (1985). If it changes it must be a process: study of emotion and coping during three stages of a college examination. *Journal of Personality and Social Psychology, 48*(1), 150-170.

Folkman, S. and Moskowitz, J. T. (2004). Coping: Pitfalls and promise. *Annual Review of Psychology, 55,* 745-774.

Frans, Ö., Rimmö, P.A., Åberg, L.L. and Fredrikson, M.M. (2005). Trauma exposure and post-traumatic stress disorder in the general population. *Acta Psychiatrica Scandinavica, 111*(4), 291-299.

Freh, F.M., Dallos, R. and Chung, M.C. (2012). An exploration of PTSD and coping strategies: Response to the experience of being in a bomb attack in Iraq. *Traumatology, 19*(2), 87-94.

Freyd, J. (1994). Betrayal trauma: Traumatic amnesia as an adaptive response to childhood abuse. *Ethics and Behavior, 4*(4), 307-329.

Galovski, T.E., Mott, J., Young-Xu, Y. and Resick, P.A. (2011). Gender differences in the clinical presentation of PTSD and its concomitants in survivors of interpersonal assault. *Journal of Interpersonal Violence, 26*(4), 789-806.

Gavranidou, M. and Rosner, R. (2003). The weaker sex? Gender and post-traumatic stress disorder. *Depression and anxiety, 17*(3), 130-139.

Goenjian, A. K., Steinberg, A. M., Najarian, L. M., Fairbanks, L. A., Tashjian, M. and Pynoos, R. S. (2000). Prospective study of posttraumatic stress, anxiety, and depressive reactions after earthquake and political violence. *The American Journal of Psychiatry, 157*(6), 911-916.

Grasso, D.J., Cohen, L.H., Moser, J.S., Hajcak, G., Foa, E.B. and Simons, R.F. (2012). Seeing the silver lining: Potential benefits of trauma exposure in college students. *Anxiety, Stress, and Coping, 25*(2), 117-136.

Green, B.L., Krupnick, J.L., Stockton, P., Goodman, L., Corcoran, C. and Petty, R. (2001).

Psychological outcomes associated with traumatic loss in a sample of young women. *American Behavioral Scientist, 44*(5), 817-837.

Green, B.L., Krupnick, J.L., Stockton, P., Goodman, L., Corcoran, C. and Petty, R. (2005). Effects of adolescent trauma exposure on risky behavior in college women. *Psychiatry: Interpersonal and Biological Processes, 68*(4), 363-378.

Gross, J. J. and John, O. P. (2003). Individual differences in two emotion regulation processes: Implications for affect, relationships, and well-being. *Journal of Personality and Social Psychology, 85*(2), 348-362.

Han, Y., Hu, D., Liu, Y., Lu, C., Luo, Z., Zhao, J., Lopez, V. and Mao, J. (2014). Coping styles and social support among depressed Chinese family caregivers of patients with esophageal cancer. *European Journal of Oncology Nursing, 18,* 571-577.

Hanson, T. C., Hesselbrock, M., Tworkowski, S. H. and Swan, S. (2002). The prevalence and management of trauma in the public domain: An agency and clinician perspective. *The Journal of Behavioral Health Services and Research, 29*(4), 365-380.

Hassija, C. M., Luterek, J. A., Naragon-Gainey, K., Moore, S. A. and Simpson, T. (2012). Impact of emotional approach coping and hope on PTSD and depression symptoms in a trauma exposed sample of veterans receiving outpatient VA mental health care services. *Anxiety, Stress and Coping, 25*(5), 559-573.

Held, P., Owens, G. P., Schumm, J. A., Chard, K. M. and Hansel, J. E. (2011). Disengagement coping as a mediator between trauma-related guilt and PTSD severity. *Journal of Traumatic Stress, 24*(6), 708-715.

Hetzel-Riggin, M.D. and Lindemann, D.F. (2012, November). *Preliminary evidence for emotion regulation training for incoming freshman college students.* Poster presented at the annual meeting of the Association for Behavioral and Cognitive Therapies, Baltimore, MD.

Hetzel-Riggin, M.D. and Roby, R.P. (2013). Trauma type and gender effects on PTSD, general distress, and peritraumatic dissociation. *Journal of Loss and Trauma, 18*(1), 41-53.

Holahan, C. J., Moos, R. H., Holahan, C. K., Brennan, P. L. and Schutte, K. K. (2005). Stress generation, avoidance coping, and depressive symptoms: a 10-year model. *Journal of Consulting and Clinical Psychology, 73*(4), 658-666.

Irish, L.A., Fischer, B., Fallon, W., Spoonster, E., Sledjeski, E.M. and Delahanty, D.L. (2011). Gender differences in PTSD symptoms: An exploration of peritraumatic mechanisms. *Journal of Anxiety Disorders, 25*(2), 209-216.

Janoff-Bulman, R. (1992). *Shattered assumptions: Towards a new psychology of trauma.* New York, NY: Free Press.

Karstoft, K. I., Armour, C., Elklit, A. and Solomon, Z. (2015). The role of locus of control and coping style in predicting longitudinal PTSD-trajectories after combat exposure. *Journal of Anxiety Disorders, 32,* 89-94.

Kelley, L.P., Weathers, F.W., McDevitt-Murphy, M.E., Eakin, D.E. and Flood, A.M. (2009). A comparison of PTSD symptom patterns in three types of civilian trauma. *Journal of Traumatic Stress, 22*(3), 227-235.

Kessler, R.C. (2000). Posttraumatic stress disorder: The burden to the individual and to society. *Journal of Clinical Psychiatry, 61*(Suppl 5), 4-14.

Kessler, R. C., Sonnega, A., Bromet, E., Hughes, M. and Nelson, C. B. (1995). Posttraumatic stress disorder in the National Comorbidity Survey. *Archives of General Psychiatry, 52*(12), 1048-1060.

Kilpatrick, D.G., Acierno, R., Resnick, H.S., Saunders, B.E. and Best, C.L. (1997). A 2-year longitudinal analysis of the relationships between violent assault and substance use in women. *Journal of Consulting and Clinical Psychology, 65*(5), 834-847.

King, D. W., King, L. A., Foy, D. W. and Gudanowski, D. M. (1996). Prewar factors in combat-related posttraumatic stress disorder: structural equation modeling with a national sample of female and male Vietnam veterans. *Journal of Consulting And Clinical Psychology, 64*(3), 520-531.

King, D.W., King, L.A., Foy, D.W., Keane, T.M. and Fairbank, J.A. (1999). Posttraumatic stress disorder in a national sample of female and male Vietnam veterans: Risk factors, war-zone stressors, and resilience-recovery variables. *Journal of Abnormal Psychology, 108*(1), 164-170.

Kira, I. A., Omidy, A. Z. and Ashby, J. S. (2014). Cumulative trauma, appraisal, and coping in Palestinian and American Indian adults: Two cross-cultural studies. *Traumatology, 20*(2), 119-133.

Kirz, J.L., Drescher, K.D., Klein, J.L., Gusman, F.D. and Schwartz, M.F. (2001). MMPI-2 assessment of differential post-traumatic stress disorder patterns in combat veterans and sexual assault victims. *Journal of Interpersonal Violence, 16*(7), 619-639.

Kolassa, I. T., Ertl, V., Eckart, C., Kolassa, S., Onyut, L. P. and Elbert, T. (2010). Spontaneous remission from PTSD depends on the number of traumatic event types experienced. *Psychological Trauma: Theory, Research, Practice, and Policy, 2*(3), 169-174.

Krupnick, J.L., Green, B.L., Stockton, P., Goodman, L., Corcoran, C. and Petty, R. (2004). Mental health effects of adolescent trauma exposure in a female college sample: Exploring differential outcomes based on experiences of unique trauma types and dimensions. *Psychiatry: Interpersonal and Biological Processes, 67*(3), 264-279.

Kubany, E. S., Haynes, S. N., Leisen, M. B., Owens, J. A., Kaplan, A. S., Watson, S. B. and Burns, K. (2000). Development and preliminary validation of a brief broad-spectrum measure of trauma exposure: the Traumatic Life Events Questionnaire. *Psychological Assessment, 12*(2), 210-224.

Laufer, A. and Solomon, Z. (2006). Posttraumatic symptoms and posttraumatic growth among Israeli youth exposed to terror incidents. *Journal of Social and Clinical Psychology, 25*(4), 429-447.

Lazarus, R.S. and Folkman, S. (1984). Stress, appraisal, and coping. New York, NY: Springer.

Leiva-Bianchi, M., Baher, G. and Poblete, C. (2012). The effects of stress coping strategies in post-traumatic stress symptoms among earthquake survivors. an explanatory model of post-traumatic stress. *Terapia Psicológica, 30*(2), 51-59.

Lilly, M. M. and Valdez, C. E. (2012). Interpersonal trauma and PTSD: The roles of gender and a lifespan perspective in predicting risk. *Psychological Trauma: Theory, Research, Practice, and Policy, 4*(1), 140-144.

Littleton, H., Horsley, S., John, S. and Nelson, D. V. (2007). Trauma coping strategies and psychological distress: a meta-analysis. *Journal of Traumatic Stress, 20*(6), 977-988.

Luthra, R., Abramovitz, R., Greenberg, R., Schoor, A., Newcorn, J., Schmeidler, J., et al., (2009). Relationship between type of trauma exposure and posttraumatic stress disorder among urban children and adolescents. *Journal of Interpersonal Violence, 24*(11), 1919-1927.

Luxton, D.D., Skopp, N.A. and Maguen, S. (2010). Gender differences in depression and PTSD symptoms following combat exposure. *Depression and Anxiety, 27*(11), 1027-1033.

Macdonald, A., Danielson, C. K., Resnick, H. S., Saunders, B. E. and Kilpatrick, D. G. (2010). PTSD and comorbid disorders in a representative sample of adolescents: The risk associated with multiple exposures to potentially traumatic events. *Child Abuse and Neglect, 34*(10), 773-783.

Maguen, S., Ren, L., Bosch, J. O., Marmar, C. R. and Seal, K. H. (2010). Gender differences in mental health diagnoses among Iraq and Afghanistan veterans enrolled in veterans affairs health care. *American Journal of Public Health, 100*(12), 2450-2456.

McManis, M. H., Bradley, M. M., Berg, W. K., Cuthbert, B. N. and Lang, P. J. (2001). Emotional reactions in children: Verbal, physiological, and behavioral responses to affective pictures. *Psychophysiology, 38*(2), 222-231.

Monet, A. and Lazarus, R.S, eds. (1985). *Stress and coping: An anthology* (2nd ed.). New York, NY: Columbia University Press.

Moser, J.S., Hajcak, G., Simons, R.F. and Foa, E.B. (2007). Posttraumatic stress disorder symptoms in trauma-exposed college students: The role of trauma-related cognitions, gender, and negative affect. *Journal of Anxiety Disorders, 21*(8), 1039-1049.

Muldoon, O. T. and Trew, K. (2000). Children's experience and adjustment to political conflict in Northern Ireland. *Peace and Conflict: Journal of Peace Psychology, 6*(2), 157.

Niedźwieńska, A. (2003). Gender differences in vivid memories. *Sex Roles, 49*(7-8), 321-331.

Nelson, K. and Fivush, R. (2004). The emergence of autobiographical memory: A social cultural developmental theory. *Psychological Review, 111*(2), 486-511.

Norris, F. H., Foster, J. D. and Weisshaar, D. L. (2002). The epidemiology of sex differences in PTSD across developmental, societal, and research contexts. In R. Kimerling, P. Ouimette, and J. Worlfe's (eds.). *Gender and PTSD* (pp. 3-42). New York, NY: Guilford.

Nuttman-Shwartz, O. and Dekel, R. (2009). Ways of coping and sense of belonging in the face of a continuous threat. *Journal of Traumatic Stress, 22*(6), 667-670.

Orcutt, H. K., Pickett, S. M. and Pope, E. B. (2005). Experiential avoidance and forgiveness as mediators in the relation between traumatic interpersonal events and posttraumatic stress disorder symptoms. *Journal of Social and Clinical Psychology, 24*(7), 1003-1029.

Ozer, E. J., Best, S. R., Lipsey, T. L. and Weiss, D. S. (2003). Predictors of posttraumatic stress disorder and symptoms in adults: A meta-analysis. *Psychological Bulletin, 129*(1), 52-73.

Parker, H. A. and McNally, R. J. (2008). Repressive coping, emotional adjustment, and cognition in people who have lost loved ones to suicide. *Suicide and Life-Threatening Behavior, 38*(6), 676-687.

Pereira, A. (2002). Combat trauma and the diagnosis of post-traumatic stress disorder in female and male veterans. *Military Medicine, 167*(1), 23-27.

Peveler, R. C. and Fairburn, C. G. (1990). Measurement of neurotic symptoms by self-report questionnaire: validity of the SCL-90R. *Psychological medicine, 20*(4), 873-879.

Prati, G., Pietrantoni, L. and Cicognani, E. (2011). Coping strategies and collective efficacy as mediators between stress appraisal and quality of life among rescue workers. *International Journal of Stress Management, 18*(2), 181-195.

Rasmusson, A.M., Vythilingam, M. and Morgan, C. (2003). The neuroendocrinology of posttraumatic stress disorder: New directions. *CNS Spectrums, 8*(9), 651-667.

Read, J. P., Ouimette, P., White, J., Colder, C. and Farrow, S. (2010). Rates of DSM–IV–TR trauma exposure and posttraumatic stress disorder among newly matriculated college students. *Psychological Trauma: Theory, Research, Practice and Policy, 3*(2), 148-156.

Rosenheck, R. and Fontana, A. (1994). Utilization of mental health services by minority veterans of the Vietnam era. *The Journal of Nervous and Mental Disease, 182*(12), 685-691.

Schnider, K.R., Elhai, J.D. and Gray, M.J. (2007). Coping style use predicts posttraumatic stress and complicated grief symptom severity among college students reporting a traumatic loss. *Journal of Counseling Psychology, 54*(3), 344-350.

Smyth, J.M., Hockemeyer, J.R., Heron, K.E., Wonderlich, S.A. and Pennebaker, J.W. (2008). Prevalence, type, disclosure, and severity of adverse life events in college students. *Journal of American College Health, 57*(1), 69-76.

Shakespeare-Finch, J. and Armstrong, D. (2010). Trauma type and posttrauma outcomes: Differences between survivors of motor vehicle accidents, sexual assault, and bereavement. *Journal of Loss and Trauma, 15*(2), 69-82.

Somer, E., Ruvio, A., Sever, I. and Soref, E. (2007). Reactions to repeated unpredictable terror attacks: relationships among exposure, posttraumatic distress, mood, and intensity of coping. *Journal of Applied Social Psychology, 37*(4), 862-886.

Stein, M. B., Walker, J. R. and Forde, D. R. (2000). Gender differences in susceptibility to posttraumatic stress disorder. *Behaviour Research and Therapy, 38*(6), 619-628.

Taylor, S.E., Klein, L., Lewis, B.P., Gruenewald, T.L., Gurung, R.R. and Updegraff, J.A. (2000). Biobehavioral responses to stress in females: Tend-and-befriend, not fight-or-flight. *Psychological Review, 107*(3), 411-429.

Tolin, D. F. and Foa, E. B. (2006). Sex differences in trauma and posttraumatic stress disorder: A quantitative review of 25 years of research. *Psychological Bulletin, 132*(6), 959-992.

Ullman, S. E., Peter-Hagene, L. C. and Relyea, M. (2014). Coping, emotion regulation, and self-blame as mediators of sexual abuse and psychological symptoms in adult sexual assault. *Journal of Child Sexual Abuse, 23*(1), 74-93.

Watson, C. G., Juba, M. P., Manifold, V., Kucala, T. and Anderson, P. E. (1991). The PTSD interview: Rationale, description, reliability, and concurrent validity of a DSM-III-based technique. *Journal of Clinical Psychology, 47*(2), 179-188.

Webb, R.E. and Widseth, J.C. (2009). Traumas with and without a sense of agency. *Journal of Aggression, Maltreatment and Trauma, 18*(5), 532-546.

Yehuda, R. (2002). Post-traumatic stress disorder. *The New England Journal of Medicine, 346*(2), 108-114.

Zeidner, M. and Endler, N. S. (1996). *Handbook of coping: Theory, research, applications* New York, NY: John Wiley and Sons.

In: Psychological Distress
Editors: A. Compare, C. Elia, A. G. Simonelli et al.
ISBN: 978-1-63485-405-4

Chapter 5

SPSD - A NEW RATING SCALE FOR PSYCHOLOGICAL DISTRESS IN ADOLESCENCE: A VALIDATION STUDY ON A NATIONWIDE ITALIAN COHORT OF 31,661 ADOLESCENTS

Enzo Grossi*[1]*, Gabriele Manella*[2]*, Giovanni Pieretti*[2]*,
***Bruno Genetti*[3]*, Milena Sperotto*[3] *and Paolo Vian*[3]**
[1]Villa Santa Maria Institute, Milan, Italy
[2]Department of Sociology - University of Bologna, Italy
[3]EXPLORA – Research and Statistical Analysis,
Vigodarzere (Padua), Italy

ABSTRACT

In this paper we present a new rating scale for adolescent psychological distress based on an Italian population study carried out in a cohort of 31,661 adolescents, and analyzed with Rasch Analysis in addition to the traditional tests.

The Italian epidemiological survey on drug use in the school population was conducted by the Department of Anti Drug Policies in the first six months of 2014. It was based on a methodology of the European Monitoring Centre for Drugs and the Drug Addiction (EMCDDA - European School Survey Project on Alcohol and Other Drugs - ESPAD). The questionnaire and the survey procedures were taken from ESPAD and adjusted modified in order to address the specific characteristics of to the Italian school system.

The total population sample consisted on 31,661 15-19 years old students who attended Italian public high schools.

Among the items in the source scale we have selected nine items belonging to three dominions (Energy, Emotional Stability, Impulsivity and Risk-Taking) from which we expected the maximal indirect relation to wellbeing state and therefore as complement, to distress. To evaluate the psychometric properties of distress scale we carried out the homogeneity analysis or internal consistency of the scale, using the Cronbach's alpha coefficient, and analysis of the validity of the scale, using the Gamma coefficient of

Goodman and Kruskal - index rank correlation. The data dimensionality was explored using Rasch Analysis and factor analysis.

The Cronbach's alpha obtained considering all items was to 0.694, making it quite satisfactory and meeting the standards criteria of acceptability. Rasch analysis confirmed the items validity and that the items distribution remains in the area of the tolerance defined.

A very good distribution emerges with a complete absorption of possible values along the scale range; neither ceiling or floor effect is observed.

Whereas the level of distress measured by the scale is higher the lower the score detected, it is observed a significantly higher level of distress in females than in males (52.59 vs 59.61).

For all psychotropic substances analyzed,significantly higher levels of distress in consumers than non-consumers have been found. In addition,the level of distress as measured by the scale appears to increase going from users of "soft" drugs to users of "hard" drugs: - 57.18 is the mean value obtained in the distress scale from the group of students who say they have never used any illegal drug; - 53.00 is the mean value obtained in the distress scale from the group of students who report use of cannabis at least once in their life; - 50.18 is the mean value obtained in the distress scale from the group of students who report use of cocaine at least once in their life; - 47.95 is the mean value obtained in the distress scale from the group of students who report use of heroin at least once in their life. This survey has detected several factors/conditions associated to the use of substances, which can be considered a reliable proxy of psychological distress: family background seems to be very important as well as the relationship with parents; this emerged as regards the presence of rules on behavior outside the home, the quality of relationships with prominent adult figures (particularly the father), their leadership role, and the family harmony.

Keywords: adolescents, distress, well-being, SPSd scale

INTRODUCTION

The literature about quality of life has growth exponentially in the last 40 years. Health related quality of life has attracted the interest of scholars and has been increasingly used as outcome measure in many settings, including clinical research, population health surveys, and clinical practice. Most of these studies regarded adults populations, even if the number of tools available for adolescents has also increased; a 2008 review identified 30 generic and 64 disease-specific tools available for use in children and adolescents (Solans et al. 2008).

While adult definitions of Quality of Life (QoL) can be applied to adolescents, other factors can affect QoL in children and adolescents (Matza et al. 2004). Despite recent developments, instruments used to assess QoL in children and adolescents still show problems relating of international comparability and may not take into account different cultural perspectives during their construction (WHO 1994).

Another problem is the psychometric validation, frequently carried out in samples of small size. The only exception is the Kidscreen, which has been validated in a sample of 22,827 children and adolescents from 13 European countries (Ravens-Sieberer et al. 2014) and has showed excellent psychometric properties as a result of a rigorous development process. Very seldom however the psychometric validation has considered the use of Rasch Analysis as methodological approach (Rasch 1980).

In this paper we present a new rating scale for adolescent psychological distress based on a Italian general population study carried out in a cohort of 31,661 adolescents and analyzed with Rasch Analysis in addition to traditional tests.

The Rasch model, named after the statistician Georg Rasch, is a psychometric model for categorical data, such as answers to questions on a reading assessment or questionnaire responses, as a function of the trade-off between (a) the respondent's abilities, attitudes or personality traits and (b) the item difficulty (Bezruczko 2005). For example, they may be used to estimate a student's reading ability, or a person's attitude to capital punishment from responses on a questionnaire. In addition to psychometrics and educational research, the Rasch model and its extensions are used in other areas, including the health profession (Bezruczko 2005) and market research (Bechtel 1985) because of their general applicability (Wright 1977).

The mathematical theory underlying Rasch models is a special case of item response theory and, more generally, a special case of a generalized linear model. However, there are important differences in the interpretation of the model parameters and its philosophical implications (Linacre 2005), that separate proponents of the Rasch model from the item response modeling tradition. A central aspect of this divide concerns the role of specific objectivity (Rasch 1977), a defining property of the Rasch model, as a requirement for successful measurement.

MATERIALS AND METHODS

The European School Survey Project on Alcohol and Other Drugs – ESPAD in Italy

The Italian epidemiological survey on drug use in the school population was conducted by the Department of Anti Drug Policies in the first six months of 2014. It was based on a methodology of the European Monitoring Centre for Drugs and the Drug Addiction (EMCDDA - European School Survey Project on Alcohol and Other Drugs - ESPAD). The questionnaire and the survey procedures were taken from ESPAD and adjusted modified in order to address the specific characteristics of to the Italian school system.

Sampling Plan

The total population sample consisted on 15-19 years old students who attended Italian public high schools.

The following sampling units features were considered:

- basic investigation unit through self-completed online questionnaire: 15-19 years old students who attended high school institutes;
- first step sampling unit: high school institutes;
- second step sampling unit: classes activated in each type of institute.

The sampling plan can be defined as a "two-stage with stratification at the first and second step, and cluster of elementary investigation units within the sampling units of the second step."

The first step sampling units (school institutes) were stratified by geographical area (North Western Italy, North Eastern Italy, Central Italy, and Southern Italy) and by type of school (high school and former teachers training schools, technical schools, vocational schools, and art schools).

The second step sampling units (classes within each extracted school institute) have been classified by year of course activated (1st, 2nd, 3rd, 4th, and 5th). The following stratification criteria were used:

- geographical area of the school institute;
- the type of school institute;
- the year of the course of classes (cluster of students) to be selected (one class for each year activated in every school of the sample, a criterion strongly correlated with the age of students).

The choice of these criteria was based on their relation with the variability of the characteristics of the group subject to estimation or hypothesis testing, as it also emerged from previous editions of this survey.

Questionnaire

In order to collect information comparable with other European Union states countries, the questionnaire was prepared through the European protocol, which was slightly changed to addresses the Italian case. The 2014 survey was supported by computer technology through the C.A.S.I. method (Computer-Aided Self-Completed Interview), which made possible to fill out the questionnaire through an online access code that was anonymous and not replicable. Online version provides more privacy than paper version; this aspect was stressed to students before they filled out their questionnaire, in order to get them free to express their opinion and personal experience.

The questionnaire consisted of 420 questions, which could be 238 in case of no substance use. The questions were direct and simple, and implemented on-line sequentially. The online administration requested 30-45 minutes for each student.

The questionnaire consisted of nine sections:

1. demographic data and leisure time activities, school performance and regularity in support to the family;
2. experience about tobacco use;
3. experience about alcohol use;
4. use of tranquilizers or sedatives with a medical prescription;
5. drug use by type, frequency, quantity, age of first use, place of recruitment, knowledge about drugs and how to find them;

6. CAST - Cannabis Abuse Screening Test and SDS - Severity of Dependence Scale (Beck and Legleye 2003), to detect problem cannabis use and the degree of psychological dependence;
7. amount of money spent during the last 30 days for purchasing psychotropic substances, peers and brothers/sisters behavior about this use, and risk perception about this use;
8. family background and opinion about family atmosphere;
9. self-perception, impulsive behaviors, and risk behaviors.

Construction of the Wellbeing-Distress Scale

Among the items present in the source scale we have selected the following nine items belonging to three dominions from which we expected the maximal indirect relation to wellbeing state and therefore as complement, to distress:

Energy

1. I am an active and vigorous person
2. I put a lot of energy in the things I do

Emotional Stability

3. I am a relaxed person
4. I can dominate the states of anxiety
5. My mood is rather stable
6. I seldom enter the agitation for something

Impulsivity and Risk-Taking

7. I act on impulse of the moment
8. Other people would call me impulsive
10. I often say and do things without considering the consequences

Each item has the following possible answers: Completely disagree, Partially disagree, Nether agree nor disagree, Partially agree, Completely agree.

Participation in the Survey

438 secondary school institutes took part to the survey; it was the 70.8% of the 619 included in the sampling plan. The participation was lower in Central Italy (61.9%) and Southern Italy (66.8%), while it was higher in North Eastern Italy (83.7%). As regards the type of institute, technical schools and high schools reported the highest participation rate (74.5% and 72.7% respectively), while art schools reported the lowest one (59.0%).

The participation rate has also been assessed through the percentage of completed questionnaires compared to the questionnaires expected. The study plan included an entire career for each school, from the first to the fifth class, for approximately 80 students. 34,922 students filled out the questionnaire, for a participation rate of 70.5%. This value, however, was affected for defect by the absence of full careers in some institutes, especially in the art schools. Many institutes, in particular the vocational schools, do not always activate five-year courses in favor of two-year or three-year courses; as a consequence, the average number of entries students enrolled is lower as well as the number of survey participants.

The participation rate was lower in art schools and vocational schools (57.7% and 60.2%) compared to technical schools and high schools (75.0% and 76, 9%).

Quality Analysis of the Data Collected

The computer version of the questionnaire included the activation of automatic system filters for some answers given by students. This structure of detection guaranteed high quality of consistency of the answers.

The quality analysis of collected data was also done through some exclusion criteria. The step 1 was the exclusion of questionnaires filled out by under 15 and over 19 year old students (2,700 questionnaires). The step 2 was the exclusion of questionnaires with unreliable answers about drug use (447 questionnaires).The step 3 consisted in eliminating the questionnaires where students said to use the "drug owl" (a drug that does not exist), alone or in combination with other psychotropic substances (114 questionnaires).

At the end of this procedure, 31,661 questionnaires remained as valid for the analysis (the 90.7% of the collected ones).

Statistical Analysis

To evaluate the psychometric properties of distress scale we carried out the homogeneity analysis or internal consistency of the scale, using the Cronbach's alpha coefficient, and analysis of the validity of the scale, using the Gamma coefficient of Goodman and Kruskal - index rank correlation. This analysis was performed through the SPSS software package release 18.0 (SPSS Inc. 2009).

The data dimensionality was explored using Rasch Analysis and factor analysis.

Initially, we performed a Rasch Analysis on the data encoded with a score from 0 to 4. The Rating Scale analysis (the items always have the same scale) was performed using the WINSTEPS and Facets Rasch (Linacre 2005).

Rasch measurement takes ordinal level data and converts the probability of endorsing an item to a logit. If the items satisfy the expectations of the Rasch model, scale score can be transformed into internal level measurement and it is possible to provide a total score by summing up the scale item scores.

The WINSTEPS reliability estimated was executed to provide an estimate of cohesion of the items (person and item reliability estimates). More importantly, the fit of each item to the model can also be investigated. There are two fit measures, Infit and Outfit, which both reflect the ratio of the observed variance to what we would expect from Rasch model. The

Rach analysis also provides the Differential item functioning (DIF) to compare item responses for different groups (e.g., for male and female participants), so that we can be sure that the scale is not biased towards either sex or other variables (Allisona et al. 2015).

Lastly, factor analysis has also been used to examine the factor structure of items that fit the Rasch model and to determine factor weights to be assigned to each item: factorial analysis is precisely the results of the analysis and the procedure used to calculate the factor loadings, reference for the definition of the indicator of synthesis for the distress scale. Factor analysis was performed using the Mplus 5.21 software (Muthen and Muthen 1998).

The underlying hypothesis of factor analysis is that the observed item responses are designed to measure a theoretically continuum construct. The most common method of estimation is Maximum Likelihood (ML), a technique which assumes that the observed variables are continuous and normally distributed. Polychoric correlation can be used as input for algorithms in case of discrete variables (Rasch 1980). The explorative factor analysis (EFA) was carried out on about 70% of the whole sample without missing values; followed by a confirmatory factor analysis (CFA) on the remaining set (30%).

The non-parametric Wilcoxon-Mann Whitney's rank-sum test (for two samples) and the non-parametric Kruskal-Wallis test (for more than two samples) have been used for comparing mean values of the distress scale between the different groups object of analysis, due to the non-Normal distribution of these scores, performed using the SPSS software package release 18.0 (SPSS Inc. 2009). When the latter was used, the Bonferroni adjustment was applied in order to know which pairs of groups or conditions were significantly different.

General Data about Participating Students: Sample Profile

The 31,661 students who took part in the survey are equally distributed by gender and age (Table 1) with a slight decrease in 15 years old and 19 years old (this is also due to a higher proportion of participating students from these cohorts who were excluded by the analysis, in particular in the fifth class).

Table 1. Absolute and percentage distribution of students who filled out the questionnaire by gender and age, 2014

GENDER	AGE											
	15 years old		16 years old		17 years old		18 years old		19 years old		Total	
	N	%	N	%	N	%	N	%	N	%	N	% col
Males	3,165	20.2	3,283	20.9	3,297	21.0	3,127	19.9	2,817	18.0	15,689	49.6
Females	2,962	18.5	3,250	20.3	3,325	20.8	3,439	21.5	2,996	18.8	15,972	50.4
Total	**6,127**	**19.4**	**6,533**	**20.6**	**6,622**	**20.9**	**6,566**	**20.7**	**5,813**	**18.4**	**31,661**	**100.0**

Source: SPS-DPA 2014 survey – Department for Anti Drug Policies.

The distribution of the sample in relation to the type of institute is: 40.1% of participating students came from High schools and former teacher training schools, 33.6% from Technical schools, 16.0% from Vocational schools, and 10.3% from Art schools. As regards the geographical areas, 39.6% of students attended schools in Southern Italy, 25.0% in North

Western Italy, 18.9% in North Eastern Italy, and 16.5% in Central Italy. There are no significant gender or age differences in these geographical areas (Table 2).

Table 2. Absolute and percentage distribution of students who filled out the questionnaire, by geographical area and type of school, 2014

GEOGRAPHIC AREA	TYPE OF SCHOOL									
	High School and former teacher training schools		Technical schools		Vocational schools		Art schools		Total	
	N	%	N	%	N	%	N	%	N	%
North Western Italy	3,504	44.0	2,643	33.4	1,050	13.3	715	9.0	7,912	25.0
North Eastern Italy	2,109	35.2	1,930	32.2	1,223	20.4	729	12.2	5,991	18.9
Central Italy	1,679	32.2	2,101	40.3	842	16.1	597	11.4	5,219	16.5
Southern Italy	5,397	43.0	3,952	31.5	1,957	15.6	1,233	9.8	12,539	39.6
Total	**12,689**	**40.1**	**10,626**	**33.6**	**5,072**	**16.0**	**3,274**	**10.3**	**31,661**	**100.0**

Source: SPS-DPA 2014 survey – Department for Anti Drug Policies.

Psychometric Characteristics of the Items of SPDd Scale

Table 3 shows the absolute and percentage frequency according to the degree of agreement / disagreement assigned by the students interviewed on the 9 items selected for the construction of the distress scale.

The highest level of agreement is observed in the items that measure the personality trait related to energy: 1.I am an active and vigorous person (66.7% Partially or Completely agree), 5.I put a lot of energy in the things I do (64.7%). The lowest agreement has been assigned, instead, to the items concerning impulsivity, and in particular 8.Other people would call me impulsive (29.7%), 9.I often say and do things without considering the consequences (28.5%).

The level of agreement of all items that measure the trait of personality related to emotional stability, was significantly higher in male students than female students: 2.I am a relaxed person (61.9% in males VSvs 48.7% in females), 3.I can dominate the states of anxiety (53.5% in males vs 38.7% in females), 4.My mood is rather stable (54.4% in males vs 39.3% in females), 6.I seldom enter the agitation for something (42.2% in males vs 32.5% in females). Contrarily, the level of agreement of all the items that measure the impulsiveness is higher in female students, in particular: 7.I act on impulse of the moment (40.1% in males vs 48.7% in females), 8.Other people would call me impulsive (25.7% in males vs 33.7% in females).

There are no significant differences in the percentages of agreement by the age of the students, in all the nine items selected for the construction of distress scale; a slight increase with age emerges only in the item 8.Other people would call me impulsive: 27.1% in 15 years old, 29.8% in 17 years old and 32.8% in 19 years old.

Table 3. Distribution (absolute and %) of students by items of the distress scale, 2014

Item	Completely disagree	Partially disagree	Nether agree nor disagree	Partially agree	Completely agree	No response
1.I am an active and vigorous person	1,809 (5.7%)	2,370 (7.5%)	5,503 (17.4%)	11,872 (37.5%)	9,255 (29.2%)	852 (2.7%)
2.I am a relaxed person	2,948 (9.3%)	3,944 (12.5%)	6,391 (20.2%)	11,084 (35.0%)	6,442 (20.3%)	852 (2.7%)
3.I can dominate the states of anxiety	4,286 (13.5%)	5,040 (15.9%)	6,855 (21.7%)	8,897 (28.1%)	5,731 (18.1%)	852 (2.7%)
4.My mood is rather stable	4,297 (13.6%)	4,539 (14.3%)	7,126 (22.5%)	9,602 (30.3%)	5,245 (16.6%)	852 (2.7%)
5.I put a lot of energy in the things I do	1,584 (5.0%)	1,968 (6.2%)	6,772 (21.4%)	11,199 (35.4%)	9,286 (29.3%)	852 (2.7%)
6.I seldom enter the agitation for something	5,494 (17.4%)	5,829 (18.4%)	7,645 (24.1%)	7,322 (23.1%)	4,519 (14.3%)	852 (2.7%)
7.I act on impulse of the moment	3,948 (12.5%)	4,323 (13.7%)	8,307 (26.2%)	9,152 (28.9%)	4,897 (15.5%)	1,034 (3.3%)
8.Other people would call me impulsive	6,748 (21.3%)	5,445 (17.2%)	9,039 (28.5%)	5,703 (18.0%)	3,692 (11.7%)	1,034 (3.3%)
9.I often say and do things without considering the consequences	8,132 (25.7%)	5,928 (18.7%)	7,515 (23.7%)	6,031 (19.0%)	3,021 (9.5%)	1,034 (3.3%)

Source: SPS-DPA 2014 survey – Department for Anti Drug Policies.

Table 4. Percentages of observed agreement by items of the distress scale, by gender, age, geographical area and type of school, 2014

	1.I am an active and vigorous person	2.I am a relaxed person	3.I can dominate the states of anxiety	4.My mood is rather stable	5.I put a lot of energy in the things I do	6.I seldom enter the agitation for something	7.I act on impulse of the moment	8.Other people would call me impulsive	9.I often say and do things without considering the consequences
Males	68.5	61.9	53.5	54.4	65.3	42.2	40.1	25.7	27.0
Females	64.9	48.7	38.7	39.3	64.1	32.5	48.7	33.7	30.2
15 years old	67.9	39.6	45.4	49.6	65.2	39.6	43.6	27.1	29.0
16 years old	66.6	36.7	45.0	46.5	63.4	36.7	44.1	29.0	28.9
17 years old	65.5	36.1	45.6	44.5	63.8	36.1	44.8	29.8	29.5
18 years old	66.9	37.9	47.8	46,6	65.3	37.9	44.5	29.8	27.6
19 years old	66.9	36.8	47.3	47.6	66.0	36.8	44.9	32.8	27.8
North Western Italy	65.5	35.1	46.2	45.0	63.3	35.1	42.5	28.0	27.9
North Eastern Italy	64.6	33.6	45.0	44.6	60.6	33.6	42.2	27.1	27.6
Central Italy	65.9	35.6	43.9	46.5	64.9	35.6	44.0	29.2	27.2
Southern Italy	68.9	41.5	47.7	49.3	67.5	41.5	46.7	32.1	30.1
High School and former teacher training school	69.3	35.5	46.5	46.6	67.2	35.5	45.7	30.6	28.1
Technical School	67.3	39.0	47.9	49.2	64.2	39.0	43.6	28.6	28.6
Vocational School	62.4	38.2	44.3	45.8	60.5	38.2	42.5	29.1	29.1
Art School	61.9	38.3	42.4	42.2	63.0	38.3	44.7	30.4	29.7

Source: SPS-DPA 2014 survey – Department for Anti Drug Policies.

Table 5. Cronbach's alpha analysis for the distress scale

	Scale Mean if Item Deleted	Scale Variance if Item Deleted	Corrected Item-Total Correlation	Cronbach's Alpha if Item Deleted
1.I am an active and vigorous person	25.99	30.908	.352	.672
2.I am a relaxed person	26.33	28.821	.477	.647
3.I can dominate the states of anxiety	26.57	28.036	.495	.641
4.My mood is rather stable	26.56	27.420	.560	.627
5.I put a lot of energy in the things I do	25.98	30.718	.385	.666
6.I seldom enter the agitation for something	26.80	28.890	.423	.657
7.I act on impulse of the moment	27.00	32.378	.188	.703
8.Other people would call me impulsive	26.59	31.620	.224	.698
9.I often say and do things without considering the consequences	26.45	31.308	.240	.695

Table 6. Goodman and Kruskal's Gamma cograduation coefficients for the distress scale

		1. I am an active and vigorous person	2. I am a relaxed person	3. I can dominate the states of anxiety	4. My mood is rather stable	5. I put a lot of energy in the things I do	6. I rarely enter in agitation for something	7. I act on impulse of the moment	8. Other people would call me impulsive
2. I am a relaxed person	Valore	.321**							
	P value	.000							
3. I can dominate the states of anxiety	Valore	.301**	.390**						
	p-value	.000	.000						
4. My mood is rather stable	Valore	.313**	.405**	.395**					
	P value	.000	.000	.000					
5. I put a lot of energy in the things I do	Valore	.453**	.249**	.286**	.415**				
	P value	.000	.000	.000	.000				
6. I rarely enter in agitation for something	Valore	.230**	.318**	.402**	.402**	.279**			
	P value	.000	.000	.000	.000	.000			
7. I act on impulse of the moment	Valore	.134**	.013**	.015**	.005	.140**	.036**		
	P value	.000	.005	.001	.254	.000	.000		
8. Other people would call me impulsive	Valore	.109**	.028**	.000	.034**	.091**	.027**	.632**	
	P value	.000	.000	.956	.000	.000	.000	.000	
9. I often say and do things without considering the consequences	Valore	.012*	.028**	.040**	.065**	.020**	.009*	.413**	.414**
	pvalue	.013	.000	.000	.000	.000	.043	.000	.000

*Correlation is significant at the 0.05 level (2-tailed).

**Correlation is significant at the 0.01 level (2-tailed).

As regards geographical areas, the highest degree of agreement, for all the selected items, was found for students from institutes in Southern Italy. The high schools and former teacher training schools have the highest level of agreement over the items that measure the personality trait related to energy: 1.I am an active and vigorous person (69.3%), 5.I put a lot of energy in the things I do (67.2%).

Albeit with slight differences, students from technical schools show, however, the highest level of agreement in all the items measuring emotional stability: 2.I am a relaxed person (39.0%), 3.I can dominate the states of anxiety (47.9%), 4.My mood is rather stable (49.2%), 6.I seldom enter the agitation for something (39.0%).

The Cronbach's alpha obtained considering all items was 0.694, making it quite satisfactory and meeting the standards criteria of acceptability (Bagozzi 1994) (Pedhazur and Schemelkin 1991). The column "Corrected Item-Total Correlation" (Table 5) contains the Pearson correlation coefficients between the scores obtained by that item and the sum of the scores obtained from the remaining items. As we can see, the item with the lowest correlation coefficient is the item 7 (I act on impulse of the moment).

The column "Cronbach's Alpha if Item Deleted," however, describes how the reliability of the scale is affected by each item. It shows the Cronbach's alpha coefficient in case that item is excluded from the analysis. As we can see from this column, the exclusion of any item would make a not significant increase in the coefficient.

Cograduation analysis (Goodman and Kruskal Gamma) shows that some items have high coefficients (e.g., Item8-Item7), while other have low coefficients (e.g., Item8-Item4). All coefficients are highly significant ($p < .001$), with the exception of that between Item4-Item7, Item3-Item8 and Item9-Item6 (Table 6).

Rasch Analysis

The Rasch Model can be used to evaluate the extent to which the data conform to the model. More specifically, item fit statistics (calculated as the standardized means -across all students- of the difference between observed scores and those expected by the model on every item) indicate which items are eliciting data with poor fit to the model and why the lack of fit has occurred (Pagani and Zanotti 2003).

In the case of the items of the distress scale we are not concerned only with whether an item is correct, but also on how characteristic a positive response would be for high and low "stressed." A participant with high overall scores on the distress scale would be expected to definitely agree with items that are measuring this dimension. The logic and statistical procedures, however, are the same as if the distress scale was an ability measure. In addition, the use of Differential Item Functioning (DIF) techniques to help detect item bias is also included in this category of types of validity (internal structure) evidence (Choi et. al 2006)

In order to apply the Rasch Analysis, the answer to each item were recoded into scores. Recoding for the positive items was: Completely disagree → 0, Partially disagree → 1, Nether agree nor disagree → 2, Partially agree → 3, Completely agree → 4; instead, recording for the negative items was as follows: Completely disagree → 4, Partially disagree → 3, Nether agree nor disagree → 2, Partially agree → 1, Completely agree → 0.

Goodness of Fit Analysis

Regarding the goodness of fit, we considered the following reliability tests: Person separation index and Cronbach's alpha (person separation reliability). The summary analysis shows that the item reliability was high at 1.00, which indicated that the item difficulties (in this case likelihood of agreement) were very likely to replicate if the items were given to another sample. The person reliability was acceptable (0.64), which indicated that the ordering of participants in terms of their distress was likely to replicate if they were given another parallel set of items. The Rasch Analysis can also analyze the consistency of the responses measured in each questionnaire, highlighting the inconsistent probabilistically questionnaires (MISFIT): through this analysis have been identified about 2,300 PERSON MISFIT.

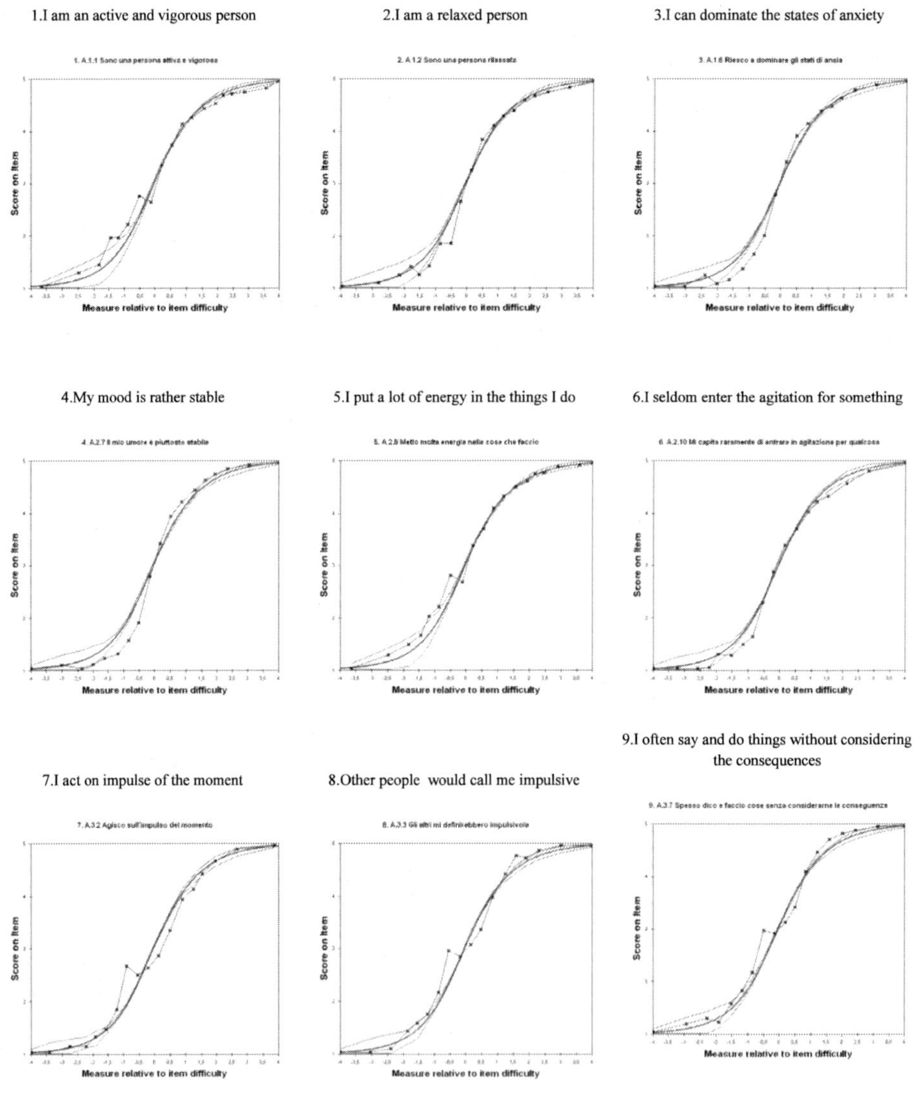

Figure 1. Item Characteristic Curve (ICC) for the items of the distress scale.

Items Validity

The estimation of item parameters location provides a "ranking" of items which allows to determine the level of agreement given to each item. The nine items present difficulties ranging from a minimum of -0.46 to a maximum of 0.47 (a difference of 1 logit), with a mean of 0 and a standard deviation of 0.29. The item for which it is easier to agree is the 7 (I act on impulse of the moment), while the one for which it is more difficult to agree is the item 5 (I put a lot of energy in the things I do).

More importantly, the fit of each item to the model can also be investigated. There are two fit measures, Infit and Outfit, which both reflect the ratio of the observed variance to what we would expect from the Rasch model. Infit, however, is weighted to reduce the effect of outliers or extreme responses. Item Infit and Outfit statistics were examined: a fit value of 1 indicates perfect fit (L).

The indexes of input and Outfit range from a minimum of 0.77 to a maximum of 1.26 and indicate a good fit of the model: none of the items showed measure fit out of the range (0.6-1.4 for Likert scale). In detail, item 7, 8, and 9 show a fit of 1.26, which indicates 26% of higher variation in observed data in comparison to that predicted by Rasch model while item 4 shows a fit of 0.77, showing 23% of lower variation in observed data in comparison to that predicted by Rasch model.

Graphically the misfit of the items can be appreciated by Item Characteristic Curve (ICC). Figure 1 shows ICC for the nine items: on the whole we can see a good fit to the Rasch model for all items. For some items (1 and 9) is noted, however, that the observed probabilities (blue asterisks) are higher than would be expected (red curve) for the smaller skills and lower than those expected for the larger skills. It is a typical example where the item does not discriminate sufficiently between individual skills (under discrimination) and the cause is often linked to a violation of the hypothesis of one-dimensionality (the item goes to grasp not only the object variable of the measurement but also another variable). For other items (3 and 4), we can see the opposite case: the values observed are arranged in the most inclined manner to what would require the model. It is a typical case of over discrimination, that is a case where the item discriminates too much between students' skills (small variations of skill produce large variations in the frequency of correct answers), often linked to a response dependence problem (item responses also depend on how a student responded to other items).

The bubble-chart in Figure 2, confirms that the items distribution remains in the area of the tolerance defined by the Rasch model (validity range), thus showing that all items fit well in the Rasch model prediction. Consider that the greater the dispersion of the items with respect to the central axis and minor is the coherence of the whole model (model validity). It is noted that the item 4 (My mood is rather stable) is placed in the space at a lower consistency while the items are 8 and 9 are situated in the opposite outer space.

In the bubble-chart we can see the overlap of the estimates of the parameters of the items position on the continuum (measures), which might correspond to a conceptual overlap: the items 8 and 9 on the one hand, as well as the items 1 and 5 on the other, could be the same measure of a single aspect of the distress scale. In either case, under review of the measuring instrument, it would probably be appropriate to replace these items with only two sets of items, which are then "redundant." After careful analysis, although it is clear the overlap of the above item, below and to the right of the graph shows that precisely these two blocks of items represent two important components of the distress scale: impulsiveness and energy, which together to stability emotional (another aspect represented by other items), allow a better reading of the phenomenon and a better understanding of the different areas investigated.

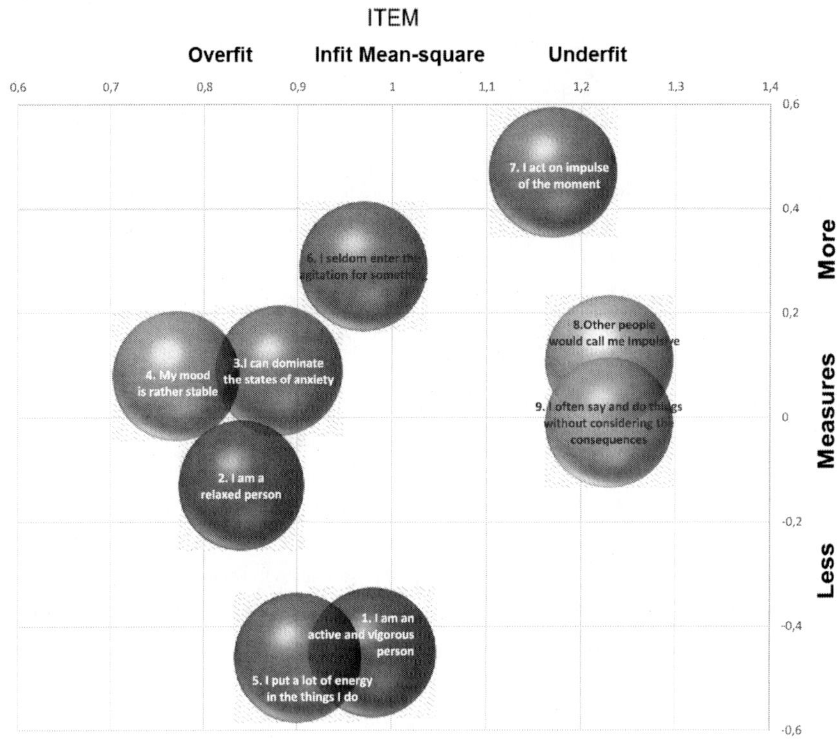

Figure 2. Graphical "bubbles" representation of the items distribution in the interior and exterior space to the validity of the model.

Differential Item Functioning (DIF)

Differential Item Functioning (DIF) in psychometric tests has been recognized as a potential source of bias in person measurement. Originally called `item bias', the analysis of DIF is concerned with the identification significant differences, across group membership, of the proportion of individuals at the same apparent ability level who answer a given item correctly (or can do a particular task). If an item measures the same ability in the same way across groups then, except for random variations, the same success rate should be found irrespective of the nature of the group. Items that give different success rates for two or more groups, at the same ability level, are said to display DIF (Bechtel 1985).

DIF can be investigated with Rasch Analysis by comparing item difficulty measures (in this case likelihood of agreement) from different groups; it indicates that one group of respondents is scoring better than another group of respondents on an item. One method of comparing item functioning is to conduct a t test comparison of item measure scores from this group of respondents.

In the Figure 3, graphics DIF related to four groups were represented: gender, age, type of institute and geographical areas. Were highlighted the items that have a t> | 4 | for at least one pair inside the specific group. It emerges that both gender differences and differences by type of institute are transversal to all items. As regards analysis by age, however, the differences among the item difficulty measures mainly concern item 3 (I can dominate the states of anxiety) and item 8 (Other people would call me impulsive). As regards geographical areas, differences emerge especially in items related to impulsivity (7.I act on impulse of the moment; 8.Other people would call me impulsive; 9.I often say and do things without considering the consequences).

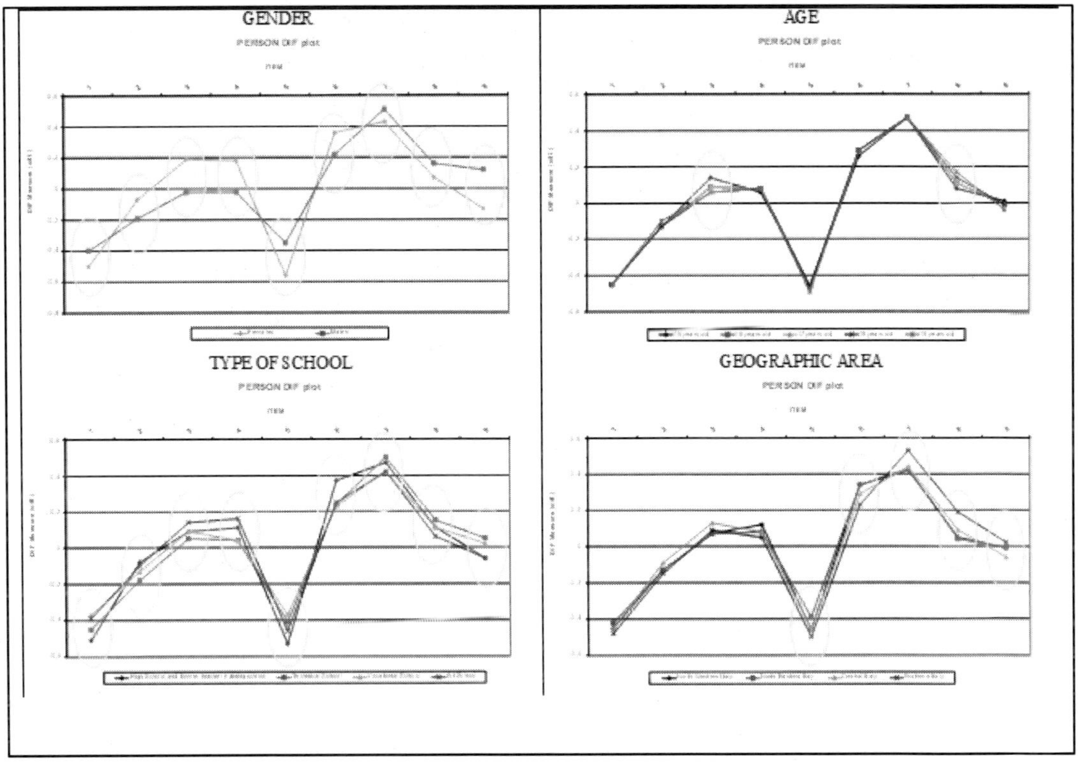

Legend: 1.I am an active and vigorous person; 2.I am a relaxed person; 3.I can dominate the states of anxiety; 4.My mood is rather stable; 5.I put a lot of energy in the things I do; 6.I seldom enter the agitation for something; 7.I act on impulse of the moment; 8.Other people would call me impulsive; 9.I often say and do things without considering the consequences.

Figure 3. Differential Item Functioning (DIF) by items of the distress scale, by gender, age, geographical area and type of school.

Factor Analysis

The analytical approach chosen is based on a factor analysis aimed at highlighting the correlation between the considered statements about personality. The purpose is to summarize and simplify the information on the relationships among statements: the factorial analysis is a multivariate statistical technique that allows, in fact, to obtain a reduction of the complexity of the phenomenon. The aim, therefore, is determining a lower number of "latent" factors with respect to the number of starting variables, which allow to calculate a synthetic indicator of distress, obtained from the final weights associated with the variables.

In order to perform this analysis of the distress scale, from the sample with 31,661 records, we deleted the records with missing values in at least one item considered and the questionnaires of the students that result PERSON MISFIT from the Rasch Analysis (as a result, final records were 28,334).

An exploratory factor analysis (EFA) of performance scores was performed on 19,842 questionnaires (70% of the sample). The reliability analysis performed in the EFA sub-sample shows a Cronbach's Alpha of 0.689, indicating an acceptable internal consistency.

Through the scree-test, we have derived principal components and eigenvalues. The solution found by Mplus is the two-factor solution (eigenvalues greater than 1). There are two eigenvalues greater than 1 (Table 7), for which are extracted two main components that explain, together, 63% of the variance.

Table 7. Eigenvalues for Exploratory Factor Models of the distress scale

Factors	Initial Eigenvalues		
	Total	% Variance	Cumulative %
1	2.919	32.43	32.43
2	2.188	24.31	56.74
3	0.938	10.42	67.16
4	0.720	8.00	75.16
5	0.590	6.55	81.71
6	0.541	6.01	87.72
7	0.490	5.44	93.17
8	0.366	4.07	97.23
9	0.249	2.77	100.00

Table 8. CFA results for the two-factors solution: STD Standardization

Items	Estimate	S.E.	EST./S.E.	p-value (t-student)
Factor 1				
2.I am a relaxed person	0.598	0.008	72.020	0.000
3.I can dominate the states of anxiety	0.649	0.008	83.074	0.000
4.My mood is rather stable	0.731	0.007	104.533	0.000
6.I seldom enter the agitation for something	0.598	0.008	72.006	0.000
1.I am an active and vigorous person	0.561	0.009	61.993	0.000
5.I put a lot of energy in the things I do	0.609	0.008	75.149	0.000
Factor 2				
7.I act on impulse of the moment	0.864	0.007	130.030	0.000
8.Other people would call me impulsive	0.855	0.007	128.148	0.000
9.I often say and do things without considering the consequences	0.581	0.008	72.792	0.000
Factor 1 with Factor 2	0.042	0.012	3.382	0.001

CFI (0.986) and TLI (0.977) indicated good fit, as well as RMSEA (0.067) that was lower than 0.1 and SRMR (0.020) that is lower than 0.9.

Confirmatory factor analysis (CFA) was performed on 8,492 students (30% of the sample) (Table 8). Confirmatory factor analysis of capacity scores suggested that two dimension was an acceptable model of the distress scale. Althought CFI (0.929) and TLI (0.934) measures showed a good fit, RMSEA was 0.116 (higher than 0.1), suggesting poor fit (Linleya et al. 2009).

Finally, all unstandardized and standardized factor loadings are were statistically significant ($p < .000$). The R-square output (Table 9) showed that large amounts of variance were accounted for by the item 7 (I act on impulse of the moment) and the item 8 (Other people would call me impulsive). All the other variables had a R-square with values between 0.3 and 0.75 (Pryor et al. 2008).

Table 9. CFA results for the two-factors solution: R-SQUARE values

Items	Estimate	Residual Variance
1.I am an active and vigorous person	0.315	0.685
2.I am a relaxed person	0.358	0.642
3.I can dominate the states of anxicty	0.421	0.579
4.My mood is rather stable	0.535	0.465
5.I put a lot of energy in the things I do	0.371	0.629
6.I seldom enter the agitation for something	0.358	0.642
7.I act on impulse of the moment	0.747	0.253
8.Other people would call me impulsive	0.732	0.268
9.I often say and do things without considering the consequences	0.337	0.663

Application of the Distress Scale to the Students Sample

After the factor analysis, a synthetic indicator was built: as coefficients of the model, they were used the final weights, obtained starting from the factor weights associated with each item and the respective contributions of the two factors to explanation of variability. The score so obtained has been transformed dividing by the constant (100/4), so as to obtain final scores varying from 0 to 100.

Figure 4 shows the distribution of the total score in the surveyed sample. A very good distribution emerges with a complete absorption of possible values along the scale range; neither ceiling or floor effect is observed.

The Table 10 presents the results of distress scale, constructed according to the method of calculation described above, in sub-groups of students surveyed, identified on the basis of certain characteristics: gender, age, area of residence, type of institute, consumption of psychotropic substances in the last month or at least once in life.

Whereas the level of distress measured by the scale is higher the lower the score detected, it is observed a significantly higher level of distress in females than in males (52.59 vs 59.61).

Table 10. Descriptive statistics of the distress scale between the different groupings object of analysis and significance of the non-parametric tests

	N	Mean Score	95% Confidence Interval for Mean Lower Bound	95% Confidence Interval for Mean Upper Bound	Median	Std. Deviation	p-value
Total sample	28,334	**56.00**	55.81	56.19	56.25	16.25	-
Males	14,570	**52.59**	52.32	52.87	52.75	16.84	0.000*
Females	13,764	**59.61**	59.36	59.86	59.25	14.76	
15 years old	5,478	**57.05**	56.62	57.48	57.25	16.23	0.000**
16 years old	5,875	**55.57**	55.15	55.99	56.00	16.47	
17 years old	5,916	**55.44**	55.03	55.85	55.50	16.18	
18 years old	5,860	**56.26**	55.84	56.67	56.50	16.02	
19 years old	5,205	**55.74**	55.30	56.18	56.25	16.29	
North Western Italy	7,124	**55.46**	55.07	55.84	55.75	16.45	0.000**
North Eastern Italy	5,409	**55.62**	55.19	56.05	56.00	16.02	
Central Italy	4,652	**55.84**	55.38	56.30	56.13	16.04	
Southern Italy	11,149	**56.61**	56.30	56.91	56.75	16.29	
High School and former teacher training school	11,762	**55.74**	55.43	56.04	56.25	16.83	0.000**
Technical School	9,404	**56.83**	56.52	57.14	56.75	15.47	
Vocational School	4,231	**55.79**	55.32	56.26	56.00	15.63	
Art School	2,937	**54.70**	54.09	55.32	55.00	17.02	
No tobacco use during the last 30 days	17,638	**58.21**	57.97	58.44	58.25	15.95	0.000*
Tobacco use during the last 30 days	10,696	**52.37**	52.06	52.67	52.75	16.07	
No alcohol use during the last 30 days	11,211	**57.91**	57.60	58.22	58.00	16.66	0.000*
Alcohol use during the last 30 days	17,123	**54.75**	54.51	54.99	55.25	15.85	
No getting drunk during the last 30 days	23,758	**56.71**	56.51	56.92	56.75	16.28	0.000*
Getting drunk during the last 30 days	4,576	**52.31**	51.86	52.76	52.75	15.54	
No Binge-Drinking during the last 30 days	20,084	**56.97**	56.75	57.20	57.00	16.32	0.000*
Binge-Drinking during the last 30 days	8,250	**53.64**	53.30	53.98	54.00	15.83	
No use of illegal drugs in life	20,386	**57.18**	56.96	57.40	57.25	16.19	0.000*
Use of illegal drugs at least once in life	7,948	**52.97**	52.62	53.33	53.50	16.01	
Cannabis use at least once in life	7,591	**53.00**	52.64	53.36	53.50	16.00	
Ecstasy use at least once in life	443	**49.80**	48.15	51.45	49.75	17.69	
Amphetamines use at least once in life	281	**49.74**	47.65	51.84	50.00	17.81	
Heroine use at least once in life	73	**47.95**	44.18	51.71	47.25	16.14	
Cocaine use at least once in life	557	**50.18**	48.87	51.48	51.25	15.67	
Stimulants use at least once in life	577	**49.64**	48.23	51.05	50.00	17.25	
Hallucinogens use at least once in life	760	**51.87**	50.67	53.07	51.75	16.84	
No risk	2,766	**55.10**	54.52	55.69	55.75	15.68	0.000**
Low risk	1,494	**52.52**	51.71	53.33	53.00	15.96	
Moderate risk	1,714	**51.17**	50.39	51.94	51.63	16.33	
High risk	623	**49.54**	48.30	50.77	50.25	15.73	
No psychological dependence	5,629	**53.55**	53.13	53.97	54.00	16.05	0.000**
Mild psychological dependence	883	**49.86**	48.84	50.88	50.75	15.44	
Severe psychological dependence	85	**46.72**	43.22	50.23	46.00	16.25	

* Mann-Whitney Test - ** Kruskal-Wallis Test.

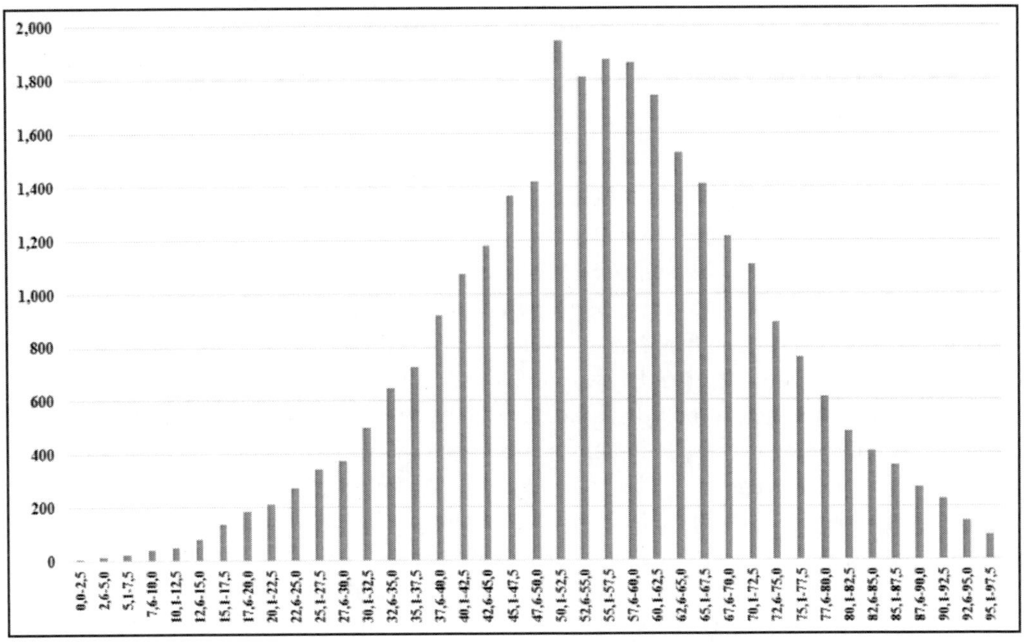

Figure 4. Distress scale scores distribution in the general population of thc survey.

For all psychotropic substances analyzed, significantly higher levels of distress in consumers than non-consumers have been found. In addition,the level of distress as measured by the scale appears to increase going from users of "soft" drugs to users of "hard" drugs:

- 57.18 is the mean value obtained in the distress scale from the group of students who say they have never used any illegal drug;
- 53.00 is the mean value obtained in the distress scale from the group of students who report use of cannabis at least once in their life;
- 50.18 is the mean value obtained in the distress scale from the group of students who report use of cocaine at least once in their life;
- 47.95 is the mean value obtained in the distress scale from the group of students who report use of heroin at least once in their life.

Discussion

Children's and adolescents' wellbeing is a topic that concerns many stakeholders: families above all, but also educators, researchers and policy makers. Only after 1990s nineties' scholars have started to work intensively on methodologies and instruments able to describe the psychological status of children and adolescents in term of wellbeing or distress, despite the emergence of positive psychology. This is rather surprising since happiness is one of the first emotions experienced by children (Pollak and Sinha 2002) and that it entails positive benefits for their well-being. Generally speaking, wellbeing has been described as global life satisfaction, the presence of positive emotions and the relative absence of negative emotions, and in a specular manner distress. Being typically a multidimensional construct historically there has been little agreement on the assessment of wellbeing-distress, leading researchers to use multiple different measures, to better capture the distinct facets that cover this construct.

The Psychological General Well-Being Index (Dupuy 1990) is one of the most popular instrument and is a measure of the level of subjective psychological wellbeing. In detail it assesses self-representations of intra-personal affective or emotional states reflecting a sense of subjective well-being or distress, and thus captures what we could call a subjective perception of well-being. By standardized 22-items, the tool produces a singles measure of psychological well-being and, for the long form, its components: anxiety, depression, positive wellbeing, self-control, general health and vitality.

Six items short version of PGWBI was developed by Grossi et al. in 2006 (Grossi 2006) as part of the MiOS project, a multidisciplinary initiative to study in depth different kinds of subjective outcome measures for the health assessment, on a representative sample of 1,129 Italian citizens above 15 years old. The main objective of this study was to reduce the number of items of the original 22-item PGWBI while keeping adequate validity of the instrument. The purpose of the item reduction was to increase the compliance of the questionnaire so that it could be administered in relatively short time and by phone. Based on these data, the twenty-two items of the questionnaire were analyzed in a linear multiple regression model with the objective to find the combination of items most relevant for the description of the summary measure. The items were identified by a step-wise selection starting with the item that would explain alone the highest degree of variance of the original PGWBI and in combination at least 90% of the variance. In the model the items were matched to find out which of their combination would best reproduce the average score for the summary measure. The most predictive items were selected to be part of the new structure of the questionnaire PGWB-S.

Despite the number of studies cross-sectional and longitudinal which have highlighted the strong psychometric properties of the instrument and its correlation with a large number of other indices of medical, mental health and in different contexts (communities, institutions, hospitals) (e.g., Wiklund et al. 1991; Omvik et al. 1993; Havelund et al. 1999; Boman et al. 2001) PGWBI has been confined to adults with the exception of few studies dealing with adolescents above 15 years old.

Also the Oxford Happiness Questionnaire–Short Form (Hills and Argyle 2002) is frequently used to assess children's and adolescents' happiness or well-being. Despite being widely used (e.g., Egan et al. 2014), it has received some criticisms because it may overlap with other constructs such as extraversion and agreeableness (Kashdan 2004).

The questionnaire developed and presented in this study seems very promising for a number of reasons.

The construct we followed in selecting the items of the instrument is rather new. Instead to work on items directly expressing the perception of positive emotions, life satisfaction or positive wellbeing, we rather sampled the psychological state of the adolescent subject indirectly, asking questions about Energy (2 items), Emotional Stability (4 items) and Impulsivity and risk-taking (3 items).

Another point of strength is the remarkable dimension of the sample size of the survey, which is one of the largest in all literature.

This survey took place in Italian high schools through an online questionnaire widely used in Europe (ESPAD, 2011) focusing the use of drugs among 31,661 students and the associated risk factors, namely socio-economic determinants for substance use.

This survey has detected several factors/conditions associated to the use of substances, which can be considered a reliable proxy of psychological distress: family background seems to be very important as well as the relationship with parents; this emerged as regards the presence of rules on behavior outside the home, the quality of relationships with prominent adult figures (particularly the father), their leadership role, and the family harmony. Living with just one parent or no parents, spending money without parental control and, above all, the lack of interest by parents on places and friends frequented: all these indicators are possibly associated to drug use. In general, boys have less parental control than their females peers have, and this can lead to a greater possibility of involvement in a possible drug use by friends. Other studies show that adolescents with unsatisfactory relationships with their parents are more inclined to try illegal substances, increasing the risk of developing problem behaviors.

The size makes feasible and reliable a number of statistical analyses necessary to outline and validate the psychometric properties of the instrument. A part from classical approaches like Cronbach's alpha, the Rasch analysis deserve major attention since it is a unique approach of mathematical modeling based upon a latent trait and accomplishes both stochastic (probabilistic) and conjoint additivity. The model assumes that the probability of a given person/item interaction (in terms of rating high or low) is only governed by the difficulty of the item and the ability of the person, that are determined by the item locations on the presumed latent variable along with the rating scale structure.

One interesting result emerging from this survey is the gender differences between males and females highlighted by our data. This finding it is not surprising: non-medical research on SWB (Ahuvia 2002; Bell 2006; Diener and Lucas 2000; Diener and Suh 2000) has repeatedly supported the notion that there are no significant gender differences when it comes to the indicators of subjective well-being (Andrews and Withey 1976; Barnes and Kaase 1979; Myers and Diener 1995) other surveys have also shown the opposite trend.

The gap however is clearly shown by instruments such as the PGWBI used in medical research though being originated from the social sciences. For example, a survey performed on a large Italian sample aiming to norm the national Italian version of the PGWBI (Grossi et al. 2002) showed an average gender difference in the total score of the PGWBI between the two genders in favor of males ($P = 0.000$). and Such finding were replicated in a recent 2011 research with an 1,500 Italian sample (Grossi et al. 2011) besides of as well as in the present this study.

A similar gender differential can be seen in data produced by other psycho-social instruments used in medical research such as in those relative to the Mental Health domain both in the Italian norming survey of the SF-36 (Apolone et al. 1997) and on that the US version of the SF-36 in 1998.

A recent study published by Grossi et al. regarding the population living in Milano, confirms this finding. In that study the impact profile of nine major determinants on subjective well-being resulted to be clearly different in the two genders. Health status dominates in both, but its impact is higher in females than in males. The obtained results remained substantially unchanged also when the two gender groups were matched according to civil status and income level distribution. Whatever the difference in constructs between types of SWB, the instruments' data shown in this article seem to be sound and reasonable since they confirm the hypothesis underlying this work (Grossi et al. 2013).

Obviously, some limitations of this survey must be considered. First, as in other national prevalence studies, the results are based on self-reported information of participating students; this may underestimate the adolescent substance use. Second, the sample did not include people from 15 to 19 years old who already dropped school, and they could be more at risk of drug use. Third, the on-line version could affect more the results than the paper version does, in particular for the different perception of anonymity of the information provided. Caution is requested, then, to compare these results with the ones of other national surveys.

One limitation of the present work is that the validity of the results is exclusively confined to the Italian setting. It might be anticipated that further analyses of foreign data from other countries could ultimately lead to a different item selection. As a result, this method might help to identify country-specific questionnaires which could be used in national and international environment.

References

Allisona, C., Baron-Cohen, S, Stone, M. H. and Muncera, S. J. (2015). Rasch Modeling and Confirmatory Factor Analysis of the Systemizing Quotient-Revised (SQ-R) Scale. *The Spanish Journal of Psychology*/Volume 18/2015, e16, 1-11.

Andrews, F. M. and Withey, S. B. (1976). Social indicators of well-being: Americans' perceptions of life quality. New York: Plenum.

Ahuvia, A. C. (2002). Individualism/collectivism and cultures of happiness: A theoretical conjecture on the relationship between consumption, culture and subjective well-being at the national level. *Journal of Happiness Studies,* 3, 23–36.

Barnes, S. H. and Kaase, M. (1979). Political action: Mass participation in five western democracies. Beverly Hills. CA: Sage Publications.

Bagozzi, R. P. (1994). Measurement in marketing research: Basic principles of questionnaire design. In Principles of marketing research, edited by Bagozzi, R. P., 1-49. Cambridge. MA: Blackwell.

Bechtel, G. G. (1985). Generalizing the Rasch model for consumer rating scales. Marketing Science, 4(1), 62-73, doi:10.1287/mksc.4.1.62.

Beck, F. and Legleye, S. (2003). Drogues et adolescence. Usages de drogues et contextes d'usage entre 17 et 19 ans, évolutions récentes. *ESCAPAD* 2002, Rapport OFDT.

Bell, D. (2006). Review of research into subjective wellbeing and its relation to sport and culture. In Scottish Executive (Ed.), Quality of life and wellbeing: Measuring the benefits of culture and sport: Literature review and thinkpiece, Annex 1. Edinburgh: Scottish Executive.

Boman, U. W., Bryman, I., Halling, K. and Moller, A. (2001). Women with Turner syndrome: psychological well-being, self-rated health and social life. *J Psychosom Obstet Gynaecol*, 22 (2), 113-22.

Bezruczko, N. (2005). Rasch measurement in health sciences. Maple Grove. MN: Jam Press.

Choi, Y., Mericle, A. and Harachi, T. W. (2006). Using Rasch Analysis to Test the Cross-Cultural Item Equivalence of the Harvard Trauma Questionnaire and the Hopkins

Symptom Checklist Across Vietnamese and Cambodian Immigrant Mothers. *J Appl Meas*, 7(1), 16-38.

Diener, E. and Lucas, R. E. (2000). Explaining differences in societal levels of happiness: Relative standards, needs fulfillment, culture, and evaluation theory. *Journal of Happiness Studies*, 1, 41-78.

Diener, E. and Suh, E. M. (eds.). (2000). Culture and subjective well-being. Cambridge, MA: Mit Press.

Dupuy, H. J. (1990). The Psychological General Well-being (PGWB) index. In Assessment of quality of life in clinical trials of cardiovascular therapies, edited by Wenger, N. K., Mattson, M. E., Furburg, C. D. and Elinson, J., 170-183. New York: Le Jacq Publishing.

Egan, V., Chan, S. and Shorter, G., (2014). The Dark Triad, happiness, and subjective well-being. *Personality and Individual Differences*, 67, 17–22.

Flora, D. B. and Curran, P. J. (2004). An empirical evaluation of alternative methods of estimation for confirmatory factor analysis with ordinal data. *Psychological Methods*, 9, 466-491.

Grossi, E., Compare, A., Lonardi, C., Cerutti, R., Callus, E. and Niero, M. (2013). Gender-related Effect of Cultural Participation in Psychological Well-being: Indications from the Well-being Project. *In Municipality of Milan Social Indicators Research*, 114:2, 255-271.

Grossi, E., Tavano Blessi, G., Sacco, P. L. and Buscema, M. (2012). The interaction between culture healthand psychological well-being: Data mining from the Italian culture and well-being project. *Journal of Happiness Studies*, 13(1), 129–148.

Grossi, E., Sacco, P. L., Tavano Blessi, G. and Cerutti, R, (2011). The impact of culture on the individual subjective well-being of the Italian population: An exploratory study. *Applied Research Quality Life*, 6, 387–410.

Grossi, E., Mosconi, P., Groth, N., Niero, M. and Apolone, G. (2002). IL Questionario Psychological General Well Being. Questionario per la valutazione dello stato generale di benessere psicologico. Versione Italiana. Istituto di Ricerche Farmacologiche "Mario Negri," Milan.

Havelund, T., Lind, T., Wiklund, I., Glise, H., Hernqvist, H., Lauritsen, K., Lundell, L., Pedersen, S. A., Carlsson, R., Junghard, O., Stubberod, A. and Anker-Hansen, O. (1999). Quality of life in patients with heartburn but without esophagitis: effects of treatment with omeprazole. *J Gastroenterol,* 94 (7), 1782-9.

Linacre, J. M., (2010). WINSTEPS® Rasch measurement computer program. Beaverton. Oregon: Winsteps.com.

Linacre, J. M., (2005). Rasch dichotomous model vs. One-parameter Logistic Model. *Rasch Measurement Transactions*, 19:3, 1032.

Linleya, P. A., Maltbyb, J., Woodc, A. M., Osborned, G. and Hurlingd, R. (2009). Measuring happiness: The higher order factor structure of subjective and psychological well-being measures. *Personality and Individual Differences,* Volume 47, Issue 8, 878-884.

Matza, L. S., Swensen, A. R., Flood E. M., Secnik, K. and Leidy, N. K. (2004). Assessment of health-related quality of life in children: a review of conceptual. methodological. and regulatory issues. *Value in Health*, 7(1). 79-92, doi:10.1111/j.1524-4733.2004.71273.x.

Myers, D. G. and Diener, E. (1995). Who is happy? *Psychological Science*, 6, 10–19.

Muthén, L. K. and Muthén, B. O. (1998-2009). Mplus Version 5.21. Base Program and Combination Add-On.

Kashdan, T. B. (2004). The assessment of subjective well-being (issues raised by the Oxford Happiness Questionnaire). *Personality and Individual Differences,* 36, 1225-1232.

OECD. (2008). Handbook on Constructing Composite Indicators METHODOLOGY AND USER GUIDE. OECD.

Omvik, P., Thaulow, E., Herlan, O. B., Eide, I., Midha, R. and Turner, R. R. (1993). Double-blind, parallel, comparative study on quality of life during treatment with amlodipine or enalapril in mild or moderate hypertensive patients: a multicenter study. *J Hypertens*, 11: 103-113.

Pedhazur, E. J. and Schmelkin. L. (1991). Measurement. design and analysis. An integrated approach. New York: Erlbaum.

Pollak, S. D. and Sinha, P. (2002). Effects of early experience on children's recognition of facial displays of emotion. *Developmental Psychology*, 38, 784–791.

Pryor, L. R., Miller, J. D. and Gaughan, E. T. (2008). A comparison of the psychological entitlement scale and the narcissistic personality inventory's entitlement scale: Relations with general personality traits and personality disorders. Journal of Personality, *Assessment*, 90, 517-520.

Rasch, G. (1980). Probabilistic models for some intelligence and attainment tests. Copenhagen. Danish Institute for Educational Research Expanded edition: The University of Chicago Press.

Rasch, G. (1977). On Specific Objectivity: An attempt at formalizing the request for generality and validity of scientific statements. The Danish Yearbook of Philosophy, 14, 58-93.

Ravens-Sieberer, U., Herdman, M., Devine, J., Otto, C., Bullinger, M., Rose, M. and Klasen, F. (2014). The European KIDSCREEN approach to measure quality of life and well-being in children: development, current application, and future advances. *Qual Life Res*, 3:791-803, doi: 10.1007/s11136-013-0428-3.

Smith, R. M., Schumacker, R. E. and Bush, M. J. (1998). Using item mean squares to evaluate fit to the Rasch model. *J Outcome Meas*, 2:66-78.

Solans, M., Pane, S., Estrada, M.-D., Serra-Sutton, V., Berra, S., Herdman, M., Alonso, J. and Rajmil, L. (2008). Health-related quality of life measurement in children and adolescents: A systematic review of generic and disease-specific instruments. *Value in Health*, 11(4), 742-764.

SPSS Inc. (Released 2009). PASW Statistics for Windows, Version 18.0. Chicago: SPSS Inc.

Whiteneck, G. and Dijkers, M. P. (2009). Difficult to measure constructs: conceptual and methodological issues concerning participation and environmental factors. Arc Phys Med Rehab, 90 (Suppl. 1): S22-S35.

Wiklund, I. and Karlberg, J. (1991). Evaluation of quality of life in clinical trials: selecting quality of life measures. *Controlled Clin Trials*, 12: S204-16.

World Health Organization-Division of Mental Health (1994). Measurement of quality of life in children. MNH/PSF/94.5. Geneva: World Health Organization.

Wright, B. D. (1977). Solving measurement problems with the Rasch model. *Journal of Educational Measurement*, 14(2), 97-11.

In: Psychological Distress
Editors: A. Compare, C. Elia, A. G. Simonelli et al.
ISBN: 978-1-63485-405-4

Chapter 6

PSYCHOLOGICAL INTERVENTIONS TO REDUCE DISTRESS AND IMPROVE QUALITY OF LIFE IN FAMILIES WITH AUTISTIC CHILDREN

Cristina Zarbo[1], Angelo Compare[1], Sara Melli[2] and Enzo Grossi[2]

[1]Human and Social Science Department, University of Bergamo, Bergamo, Italy

[2]Villa Santa Maria, Tavernerio (CO), Italy

ABSTRACT

The experience of childbirth and becoming a parent can become particularly distressing when newborn has a severe chronic disability, like Autism Spectrum Disorder (ASD). Families with autistic children face an overload of their adaptive capacities and crisis situations that can in turn lead to various negative psychological consequences on each parent, the couple, children, and the whole family. Indeed, parents of autistic children show high incidence of psychological distress and mental disorders (e.g., anxiety disorders, depressive symptoms). Evidence suggests that parents of children with ASD may benefit of comprehensive and flexible psychological interventions to reduce parental distress and promote the wellbeing and improve the quality of life of the family.

Keywords: parental distress, autism spectrum disorder, parents, psychological interventions

INTRODUCTION

Becoming a parent and raising a child is probably one of the most important developmental task in a life of a single subject and the couple. This difficult task could be exacerbated if new child has a developmental disease, like Autism Spectrum Disorder (ASD).

Parents of children with Autism Spectrum Disorder (ASD) show high incidence of distress that could, in turn, affect the development of the child, as well as the wellbeing of the family. Distress is the negative side of stress, that is a subjective state in which the person, for a prolonged period of time, has to face an overload of physical, intellectual or emotional energy higher than the level he considers acceptable for himself (Antonovsky 1979). Distress is often linked to excessive physiological and psychological responses as well as the onset and maintenance of medical diseases (Antonovsky 1979).

Given the important role played by parents in the child raising, assessment and treatment shouldn't focus only on the child or adolescent with the disease (e.g., its impairments and restrictions), but they should take into consideration also family as a system. Parents, in order to effectively cope with stressful situation, need skills and abilities that are often not easily available. Parental resources and skills should be kept into consideration in order to guarantee a comprehensive and effective support and treatment to the family. This chapter describes the most effective evidence-based psychological interventions to reduce parental distress and improve quality of life in families with ASD children.

The Challenge of Parenthood

Family has been defined as a multigenerational system that includes emotional systems of at least three generations, each other interrelated by legal, emotional and blood constraints. The nuclear family is a subsystem that is influenced by past, present and future relationships (McGoldrick, Heiman, and Carter 1993).

During his life path, every family faces with common phases and developmental tasks that require a reorganization of the system itself. Families differ each other by the way they face with developmental tasks. During these phases, family should change and grow to face with its developmental needs and, at the same time, preserve a sense of identity and continuity through time. Family should be able to adapt to continuous transformation as well as maintain its stability and identity (Anderson and Sabatelli 2003). The adaptability measures the ability of the family to change in response to a stressful situation. During the adaptation phase families try to maintain or restore the homeostasis, acquire new resources and activate useful behaviors, or change the meanings due to the situation, the family itself or the world. A crisis emerges in the family system when environmental requests exceed the existing resources and this imbalance persists over time.

One of the most important developmental tasks in a life of a subject is becoming a parent and raising a child. It has been shown that becoming and being a parent is experienced as overwhelming for both mothers and fathers (Nystrom and Ohrling 2004). In particular, mothers want to be satisfied and confident in their role of mother as well as responsible for the child; fathers want to be confident in their role of both father and partner (Nystrom and Ohrling 2004).

New claims and challenges due to the birth of a child could lead to strain and fatigue for both parents (Nystrom and Ohrling 2004) as well as to increased couple dissatisfaction and psychological distress. Parenting stress seems to be strictly related to parental satisfaction with family, that is linked to subjective self-esteem and marital quality (Cowan and Cowan 1988). Moreover, persistent parental stress could, in turn, lead to negative development for the child (e.g., higher risk of academic and social difficulties) (Cowan, Cowan, and Mahwah 2000). Conversely, emotional, cognitive and physical development of the child is generally enhanced when parents play a supportive and sensitive role to his personal needs.

FAMILIES WITH ASD CHILDREN: CHALLENGES AND PSYCHOLOGICAL IMPLICATIONS

The common stressful condition of becoming parents and raising a child could be exacerbated if new child has a diagnosis of Autism Spectrum Disorder (ASD). Indeed, becoming a parent of a child with ASD could lead to several physical and emotional daily burdens. New parents should face with a lot of challenges, changes and stressful situations, much more than ordinary families, and could be at risk of psychological impairments as well as psychological distress and impaired quality of life. Common challenges and changes as well as psychological implications for parents of children with Autism Spectrum Disorder will be discussed in the following paragraphs (see Table 1 for a summary).

Challenges and Changes

Over life path, children with ASD and their parents face with several common, and sometimes specific, developmental tasks. Children with ASD show lower daily living skills and higher emotional and behavioural problems than children without ASD (Estes et al. 2009, Giovagnoli et al. 2015). Family should redefine tasks, responsibilities and duties, redistribute economic resources and cope with a number of new routines for meet the needs of the new child. During infancy and childhood, learning functional skills to everyday life (such as dressing or bathing) requires specific parenting interventions repeated over time in order to ensure the maintenance and generalization of results. In adolescence and early adulthood, the development of the child with ASD is characterized by new needs of contact, intimacy and sexual life as well as more autonomy, friendships and work activities. In addition, during their life path, children with ASD have extra-care needs (e.g., night care needs, medical diseases, behavioural issues) which commonly lead parents to downsize workplace and/or recreation time.

Nevertheless, it should be highlighted that parents differ in the way they face with stressful situation: being a parent of autistic child could be considered as a tragedy or a situation that could be coped. Parents could react to stressful situations with adaptive coping strategies (e.g., social support searching) or maladaptive coping strategies (e.g., rejection, overprotection) (Cigoli 1993). If they use maladaptive coping strategies, they could be at risk of impaired quality of life, psychological distress, as well as other negative psychological consequences. A significant role in health outcomes is played by emotional regulation, a type of coping strategy directed at changing owns affects. Literature has shown that emotional regulation plays a mediating role in the development of depression and physical illness; while rumination and emotion suppression seem to have an effect to depression and physiological disease's onset (Compare et al. 2014). Moreover, social support can protect subjects from the negative influence of stressful events (buffering model) or provide stability in everyday life (main-effect model) (Cohen and Wills 1985). However, it should be highlighted that benefits of social support are strictly related to his quality (due to the presence of intimacy, good communication, secure attachment and empathy) (Zarbo et al. 2013).

Psychological Implications

Psychological Outcomes

Families with autistic child face an overload of their adaptive capacities and crisis situations that can lead to distress, impaired quality of life and several negative psychological consequences on each parent, the couple, the child, and the family.

Living with a child with ASD could be a source of confusion, fatigue and distress for the entire family system. It has been demonstrated that 34,2% of parents of children with Autism Spectrum Disorder show depressive symptoms and 55% of them significant levels of general psychological distress (Gatzoyia et al. 2014). Parents of children with ASD are at greater risk for poor mental health as well as higher stress levels, parenting stress, psychological distress and anxiety symptoms (both social anxiety and social phobia) if compared to parents of children without ASD (Zablotsky, Bradshaw, and Stuart 2013, Estes et al. 2009, Baker-Ericzn, Brookman-Frazee, and Stahmer 2005, Yamada et al. 2007, Estes et al. 2013, Giovagnoli et al. 2015, Kuusikko-Gauffin et al. 2013). Moreover, they show lower levels of wellbeing than parents with children with other developmental disabilities (Abbeduto et al. 2004). Their self-reported distress seems to be confirmed by lower than average morning cortisol levels (Foody, James, and Leader 2015).

Mothers of children with Autism Spectrum Disorder seem to have higher parenting responsibility, distress, anxiety, and depression than fathers, whom show higher blood pressure and heart rate variability (Foody, James, and Leader 2015). Mothers of autistic children seem to be distressed more mentally than physically (Suzumura 2015). A recent study found that in a sample of 243 mothers of children with autism and other developmental disabilities, 85% showed significantly elevated stress, 48% were clinically depressed and 41% had anxiety disorders (Dykens et al. 2014).

However age, time since diagnosis, financial resources and children behaviour problems are significant for stress, depression and quality of life of parents of children with ASD (Dardas and Ahmad 2014, Suzumura 2015, White and Hastings 2004, Gatzoyia et al. 2014).

Coping Strategies

Mental health seems to be significantly related to the ability to cope with stressful situations. Literature has suggested that avoidant strategies (e.g., disengagement, self-blame, denial, emotional venting) contribute to depressed mood, anxiety and stress symptoms; conversely, action-oriented strategies (planning, acceptance, positive reframing) contribute to resilience, that is the ability to cope positively with difficulties (Whitehead, Dorstyn, and Ward 2015). Lower levels of emotion-focused coping and higher levels of problem-focused coping seem to be associated to better parental well-being, regardless of the level of child symptomatology (Smith et al. 2008).

Moreover, parents of children with ASD that use different problem-solving strategies, distance them, and have less escape avoidance and responsibility acceptance behaviours, tend also to have lower parental distress as well as higher parental quality of life (Dardas and Ahmad 2014).

Predictive Factors of Mental Health and Quality of Life

Literature has shown that parental mental health outcomes (e.g., wellbeing, stress level, anxiety depression, life satisfaction) are predicted by children behavioural and emotional symptoms as well as parental hardiness, social support, parental coping skills, parental vicarious futurity, parental hope and marital satisfaction (Abbeduto et al. 2004, Weiss 2002, Hartley et al. 2011, Zablotsky, Bradshaw, and Stuart 2013, Estes et al. 2013, Faso, Neal-Beevers, and Carlson 2013, Firth and Dryer 2013, Estes et al. 2009, Giovagnoli et al. 2015). Moreover, parental stress seems to be independent to the severity of autism symptoms (Giovagnoli et al. 2015).

Protective and Mediating Factors of Mental Health and Quality of Life

Social support, age of the child, time since diagnosis, parental locus of control, parental cognitive appraisal, parental religious beliefs and spirituality seem to be protective factors of parental mental health (Bekhet, Johnson, and Zauszniewski 2012). Literature has shown that they allow parents to achieve positive outcomes, diminish the effects of risk and decrease negative reactions (Bekhet, Johnson, and Zauszniewski 2012).

Table 1. Psychological implications in parents of children with ASD

Parents of children with Autism Spectrum Disorder show high level of:

- *Mental distress*
- *Depressive symptoms*
- *Anxiety Disorders*
- *Parenting stress*
- *General psychological distress*

Parents of children with Autism Spectrum Disorder show low level of:

- *Wellbeing*
- *Average morning cortisol*

Parenting distress, mental health and quality of life are related to:

- *Age*
- *Time since child's diagnosis*
- *Financial resources*
- *Children behavior problems*
- *Coping strategies*

Parental mental health outcomes are predicted by:

- *Children behavioural and emotional symptoms*
- *Hardiness*
- *Social support*
- *Coping skills*
- *Vicarious futurity*
- *Hope*
- *Marital satisfaction*

Table 1. (Continued)

Parental mental health outcomes are protected or mediated by: • *Social support* • *Age of the child* • *Time since diagnosis* • *Locus of control* • *Cognitive appraisal* • *Religious beliefs* • *Spirituality* • *Mindfulness ability* • *Mindful parenting* • *Trait mindfulness* • *Resilience* No relationship occurs between parental distress and severity of autism symptoms.

Moreover, it has been shown that general mindfulness and mindful parenting significantly mediate the relationship between child behaviours problems and maternal anxiety, depression, and stress (Jones et al. 2014). Trait mindfulness and resilience seem to be protective factor of stress in parents of autistic children (Conner and White 2014, Ruiz-Robledillo et al. 2014). Social support mediates instead the relationship between resilience and health status (Ruiz-Robledillo et al. 2014).

Psychological Interventions for Families with Autistic Children

To efficiently cope with everyday stressful situations due to being parents of ASD children, parental skills and abilities are required. Frequently, parents of children with ASD need psychological interventions in order to acquire coping skills as well as reduce distress and improve quality of life and mental health. The main effective evidence-based interventions and outcomes will be described in the following paragraphs (see Table 2 for a summary).

Stepping Stones Triple P

Stepping Stones Triple P (SSTP) is a parenting program specifically designed for families of children with a disability, provided in both small group and individual formats. Group interventions aim to teach parenting strategies, while individual sessions aim to involve observation, practice and feedbacks as well as teach strategies to increase the understanding of the disability.

Stepping Stones Triple P has been demonstrated efficient to improve child behaviours as well as several parental outcomes (i.e., parenting styles, over-reactivity, verbosity, confidence, stress, satisfaction, conflict, self-efficacy, and psychological wellbeing (Whittingham et al. 2009c, Tellegen and Sanders 2014, Hodgetts, Savage, and McConnell

2013, Roux, Sofronoff, and Sanders 2013). Improvements in wellbeing result in turn in decreased perceived need for behavioural services (Hodgetts, Savage, and McConnell 2013).

However, it has been shown that changes in parenting styles are predicted by parental attributions before the intervention (Whittingham et al. 2009b); in particular, higher rating of strategies usability seem to be predicted by the parental attribution of child's behaviours to uncontrollable factors (Whittingham, Sofronoff, and Sheffield 2006). Moreover, literature has shown that Stepping Stones Triple P seminars are effective in reduce dysfunctional parenting styles, parental conflict and child behaviour problems, with effects maintained at 3 months' follow-up (Sofronoff, Jahnel, and Sanders 2011).

Moreover, by a qualitative point of view, parents are usually satisfied with the program and consider its strategies helpful (Whittingham et al. 2009a).

Mindfulness Interventions

Mindfulness interventions aim to train parents to become mindfulness teachers of their own autistic child in order to improve the quality of their familiar and social life. Mindfulness interventions improve mindfulness ability, parental stress, health status and family quality of parents of ASD children as well as problem behaviours of children (Hwang et al. 2015, Ferraioli and Harris 2013). Mindful parenting training, combined with mindfulness training for adolescents with ASD, is effective to improve several parental outcomes (i.e., parental quality of life, social responsiveness, competence in parenting, social communication, social cognition, preoccupations and social motivation) as well as decrease rumination of ADS adolescents (de Bruin et al. 2015).

Within this promising field, several specific programs have been developed for or applied to parents of children with Autism Spectrum Disorder. Among them the most effective seem to be the Mindfulness-Based Stress Reduction (MBSR) and the Mindfulness-Based Positive Behavior Support (MBPBS).

The Mindfulness-Based Stress Reduction (MBSR) consists of: a. teaching the concept of mindfulness, stress and anxiety psychology and physiology as well as the usefulness of mindfulness in everyday life; b. exercising on mindfulness sessions; c. group and pairs discussing. Literature has shown that Mindfulness-Based Stress Reduction (MBSR) for parents of children with autism and other intellectual disabilities are efficient to reduce parental stress, depression and anxiety as well as improve sleep quality, life satisfaction and behavioural problems in children (Dykens et al. 2014, Neece 2014). Moreover, if compared to wait list-control group or other treatments (e.g., Positive Adult Development), MBSR treatment reports significantly more improvements in life satisfaction, stress, depression, anxiety, sleep and wellbeing (Neece 2014, Dykens et al. 2014).

In the end, the Mindfulness-Based Positive Behavior Support (MBPBS) is a meditation that aims to teach to parents how to apply awareness in their everyday life and in the interaction with their own child. The Mindfulness-Based Positive Behavior Support (MBPBS) seems to be effective in improve challenging behaviors of adolescent with ASD, as well as reduce stress levels in their mothers (Singh et al. 2014).

Behavioral Parent Training

Literature has shown the efficacy of behavioral parent training in reduce behavioral problems of children with ASD and parenting stress, as well as improve parental joint engagement (Johnson et al. 2015, Kasari et al. 2015). Behavioral parent training includes examination and explanation of child disability, antecedent-behaviour consequence model in changing problems, prevention strategies and consequences (reinforcement strategies, compliance procedures). Moreover, it aims to teach positive and useful strategies. It utilizes direct instruction, modeling, and role-playing as well as video vignettes modeling skills and discussions in order to promote skill acquisition (Johnson et al. 2015). In some cases, behavioural parent training sessions include their children and provide direct and personalized strategies to start an activity with them and establish engaged play routines based on join (Kasari et al. 2015).

Psychoeducation Interventions

Psychoeducation Intervention (PEI) aims to provide education and support to parents of children with ASD, through informational sessions about autism, behavioral impairments, as well as teaching new skills (Kasari et al. 2015). Psychoeducation Intervention could moreover combine psychoeducation with home-based intervention in order to vary needs of children (Patra, Arun, and Chavan 2015). Psychoeducation intervention modules for parents of children with ASD have been demonstrated efficient in improve parenting stress and knowledge about child disability (Patra, Arun, and Chavan 2015, Kasari et al. 2015).

Table 2. Main outcomes of psychological interventions for parents of children with Autism Spectrum Disorder

Psychological Interventions	Outcomes
Stepping Stones Triple P	↑ Adaptive parenting styles (parental confidence, satisfaction, self-efficacy) ↓ Dysfunctional parenting styles (Parental over-reactivity, verbosity, conflict) ↓ Parental stress ↑ Parental psychological wellbeing ↓ Parental need for services ↓ Children problem behaviours
Mindfulness Interventions	↑ Parental mindfulness ability ↓ Parental stress ↑ Parental health status ↑ Family quality ↓ Children problem behaviours
Mindful trainings for parents combined with mindfulness trainings for children with ASD	↑ Parental competence ↑ Parental quality of life ↑ Children quality of life ↑ Children social responsiveness ↑ Children social communication ↑ Children social cognition ↑ Children social motivation ↓ Children rumination

Psychological Interventions	Outcomes
Mindfulness-based stress reduction (MBSR)	↓ Parental stress ↓ Parental depression ↓ Parental anxiety ↑ Parental sleep quality ↑ Parental life satisfaction ↓ Children behaviour problems
Mindfulness-based positive behavior support (MBPBS)	↓ Parental stress ↓ Children challenging behaviours
Psychoeducation Interventions	↑ Parental knowledge about child disability ↓ Parenting stress
Behavioral Parent Training	↓ Parenting stress ↑ Parental joint engagement ↓ Children problem behaviours
Acceptance and Commitment training	↑ Parental health status ↓ Parental depression

Acceptance and Commitment Training

Literature has demonstrated that Acceptance and Commitment (ACT) Training workshops are effective in improve health status and depression of parents of children with ASD (Blackledge and Hayes 2006). Acceptance and Commitment Training group workshop aims firstly to clarify personal values. Cognitive defusion techniques, creative hopelessness discussions and several exercises are utilized to reach this aim as well as disrupt verbal aspects of negative emotions and accept negative emotions and cognitions (Blackledge and Hayes 2006).

Conclusion

Given the high rate of psychological distress in parents of children with Autism Spectrum Disorder and its significant role on the quality of life of the family as well as on children development, it is necessary to provide psychological programs in order to support parents in their difficult role in each phase of the life path.

A crucial phase, usually undervalued, is the communication of diagnosis and prognosis that should provide an accurate description of changes, challenges, possibilities, difficulties that parents will face with in the course of the development of the child with ASD. Communication should be clear and attentive to the specific needs of a family.

In each life path developmental phase, psychological interventions have been demonstrated to be effective to: a. reduce dysfunctional parenting styles (Parental over-reactivity, verbosity, conflict), parental stress, parental need for services, parental mental health (i.e., anxiety, depression); b. improve adaptive parenting styles (parental confidence, satisfaction, self-efficacy), children problem behaviours, parental mindfulness ability, parental health status, parental competence, parental sleep quality, parental life satisfaction, parental joint engagement and children social abilities. Moreover, parental and children psychological wellbeing and quality of life are positively affected by psychological interventions.

Lastly, psychological interventions should be provided also as preventive programs in order to promote general wellbeing before the onset of psychological symptoms. Preventive and supportive psychological programs could result in reduced medical costs due to the reduction of long-term psychopharmacological and psychotherapeutic treatments.

References

Abbeduto, L., Seltzer, M. M., Shattuck, P., Krauss, M. W., Orsmond, G. and Murphy, M. M. (2004). "Psychological well-being and coping in mothers of youths with autism, Down syndrome, or fragile X syndrome." *Am J Ment Retard, 109* (3), 237-54. doi: 10.1352/0895-8017(2004)109<237: PWACIM>2.0.CO; 2.

Anderson, S. A. and Sabatelli, R. M. (2003). Family interaction: A multigenerational development perspective: Allyn and Bacon.

Antonovsky, A. (1979). Health, stress and coping. San Francisco: Jossey-Bass, 1979, Jossey-Bass.

Baker-Ericzn, M. J., Brookman-Frazee, L. and Stahmer, A. C. (2005). "Stress Levels and Adaptability in Parents of Toddlers With and Without Autism Spectrum Disorders." *Research and practice for persons with severe disabilities, 30* (4), 194-204.

Bekhet, A. K., Johnson, N. L. and Zauszniewski, J. A. (2012). "Resilience in family members of persons with autism spectrum disorder: a review of the literature." *Issues Ment Health Nurs, 33* (10), 650-6. doi: 10.3109/ 01612840.2012.671441.

Blackledge, J. T. and Hayes, S. C. (2006). "Using acceptance and commitment training in the support of parents of children diagnosed with autism." *Child and Family Behavior Therapy, 28* (1), 1-18.

Cigoli, V. (1993). " Il corpo ferito. Disabilità e relazioni familiari." *Proposte terapeutiche per il ritardo mentale, 2* (1), 14-21.

Cohen, S. and Wills, T. A. (1985). "Stress, social support, and the buffering hypothesis." *Psychol Bull, 98* (2), 310-57.

Compare, A., Zarbo, C., Shonin, E., Van Gordon, W. and Marconi, C. (2014). "Emotional Regulation and Depression: A Potential Mediator between Heart and Mind." *Cardiovasc Psychiatry Neurol, 2014*, 324374. doi: 10. 1155/2014/324374.

Conner, C. M. and White, S. W. (2014). "Stress in mothers of children with autism: trait mindfulness as a protective factor." *Research in Autism Spectrum Disorders, 8* (6), 617-624.

Cowan, C. P., Cowan, P. A. and Mahwah, N. J. (2000). When partners become parents: The big life change for couples. US: Lawrence Erlbaum Associates Publishers.

Cowan, C. P. and Cowan, P. A. (1988). "Who Does What When Partners Become Parents: Implications for Men, Women, and Marriage." *Marriage and Family Review, 12* (3-4), 105-131. doi: DOI:10.1300/ J002v12n03_07.

Dardas, L. A. and Ahmad, M. M. (2014). "Psychosocial correlates of parenting a child with autistic disorder." *J Nurs Res, 22* (3), 183-91. doi: 10.1097/ jnr.0000000000000023.

de Bruin, E. I., Blom, R., Smit, F. M., van Steensel, F. J. and Bogels, S. M. (2015). "MYmind: Mindfulness training for Youngsters with autism spectrum disorders and their parents." *Autism, 19* (8), 906-14. doi: 10. 1177/1362361314553279.

Dykens, E. M., Fisher, M. H., Taylor, J. L., Lambert, W. and Miodrag, N. (2014). "Reducing distress in mothers of children with autism and other disabilities: a randomized trial." *Pediatrics 134* (2), e454-63, doi: 10.1542/peds.2013-3164.

Estes, A., Munson, J., Dawson, G., Koehler, E., Zhou, X. H. and Abbott, R. (2009). "Parenting stress and psychological functioning among mothers of preschool children with autism and developmental delay." *Autism, 13* (4), 375-87. doi: 10.1177/1362361309105658.

Estes, A., Olson, E., Sullivan, K., Greenson, J., Winter, J., Dawson, G. and Munson, J. (2013). "Parenting-related stress and psychological distress in mothers of toddlers with autism spectrum disorders." *Brain Dev, 35* (2), 133-8. doi: 10.1016/j.braindev.2012.10.004.

Faso, D. J., Neal-Beevers, A. R. and Carlson, C. L. (2013). "Vicarious futurity, hope, and well-being in parents of children with autism spectrum disorder." *Research in Autism Spectrum Disorders, 7* (2), 288-297.

Ferraioli, S. J. and Harris, S. L. (2013). "Comparative effects of mindfulness and skills-based parent training programs for parents of children with autism: feasibility and preliminary outcome data." *Mindfulness, 4* (2), 89-101.

Firth, I. and Dryer, R. (2013). "The predictors of distress in parents of children with autism spectrum disorder." *J Intellect Dev Disabil, 38* (2), 163-71. doi: 10.3109/13668250.2013.773964.

Foody, C., James, J. E. and Leader, G. (2015). "Parenting stress, salivary biomarkers, and ambulatory blood pressure: a comparison between mothers and fathers of children with autism spectrum disorders." *J Autism Dev Disord, 45* (4), 1084-95. doi: 10.1007/s10803-014-2263-y.

Gatzoyia, D., Kotsis, K., Koullourou, I., Goulia, P., Carvalho, A. F., Soulis, S. and Hyphantis, T. (2014). "The association of illness perceptions with depressive symptoms and general psychological distress in parents of an offspring with autism spectrum disorder." *Disabil Health J, 7* (2), 173-80. doi: 10.1016/j.dhjo.2013.10.008.

Giovagnoli, G., Postorino, V., Fatta, L. M., Sanges, V., De Peppo, L., Vassena, L., Rose, P. D., Vicari, S. and Mazzone, L. (2015). "Behavioral and emotional profile and parental stress in preschool children with autism spectrum disorder." *Res Dev Disabil, 45-46*, 411-21. doi: 10.1016/ j.ridd.2015.08.006.

Hartley, S. L., Barker, E. T., Seltzer, M. M., Greenberg, J. S. and Floyd, F. J. (2011). "Marital satisfaction and parenting experiences of mothers and fathers of adolescents and adults with autism." *Am J Intellect Dev Disabil, 116* (1), 81-95. doi: 10.1352/1944-7558-116.1.81.

Hodgetts, S., Savage, A. and McConnell, D. (2013). "Experience and outcomes of stepping stones triple P for families of children with autism." *Res Dev Disabil, 34* (9), 2572-85. doi: 10.1016/j.ridd.2013.05.005.

Hwang, Y. S., Kearney, P., Klieve, H., Lang, W. and Roberts, J. (2015). "Cultivating Mind: Mindfulness Interventions for Children with Autism Spectrum Disorder and Problem Behaviours, and Their Mothers." *Journal of Child and Family Studies*, 1-14.

Johnson, C. R., Foldes, E., DeMand, A. and Brooks, M. M. (2015). "Behavioral Parent Training to Address Feeding Problems in Children with Autism Spectrum Disorder: A Pilot Trial." *Journal of Developmental and Physical Disabilities, 27* (5), 591-607.

Jones, L., Hastings, R. P., Totsika, V., Keane, L. and Rhule, N. (2014). "Child behavior problems and parental well-being in families of children with autism: the mediating role of mindfulness and acceptance." *Am J Intellect Dev Disabil*, *119* (2), 171-85. doi: 10.1352/1944-7558-119.2.171.

Kasari, C., Gulsrud, A., Paparella, T., Hellemann, G. and Berry, K. (2015). "Randomized comparative efficacy study of parent-mediated interventions for toddlers with autism." *J Consult Clin Psychol*, *83* (3), 554-63. doi: 10.1037/a0039080.

Kuusikko-Gauffin, S., Pollock-Wurman, R., Mattila, M. L., Jussila, K., Ebeling, H., Pauls, D. and Moilanen, I. (2013). "Social anxiety in parents of high-functioning children with autism and Asperger syndrome." *J Autism Dev Disord*, *43* (3), 521-9. doi: 10.1007/s10803-012-1581-1.

McGoldrick, M., Heiman, M. and Carter, B. (1993). "The changing family life cycle." In Normal Family Processes, edited by F. Walsh. New York: Guilford Press.

Neece, C. L. (2014). "Mindfulness-based stress reduction for parents of young children with developmental delays: implications for parental mental health and child behavior problems." *J Appl Res Intellect Disabil*, *27* (2), 174-86. doi: 10.1111/jar.12064.

Nystrom, K. and Ohrling, K. (2004). "Parenthood experiences during the child's first year: literature review." *J Adv Nurs*, *46* (3), 319-30. doi: 10.1111/ j.1365-2648.2004.02991.x.

Patra, S., Arun, P. and Chavan, B. S. (2015). "Impact of psychoeducation intervention module on parents of children with autism spectrum disorders: A preliminary study." *Journal of Neurosciences in Rural Practice*, *6* (4), 529.

Roux, G., Sofronoff, K. and Sanders, M. (2013). "A randomized controlled trial of group Stepping Stones Triple P: a mixed-disability trial." *Fam Process*, *52* (3), 411-24. doi: 10.1111/famp.12016.

Ruiz-Robledillo, N., De Andres-Garcia, S., Perez-Blasco, J., Gonzalez-Bono, E. and Moya-Albiol. L. (2014). "Highly resilient coping entails better perceived health, high social support and low morning cortisol levels in parents of children with autism spectrum disorder." *Res Dev Disabil*, *35* (3), 686-95. doi: 10.1016/j.ridd.2013.12.007.

Singh, N. N., Lancioni, G. E., Winton, A. S., Karazsia, B. T., Myers, R. E., Latham, L. L. and Singh, J. (2014). "Mindfulness-Based Positive Behavior Support (MBPBS) for mothers of adolescents with autism spectrum disorder: effects on adolescents' behavior and parental stress." *Mindfulness*, *5* (6), 646-657.

Smith, L. E., Seltzer, M. M., Tager-Flusberg, H., Greenberg, J. S. and Carter, A. S. (2008). "A comparative analysis of well-being and coping among mothers of toddlers and mothers of adolescents with ASD." *J Autism Dev Disord*, *38* (5), 876-89. doi: 10.1007/s10803-007-0461-6.

Sofronoff, K., Jahnel, D. and Sanders, M. (2011). "Stepping Stones Triple P seminars for parents of a child with a disability: a randomized controlled trial." *Res Dev Disabil*, *32* (6), 2253-62. doi: 10.1016/j.ridd.2011.07.046.

Suzumura, S. (2015). "Quality of life in mothers of preschoolers with high-functioning pervasive developmental disorders." *Pediatr Int*, *57* (1), 149-54. doi: 10.1111/ped.12560.

Tellegen, C. L. and Sanders, M. R. (2014). "A randomized controlled trial evaluating a brief parenting program with children with autism spectrum disorders." *J Consult Clin Psychol*, *82* (6), 1193-200. doi: 10.1037/ a0037246.

Weiss, M. J. (2002). "Harrdiness and social support as predictors of stress in mothers of typical children, children with autism, and children with mental retardation." *Autism, 6* (1), 115-30.

White, N. and Hastings, R. P. (2004). "Social and Professional Support for Parents of Adolescents with Severe Intellectual Disabilities." *Journal of Applied Research in Intellectual Disabilities, 17* (3), 181-190.

Whitehead, K., Dorstyn, D. and Ward, L. (2015). "Psychological Adjustment in Families Affected by Autism Spectrum Disorder." *Journal of Developmental and Physical Disabilities, 27* (5), 703-717.

Whittingham, K., Sofronoff, K. and Sheffield, J. K. (2006). "Stepping Stones Triple P: a pilot study to evaluate acceptability of the program by parents of a child diagnosed with an Autism Spectrum Disorder." *Res Dev Disabil, 27* (4), 364-80. doi: 10.1016/j.ridd.2005.05.003.

Whittingham, K., Sofronoff, K., Sheffield, J. and Sanders, M. R. (2009a). "Behavioural Family Intervention with parents of children with ASD: What do they find useful in the parenting program Stepping Stones Triple P?" *Research in autism spectrum disorders, 3* (3), 702-713.

Whittingham, K., Sofronoff, K., Sheffield, J. and Sanders, M. R. (2009b). "Do parental attributions affect treatment outcome in a parenting program? An exploration of the effects of parental attributions in an RCT of Stepping Stones Triple P for the ASD population." *Research in Autism Spectrum Disorders, 3* (1), 129-144.

Whittingham, K., Sofronoff, K., Sheffield, J. and Sanders, M. R. (2009c). "Stepping Stones Triple P: an RCT of a parenting program with parents of a child diagnosed with an autism spectrum disorder." *J Abnorm Child Psychol, 37* (4), 469-80. doi: 10.1007/s10802-008-9285-x.

Yamada, A., Suzuki, M., Kato, M., Suzuki, M., Tanaka, S., Shindo, T., Taketani, K., Akechi, T. and Furukawa, T. A. (2007). "Emotional distress and its correlates among parents of children with pervasive developmental disorders." *Psychiatry Clin Neurosci, 61* (6):651-7. doi: 10.1111/j.1440-1819.2007.01736.x.

Zablotsky, B., Bradshaw, C. P. and Stuart, E. A. (2013). "The association between mental health, stress, and coping supports in mothers of children with autism spectrum disorders." *J Autism Dev Disord, 43* (6), 1380-93. doi: 10.1007/s10803-012-1693-7.

Zarbo, C., Compare, A., Baldassari, E., Bonardi, A. and Romagnoni, C. (2013). "In Sickness and in Health: a Literature Review about Function of Social Support within Anxiety and Heart Disease Association." *Clin Pract Epidemiol Ment Health, 9*, 255-62. doi: 10.2174/1745017901309010255.

In: Psychological Distress
Editors: A. Compare, C. Elia, A. G. Simonelli et al.
ISBN: 978-1-63485-405-4

Chapter 7

MENTAL STRESS IN PARENTS AND SIBLINGS OF AUTISTIC CHILDREN: REVIEW OF THE LITERATURE AND ORIGINAL STUDY OF THE RELATED PSYCHOLOGICAL DIMENSIONS

Sara Melli[1], Enzo Grossi[1], Cristina Zarbo[2] and Angelo Compare[2]
[1]Autism Research Unit - Villa S. Maria Institute, Tavernerio (CO), Italy
[2]Human and Social Science Department, Bergamo University, Italy

ABSTRACT

Parental mental stress is clinically common in families of autistic children and adversely affects the care of the child. Moreover, parents of autistic children frequently experience feelings of guilt, maladaptive coping styles, a lack of ability to forgive themselves and variations in mindfulness. However,it is unclear which of these dimensions is predominant in these families and their pattern of association with other components of this complex picture. While most notable in parents, this is also true of healthy siblings who intrinsically perceive more responsibility and often receive less attention than their afflicted brothers or sisters. The evidence available in the literature on the topic is quite controversial, revealing both positive and negative effects deriving from growing up with ASD siblings.

Demographic and psychological information on mental stress, feelings of guilt, ability to forgive, mindfulness and coping styles were collected through clinical interviews and self-report questionnaires in parents and siblings of autistic children. Artificial Neural Networks (Auto-CM system) were applied to parents data to highlight the associations among the variables under investigation.

Predominant dimensions in parents of autistic children indcluded low feelings of guilt, high levels of forgiveness and low levels of maladaptive coping responses. These three main dimensions were strictly related among themselves. While high parental mental stress was strictly related to high parental distress subscales, to high maladaptive coping styles, and to low self-forgiveness ability, conversely, low mental stress appeared to be marginal in relation to the other psychological dimensions.

This behavior is typical of complex nonlinear systems. The severity of the ASD was not related to parental psychological dimensions. The ADOS scores, both low and high, were in fact marginal in the connectivity map in relation to the other dimensions.

In siblings, the average distress scores level was extremely high irrespectively of ASD severity or family size. About one third of them were at risk of developing major depression. Distress appeared to be mainly related to difficulties in building a meaningful relationship with the ASD child and in managing the child's behavioral problems. In conclusione the interplay of psychological factors related to stress in parents and siblings of ASD children is complex. Understanding these relationships is the starting point to activating and enhancing parental resources essential to the wellbeing of both children and caregivers.

Keywords: parental distress, ASD, siblings

INTRODUCTION

High level of parental mental stress is clinically common in families of autistic children and adversely affects the care of the child.

Parenting stress is the occurrence of distress or discomfort related to the experience of parenting (Deater-Deckard, 1998). Some quantity of parenting stress is naturally expected, and even beneficial but significant levels of parenting stress can lead to lower parental self-efficacy, poor quality of life and compromised parent-child relationships (Rodrigue, Morgan, and Geffken,1990; Donnenberg and Baker, 1993; Hastings and Brown, 2002; Guralnick, 2006).

A considerable number of studies reported that parents of children with Autism Spectrum Disorder (ASD) experience higher levels of parenting stress, psychological distress and anxiety symptoms (both social anxiety and social phobia) than parents of children without ASD (Baker-Ericzn, Brookman-Frazee, and Stahmer, 2005; Estes et al., 2009; Estes et al., 2013; Giovagnoli et al., 2015; Kuusikko-Gauffin et al., 2013; Yamada et al., 2007). Additionally, parents of children with ASD experience higher levels of stress than parents of children with other disorders and medical conditions including Down syndrome, intellectual disability, fragile X syndrome, cystic fibrosis, cerebral palsy and developmental delay (Blacher and McIntyre, 2006; Bouma and Schweitzer, 1989; Estes et al., 2009; Hayes and Watson, 2013).

Parents of children with ASD have also shown lower levels of wellbeing than parents with children with other developmental disabilities (Abbeduto et al., 2004): 34,2% of parents of children with Autism Spectrum Disorder show depressive symptoms and 55% of them significant levels of general psychological distress (Gatzoyia et al., 2014).

Autism spectrum disorder (ASD) is a neurodevelopmental disorder with a lifelong impact on multiple domains of functioning, characterized by a profound impairment in social communication and social interaction and restricted and repetitive behavior, interest and activities (APA, 2013). Social deficits include diminished nonverbal communicative behaviors used for social interaction (e.g., eye contact, gestures, pointing), and a failure to share experiences with others, both of which result in an inability to form reciprocal relationships. Children with ASD demonstrate an inability to engage in joint attention, a lack of spontaneous imitation, limited reciprocal and imaginative play, and difficulty understanding facial expressions. Deficits in social interaction are intrinsically related to difficulties with communication. Many children with ASD show a delay in language acquisition, and some never acquire verbal communication. Other individuals typically develop structural aspects of language, but have deficits in pragmatics or social use of language. Individuals with ASD demonstrate repetitive behaviors, and/or restricted areas of intense interest and/or repetitive activities. Some individuals with ASD may exhibit stereotyped or repetitive speech (e.g., echolalia), repetitive motor movements (hand flapping, head rolling, body rocking, jumping, toe-walking, etc.), or restricted interest for a part of an object (e.g., spinning the wheels of a toy car). They often show highly restricted, fixated interests that are abnormal in intensity or focus (e.g., construction signs, train schedules, types of cars). Similarly, ASD individuals may rigidly adhere to routines or specific daily schedules. They often show ritualistic behavior, that involves an unvarying pattern of daily activities, such as an unchanging menu or a dressing ritual, and show ritualized patterns of verbal or nonverbal behavior (e.g., arranging objects in stacks or lines). Sameness (an excessive resistance to change) is another feature that characterizes ASD (e.g., insisting that the furniture not be moved or refusing to be interrupted) together with limited focus, interest, or activity (e.g., preoccupation with a single television program, toy or game). Autistic individuals may have symptoms that are independent of the diagnosis, but that can affect the individual or the family. Finally, they frequently exhibit hyper- or hypo- sensitivity to sensory input or unusual interest in sensory aspects of their environment, including certain textures (clothing, food, etc.), sounds, smells and motions.

Among individuals with ASD, there is great heterogeneity in the severity and presentation of these symptoms.

Some studies reported a significant positive correlation between autistic symptoms severity and parental stress, suggesting that the severity of autistic traits could also be related to parental stress (Baker-Ericzen et al., 2005; Hastings and Johnson, 2001; Hastings et al., 2005; Hill-Chapman et al., 2013; Osborne and Reed, 2009). However, other studies show the exact opposite (Giovagnoli et al., 2015).

Frequently, ASD can occur in comorbidity with other medical, psychiatric, and developmental disorders such as epilepsy, allergies, sleep disorders, conduct disorders, attention deficit/hyperactivity disorder (ADHD), gastro-intestinal disorders, anxiety disorders, intellectual disability and language disorders. Moreover, Autistic individuals may have symptoms that are independent of the diagnosis, but that can affect the individual or the family such as unusual eating behavior (e.g., selectivity, eating rituals and food refusal) many regulatory problems (e.g., eating, sleeping, emotion regulation) and self injury. Some research highlights the everyday management of behavioral problems and the child's characteristics (i.e., adaptive behavior, intelligence, gender, age, etc.) as a relevant source of parental stress (Dabrowska and Pisula, 2010; Davis and Carter, 2008; Estes et al., 2009, 2013; Hastings et al., 2005; Rivard et al., 2014).

Given the complexity and severity of the clinical picture, the challenges involved in raising a child with autism spectrum disorders (ASD) could certainly lead to daily physical and emotional burdens of the various family members. A child with ASD requires substantial financial investment in therapy, medical treatment, and early intervention education, increased vigilance of the child, micromanagement of the family environment to ensure minimal sensory discomfort and maintenance of a highly predictable routine and a large commitment from the family. It is empirically intuitive to assume that quality of life (QoL) is negatively influenced in these families.

Moreover, several studies have demonstrated that parents of children diagnosed with ASD experience greater amounts of anxiety, depression, stress, and strained martial relationships than parents of typically developing children or parents of children with other types of developmental delays (Dumas, Wolf, Fisman, and Culligan, 1991; Plant and Sanders, 2007).

Furthermore, parents of children with ASD frequently experience feelings of guilt, a lack of ability to forgive themselves, maladaptive coping styles and variations in mindfulness.

Parental mental health seems to be significantly determined by individual coping responses. Literature has suggested that avoidant strategies (e.g., disengagement, self-blame, denial, emotional venting) contribute to depressed mood, anxiety and stress symptoms; conversely, action-oriented strategies (planning, acceptance, positive reframing) contribute to resilience or to positively coping with difficulties (Whitehead, Dorstyn, and Ward, 2015). Lower levels of emotion-focused coping and higher levels of problem-focused coping seem to be associated with better parental well-being, regardless of the level of child symptomatology (Smith, Seltzer, Tager-Flusberg, Greenberg, and Carter, 2008).

The literature has shown that parents using different problem-solving and distance coping strategies are less likely to try and escape the problem. They also are more accepting of their responsibility and general demonstrate lower distress levels thus increasing their quality of life (Dardas and Ahmad, 2014).

Moreover, it has been shown that general awareness and mindful parenting significantly mediate the relationship between child behavioural problems and parental anxiety, depression, and stress (Jones, Hastings, Totsika, Keane, and Rhule, 2014). Trait awareness and resilience seem to be protection fromstress factors in ASD parents (Conner and White, 2014; Ruiz-Robledillo, De Andres-Garcia, Perez-Blasco, Gonzalez-Bono, and Moya-Albiol, 2014). Social support instead helps the relationship between resilience and health status (Ruiz-Robledillo et al., 2014).

In summary, several studies investigated the predictors of stress in ASD parents, identifying crucial factors such as the revelation of the ASD diagnosis, parental coping methods, as well as the aforementioned feelings of guilt, lack of ability to forgive and other family-related variables. The role of these dimensions on parental stress onset has not been clarified yet and is unclear which of these dimensions is predominant in these families and if their associations are symmetrical in quantifiable terms.

It is very important to investigate the impact of these dimensions linked to parental perceived stress and to offer support in an attempt to improve the quality of life of the whole family with more effective treatments. Some studies report that higher parental stress levels were also shown to reduce the effectiveness of early teaching intervention programs, thereby impairing the clinical improvement in intellectual and educational skills, adaptive behavior and social functioning (Osborne, McHugh, Saunders, and Reed, 2008). Thus, supporting parental stress management initiatives may make the most sense for ASD parents.

But what about ASD siblings?

Raising a child with autism places extraordinary demands on the family as a whole. Indeed, if there are siblings in the family, the ASD child often receives a disproportionate share of parental attention. The time involved in meeting the needs of a family member with autism may leave parents with little time for their healthy children. Typically developing children within an ASD household may suffer several consequences on their psychological well being and quality of life.

The current literature presents contradictory findings as to whether ASD siblings are at risk as they have been shown to do more poorly on a number of tests when compared to siblings of other developmental disabilities, or to those with only typically developing siblings. They have been shown to exhibit higher levels of internalizing and externalizing disorders (Rodrigue J. R., Geffken G. R., and Morgan S. B., 1993; Ross P. and Cuskelly M., 2006), social and behavioral adjustment problems (Orsmond G. I. and Seltzer M. M., 2007), hassles with sibling behavior (Moyson T. and Roeyers H., 2011), and distressing emotions such as guilt (Opperman S. and E. Alant E., 2003). Conversely, other researchers have found no difference in adjustment levels between siblings of individuals with ASD and those with only typically developing siblings (Kaminsky L. and Dewey D., 2002). or those with siblings with other developmental pathologies (Pilowsky T., Yirmiya N., Doppelt O., Gross-Tsur V., and Shalev R. S., 2004). Some studies have found positive effects for ASD siblings, such as increased positive self-esteem when compared to matched controls (Macks and Reeve, 2007; Rivers and Stoneman, 2003). Siblings of individuals with autism have been reported to have less conflict in the sibling relationship (Kaminsky L. and Dewey D., 2002), family resilience (Bayat M., 2007) and increased self-perceived competence (Rodrigue, J. R., Morgan, S. B. and Geffken, G., 1990; Vert´e S., Roeyers H., and Buysse A., 2003; Macks R. J. and Reeve R. E., 2007). They have also been shown to have a more positive opinion of the sibling relationship (Rivers J. W. and Z. Stoneman Z., 2003), positive psychosocial and emotional development conditional upon limited demographic risk factors (Macks R. J. and Reeve R. E., 2007), feelings of empathy for their sibling (Benderix Y. and Sivberg B., 2007), and increased maturity (Gray D.E.,1998). On the other hand, frequently siblings are the target of negative autistic behaviors, ranging from indifference to physical violence that threatens their safety and they sometimes suffer from social embarrassment caused by exposure to negative autistic behavior with consequences on their psychological well being.

Being a sibling of a child with ASD has different consequences and meanings based on the time perdiod being considered. The concerns of an adolescent sibling will be different from those of a child sibling. During childhood siblings may fail to understand a complex disability like ASD and may not understand why their brother or sister will not play with them, why their brother or sister gets different rules, and why their parents spend more time with their brother or sister, while during adolescence, teenagers begin to spend less time with siblings and family and more time with friends. They may begin to better understand ASD and feel some sense of guilt for their previous less than sympathetic behaviours toward their ASD sibling. They have usually formed strong social awareness and may become embarrassed by the disability in the family, potentially resulting in a conflict between their loyalty to their sibling and a desire to fit in with their peers.

The research on siblings of children with autism has not generally taken the different stages of upbringing into consideration. All of the studies that have included adolescent siblings have also included children as young as 5–8 years in the same sample (Bagenholm and Gillberg 1991; Gold 1993; Kaminsky and Dewey 2002; Mates 1990; Roeyers and Mycke 1995). Past research has not considered the developmental context of adolescence and specifically the challenges to sibling well-being associated with it. There are some indications that the risk of psychological and adjustment problems for siblings of individuals with ASD increases during adolescence, although findings are not unanimous. Gold (1993) found that siblings aged 7–12 reported significantly fewer depressive symptoms than siblings aged 13–17.

Despite reports that the large majority of siblings of individuals with ASD may be well adjusted, a significant proportion of the research indicates some vulnerability in behavioural and emotional dysfunction. ASD siblings may be well-behaved and report no negative effects caused by their domestic environment. This is likely due to a sense of empathy for their sibling and a desire to assist their parents, despite the risk of implicitly suffering to some extent and having to compromise.

This suggests that siblings need to be considered as important members within the family as a whole when planning ASD treatment and counselling.

Any intervention only aimed at the ASD child may be ineffective in assisting the entire family and may very well hamper the treatment's outcome. Thus, this investigation assesses the impact of children with ASD on parental stress, sibling adjustment and proper family functioning.

Considering this framework, we conducted an observational study with four primary aims:

- to evaluate stress and well-being level by self-perceived evaluation in parents and siblings of ASD children;
- to evaluate if negative psychological dimensions work in a symmetrical or asymmetrical way when they are mild or severe and to establish the hyerarchy of that relationship;
- to establish if psychological dimensions are related to ASD severity;
- to rate presence of psychopathological traits (anxiety and depression) in order to better plan early intervention.

METHODS

Participants

Family demographics have long been linked to stress outcomes in families with children with disabilities. Therefore, demographic information was collected about parents, siblings and children with ASD. Items included: gender, job, highest level of education, relationship to the child with ASD, age, family dimension and current marital status of the parents.

We measured parental stress, mindfulness, coping strategies, self-forgiveness, guilt and psychological well being.

In Siblings we assessed the presence of depressive and anxious symptoms, Attachment styles, psychological well-being and level of perceived stress. The scales utilized are described in the following section.

Parenting Stress Index Short Form PSI–SF

The PSI–SF(Abidin, 1995) is a 36- item questionnaire designed to measure stress in the parent–child system and identify those families most in need of follow-up services. The PSI–SF consists of three subscales: Parental Distress, Parent–Child Dysfunctional Interaction, and

Difficult Child. Each subscale consists of 12 items rated from 1 (strongly disagree) to 5 (strongly agree). Subscale scores therefore range from 12 to 60, whereas the total score ranges from 36 to 180. High scores on the subscales and PSI–SF total score indicate greater levels of stress. The Parental Distress subscale reflects a parent's perception of child-rearing competence, conflict with his or her spouse or partner, social support, and stresses associated with the restrictions placed on other life roles. The Parent–Child Dysfunctional Interaction subscale assesses a parent's perception that the child does not meet expectations and that interactions with the child are not reinforcing. The Difficult Child subscale surveys the parent's view of the child's temperament, defiance, noncompliance, and demandingness.

Psychological General Well Being Index (PGWBI)

The level of subjective psychological well being in siblings and parents has been measured by an index that has been validated by decades of clinical practice: The Psychological General Well Being Index (PGWBI). PGWBI has been validated and is used in many countries in large populations and specific groups studies. In 2000 the PGWBI was validated in a representative sample of 1,129 Italian citizens aged from 15 years, and its normative values are available (Grossi, E., Mosconi, P., Groth, N., Niero, M. and Apolone, G., 2005). Questions cover 6 aspects: anxiety, depressed mood, positive well-being, self-control, general health and vitality. The PGWBI has been developed as a tool to measure self-representations of intra-personal affective or emotional states reflecting a sense of subjective well-being or distress, and thus captures what we could call a subjective perception of well-being (see Dupuy 1990 for a general presentation and a historical account of its development). The original PGWBI consists of 22 self-administered items, rated on a 6-points Lykert scale, which assess psychological and general well-being of respondents in the six HRQoL domains mentioned above. Each item has six possible scores (from 0 to 5), referred to the last four weeks of the subject's lifetime. Each domain is defined by a minimum of 3 to a maximum of 5 items. The scores for all domains can be summarized into a global summary score, which reaches a theoretical maximum of 110 points, representing the best achievable level of well being (Dupuy 1990), a sort of 'state of bliss.'

Five Facet Mindfulness Questionnaire (FFMQ)

All participants completed the FFMQ (Baer et al., 2006), which assesses five facets of a general tendency to be mindful in daily life: observing, describing, acting with awareness, non reactivity to inner experience, and non-judgmental of inner experience. Items are rated on a 5-point Likert-type scale ranging from 1 (never or very rarely true) to 5 (very often or always true).

Coping Orientation to Problem Experienced—New Italian Version (COPE-NVI)

Parents completed the COPE-NVI (Coping Orientation to Problem Experienced—New Italian Version) (Sica C, Magni M, Ghisi M, Altoè G, Sighinolfi C, et al., 2008). This is a standardized and validated questionnaire, used to assess five specific coping strategies, such as: social support, avoidance, positive aptitude, orientation toward problems, and transcendent orientation. This 60-item questionnaire requires 4-mark answers measured on a Likert scale (from 1 = I do not usually do that, 4 = I almost always do that). Its administration is individual, and the subject is asked to evaluate how many times s/he activates that specific coping process in difficult and stressful situations.

State Self-Forgiveness Scale (SSFS)

To assess parents' levels of self-forgiveness, we used the State Self-Forgiveness Scale (SSFS; Wohl et al., 2008). The SSFS consists of two sub-scales: Self-Forgiving Feelings and Actions (SSFA) and Self-Forgiving Beliefs (SFB). All items were quantified on a 4-point Likert scale (from 1 = Not at all, to 4= Completely). Participants were asked to respond to questions preceded by "Since I consider what I did was wrong..." Example items include, "I punish myself" (SSFA) and "I believe I am acceptable" (SFB). All items were quantified with a four-point scale ranging from 1 (Not at All) to 4 (Completely"), with higher scores representing greater self-forgiveness.

Guilt Inventory

The Guilt Inventory (Kugler and Jones, 1992) contains 45 statements that make up three subscales (state guilt, trait guilt, and morality), but only the subscale trait guilt (10 items) was assessed in this study. Parents rate an item of the subscale trait guilt on a five-point scale (1= very untrue of me or strongly disagree, 5 = very true of me or strongly agree). Participants were classified as either low or high in trait guilt.

Center for Epidemiological Studies-Depression Scale (CES-D)

Depressive symptoms in adolescent siblings were measured with the Center for Epidemiological Studies-Depression scale (CES-D; Radloff 1977) a 20-item self report developed to assess the frequency of depressive symptoms. The scale requires responsents to indicate how often they experienced each symptom on a 4-point Likert scale consisting of ''Rarely or none of the time (less than 1 day)'' (coded as 1), ''Some or a little of the time (1-2 days)'' (coded as 2), ''Occasionally or a moderate amount of time (3-4 days)'' (coded as 3), and ''All of the time (5-7 days)'' (coded as 4). The CES-D is a well validated and reliable measure of depressive affect (Radloff 1991) that frequently has been used with adults (Steinhausen et al. 2006; Zimmerman and Coryell 1994) as well as adolescents (Dierker et al. 2001; Field et al. 2001; Lewinsohn et al. 2001; Schoenbach et al. 1982) and has been standardized for high school populations (Radloff 1991). Test–retest reliability, internal consistency, and concurrent validity are good (Schoenbach et al. 1982). Scores range from 0 to 60 and a score of 16 or higher is indicative of depressed mood.

The mean for siblings in the present sample was 14.4 (SD = 10.56; range from 3 to 47). Five siblings presented high depressive symptomatology (CES –D score > 16) and were identified as potentially at-risk siblings.

Self-Rating Anxiety Scale (SAS)

Adolescent siblings completed the Self-Rating Anxiety Scale (SAS). The SAS (Zung, 1971) is a 20-item measure developed to assess the frequency of anxiety symptoms based on diagnostic conceptualizations. It consists primarily of somatic symptoms. The respondent indicates how often he or she has experienced each symptom on a 4-point Likert scale consisting of ''none or a little of the time'' (coded as 1), ''some of the time'' (coded as 2), ''good part of the time'' (coded as 3), and ''most or all of the time'' (coded as 4). Total scores on the SAS range from 20 to 80 (20-44 Normal Range; 45-59 Mild to Moderate Anxiety Levels; 60-74 Marked to Severe Anxiety Levels; 75-80 Extreme Anxiety Level). The mean for siblings in the present sample was 35,86 (SD = 10.66; range from 26 to 71). Only one sibling presented high anxiety symptomatology (SAS > 16) and were identified as potentially at-risk siblings.

Attachment Style Questionnaire (ASQ)

This construct was assessed using the attachment style questionnaire (ASQ; Feeney et al., 1994). The ASQ is a 40-item measure, with response format: from 1 = totally disagree, to 6 = totally agree. The ASQ yields scores on five variables: confidence, need for approval, preoccupation with relationships, discomfort with closeness, and relationships as secondary. Confidence (8 items) scale assesses security of attachment (e.g., "I am confident that other people will like and respect me"). Need for approval (7 items) reflects individuals' need for acceptance and confirmation (e.g., "It is important to me to avoid doing things that others won't like"). Preoccupation with relationships (8 items) measures fears of rejection and abandonment and concerns about whether partners' feelings of love and commitment are deep and lasting (e.g., "I worry that others won't care about me as much as I care about them"). Discomfort with closeness (10 items) measures the tendency to be uncomfortable with high levels of intimacy and to have difficulty in depending on relationship partners (e.g., "I find it difficult to depend on others"). Relationships as secondary (7 items) reflects individuals' wishes to protect themselves against hurt and vulnerability by emphasizing achievement and independence (e.g., "Achieving things is more important than building relationships"). Feeney and her colleagues also reported significant associations between the ASQ scales and measures of attachment styles (secure, avoidant, and anxious/ambivalent), as well as meaningful links with measures of personality and family functioning.

The questionnaire was completed both by siblings and parents.

Autism Diagnostic Observation Schedule-2

We used ADOS 2 in order to assess severity of autistic symptoms. The Italian version of the Autism Diagnostic Observation Schedule-II (Lord at. al., 2012). Autism Diagnostic Observation Schedule, second edition was individually administered to all ASD children by a licensed clinician in order to assess autistic symptoms. The ADOS-2 is a semi-structured, standardized, play-based assessment measure designed to evaluate current autistic behaviors. Each item of the ADOS-2 is based on a 0–3 scale scores (0 = no evidence of abnormal behavior to 3 = markedly abnormal behavior) The ADOS-2 is divided into four separate modules, each of whose is aimed at a specific level of expressive language ability. Items used in the ADOS-2 are divided into two domains, Social Affect (SA) and Restricted/Repetitive Behaviors or Interests (RRB). The use of different modules reduces possible biasing effects of differences in language skills. To calculate the total cut-off, SA and RRB are combined into one score. An ASD severity scale has been developed based on 18 narrowly defined age and language cells, and the total raw scores were divided into a 10-point severity score (1 = fewer problems and 10 = more severe problems) (de Bildt et al., 2011; Gotham, Pickles, and Lord, 2009). In the present study, the raw score of the ADOS-2 severity index was used as a measure for autistic symptoms.

Data Analysis

For parents and siblings samples, descriptive statistical analyses were conducted. Measures of central tendency and measures of dispersion were used to look at the data of each scale and subscale. Since the focus of this study is on the linear relationship between quantitative variables, Pearson's correlation coefficient was used to explore the extent of linear relationships among the variables, and to quantify the strength and direction of the relationship.

Stress levels and psychological well-being indexes were compared in term of gender and family size trough t-test.

In addition, Artificial Neural Networks (Auto-CM system) were applied to parents data to highlight the associations among variables under study.

The Auto-Contractive Map (AutoCM for short) was born as a new Artificial Neural Network. It was designed by Massimo Buscema at the Semeion Research Center (Buscema M., Grossi E., 2008; Buscema M., Grossi E., Snowdon D., Antuono P., 2008; Buscema M., Sacco. PL., 2010). AutoCMs 'spatializes' the correlation among variables by building a suitable embedding space where a visually transparent and cognitively natural notion such as 'closeness' among variables accurately reflects their associations. AutoCM converts this 'closeness' into a compelling graphic-theoretical representation that picks all and only the relevant correlations and organizes them into a coherent picture. Such representation is not actually built through a cumbersome aggregation of two-by-two associations between couples of variables, but rather by building a complex global picture of the whole pattern of variation. Moreover, it fully exploits the topological meaning of graphic-theoretical representations in that actual paths connecting vertices (variables) in the representation carry a definite meaning in terms of logical interdependence in explaining the data set's variability.

The AutoCM produces a matrix of the correlations between the variables in the dataset, including information on the complex dynamics of adaptive interactions in the form of weights (w) between the variables (Buscema M., Grossi E., 2008), In this case correlation does not refer to a linear relationship between the variables, as in the Pearson product-moment correlation, but to the similarity between the binary vectors of the indicator variables described as the degree of membership of the two nodes in the same fuzzy set. The relationship between the two variables can be said to be null or very low when w .33, quite low when $0.33 < w$ 0.66, quite high when $0.66 < w$ 0.84, and very high when $w > 0.84$. Based on this definition of correlation, only positive associations between the nodes are presented in the graphs. Starting from a connected, weighted graph, linking all variables to all others, the algorithm constructs a tree with variables as nodes and their distances as edges, called the minimum spanning tree (MST) (Kruskal J.B. Jr.,1956; Fredman M.L., Willard D.E., 1990). This includes all the variables considered, linked in a way that the energy structure of the system is minimized, or if weights are correlation measures, in a way that these are maximized for all the connections in the graph. The MST algorithm does not map all the correlations present in the data but only the simplest view of the strongest correlations present between the nodes in the system in a way that all the nodes are connected to another node and only a single path is available to travel between two nodes (no loops). Also, each connection between nodes is adjusted for all the other connections between all the nodes included in the graph through an optimization of the square matrix containing all correlations between the indicator variables. In the MST, every link that is able to generate a cycle onto the graph is eliminated, irrespective of its strength of association, resulting in a simplified graph (Buscema M., Grossi E., Ieee, 2007).

RESULTS

The study utilized data collected from 39 parents and 15 siblings of individuals diagnosed with an ASD attending Villa Santa Maria Institute as residents or out-patients.

Parents ranged in age from 38 to 57 years (Mean = 45.53). 30 were mothers and 9 were fathers. Seventy nine % of parents were actually married, 64% had a job and 67% had 2 or more children.

Table 1 summarizes the demographics of the parents sample in this study.

Table 1. Caregivers of children with ASD: Demographic Findings

Caregiver variables		
Gender	Frequency	Percent
Male	9	23%
Female	30	77%
Educational level	Frequency	Percent
Middle school diploma	8	20%
High school diploma	27	69%
Bachelor's Degree	1	3%
Master's Degree	3	8%
Marital status	Frequency	Percent
Single	4	10%
Married	31	79%
Separated	1	3%
Relationship	3	8%
Job category	Frequency	Percent
Unemployed	4	10%
Freelance	4	10%
Employed	21	54%
Housewife	9	23%
Pensioner	1	3%
N. of Children	Frequency	Percent
1 child	13	33%
2 children	19	49%
3 children	2	5%
4 children	5	13%
Relationship with child	Frequency	Percent
Biological caregiver	37	95%
Non-biological caregiver	2	2%

Siblings investigated were between 10 and 18 years old (mean age 15.4 yrs). The research on siblings of children with autism has not generally taken life stage into account. A lot of studies have included adolescent siblings, and children as young as 5–8 years in the same sample (Gold 1993; Kaminsky and Dewey 2002; Mates 1990; Roeyers and Mycke 1995). We chose to consider the developmental context of adolescence, and specifically the challenges to sibling well-being. We investigated 7 sisters and 8 brothers. 73% of siblings were older than their brother or sister with ASD. Most (60%) are currently attending high school.

Table 2 summarizes the demographics of the siblings sample in this study

Table 2. Siblings of children with ASD: Demographic Findings

Siblings variables		
Gender	Frequency	Percent
Male	8	53%
Female	7	47%
Job category	Frequency	Percent
Students	14	93%
Employed	1	7%
Educational level attending	Frequency	Percent
Primary school	2	13%
Secondary school	3	20%
High school	9	60%
High school diploma	1	7%
N. of Siblings	Frequency	Percent
1 Sibling	6	40%
2 Siblings	6	40%
3 Siblings	3	20%
Order of birth	Frequency	Percent
First born	11	73%
Second born	2	13%
Third born	1	7%
Fourth born	1	7%

Table 3 summarizes the demographics of the ASD children sample in this study.

The majority of the children with ASD in the studies on parents and siblings were boys (87% and 60%). The children's average age at the time of the study was 13.05 in the study on parents and 14.06 in the study of siblings. Children included in the ASD group were diagnosed within the Autism of Spectrum Disorders conditions according to the DSM-5 criteria by experienced clinicians and confirmed by ADOS-2 assessment (Autism Diagnostic Observation Schedule second edition). The Italian version of the Autism Diagnostic Observation Schedule- second edition (ADOS-2) was individually administered to all ASD children by a licensed clinician in order to assess autistic symptoms. Table 4 summarizes data about ADOS-2 in the samples of children with ASD (Table 4).

Table 3. Children with ASD: Demographic Findings

	Parents sample		Siblings Sample	
Gender	Frequency	Percent	Frequency	Percent
Male	34	87%	9	60%
Female	5	13%	6	40%
Type of Treatment	Frequency	Percent	Frequency	Percent
Resident	13	33%	11	73%
Day- Hospital	26	67%	4	27%
Educational level attending	Frequency	Percent	Frequency	Percent
Elementary School	13	33%	3	20%
Middle school	21	53%	9	60%
Middle school degree	5	14%	3	20%
N. of Siblings	Frequency	Percent	Frequency	Percent
Only child	13	33%	0	0%
1 Sibling	19	49%	6	40%
2 Siblings	2	5%	6	40%
3 Siblings	5	13%	3	20%

Table 4. ADOS-2 severity index and modules

ADOS Severity Index				
Parents sample			Siblings Sample	
	Frequency	Percent	Frequency	Percent
High	20	51%	6	40%
Moderate	19	49%	9	60%
	Language			
No words or some words	33	85%	2	13%
Language with phrases	6	15%	13	87%

Parental and Siblings Level of Stress

Parents completed PSI -SF. The mean in the present sample was 101,5 (SD =21.04; range from 35 to 141). Of note, 78% of the parents scored above the 85th percentile ranks on all of the subscales of the PSI-SF. Total stress includes to what extent parents are experiencing stress in their role as a parent, the extent to which parents believe that his/her child does not meet their expectations and their interactions are not satisfying and how easy or difficult parents perceives his/her child.

Particularly high percentile rankings were found in the Parent-Child Dysfunctional Interaction (P-CDI) with a mean raw score of 32.07 and in Difficult Child (DC) with a mean raw score of 38.6, both placed in the 95th percentile. The lowest subscale for participants in this study was the Parental Distress, with a mean raw score of 33.75 and a percentile of 85%. Table 5 summarizes data about PSI in the samples of parents of children with ASD.

Siblings completed an adaptation of PSI -SF. The average level of distress resulted to be extremely high (PSI-SF mean = 98.33). Of note, 80% of the siblings scored above the 85th percentile ranks on all of the subscales of the PSI-SF. Distress appeared to be mainly related to difficulties in building a meaningful relationship with ASD child and in managing child's behavioral problems. Table 5 summarizes data about PSI in the samples of siblings of children with ASD.

Table 5. Breakdown of PSI-SF Total Score and Subscales

	Parents sample					Siblings sample				
	Mean Score	SD	Total Range*	Study Range	Clinically Significant (CS)	Mean Score	SD	Total Range*	Study Range	Clinically Significant (CS)
Total Score	104.5		38-186	35-141	95%	98.3		38-186	59-136	90%
PD	33.7		12-60	17-60	85%	28.6		12-60	17-36	67%
P-CDI	32.0		12-60	16-46	95%	33.6		12-60	21-47	95%
DC	38.6		12-60	16-50	95%	36.6		12-60	21-53	95%

*Based on information obtained from PSI-SF manual (Abidin, 2005).

Siblings and Parents Well-Being

The Quality of life was assessed using the PGWBI both in parents and siblings. The scores obtained from the PGWBI and the means of all the subscales were compared with the Italian general population and adolescent population scores. Total score of "well being" (ranging from 0 – 110 points, 110 being the maximum), has been divided into the following 3 broad categories (Chassany, Dimenäs, Dubois, Wu, and Dupuy, 2004): 1. Positive well-being: 73-110 (this has also been divided into other 2 categories: positive wellbeing: 96-110, non-distress 73-95 (Grossi, Mosconi, Groth, Niero, and Apolone, 2005)); 2. Moderate distress: 61-72; 3. Severe distress: 0-60. Table 7 repots PGWBI scores and means for Italian population and for study samples. Forty-six % of the parents reports a subjective state of severe or moderate distress while 54% describe themselves in a well-being state (Table 6).

Table 6. PGWBI total score in the study sample

	PGWBI Tot			
	Parents sample		Siblings Sample	
	Frequency	Percent	Frequency	Percent
Positive well-being	21	54%	2	13%
Moderate distress	9	23%	6	40%
Severe distress	9	23%	7	47%

In parents sample comparisons between PGWBI and respective normative scores showed PGWBI scores quite lower than the ones obtained by normative population (Table 7) especially in the components of self-control and vitality.

The majority of siblings (13/15, 87%) described themselves as being in a state of low psychological well-being, from moderate to severe distress (Table 6). Comparisons between PGWBI and respective normative scores showed PGWBI scores quite lower than the ones obtained by normative adolescent population (Table 7) especially in the components of anxiety, self-control and general health.

Table 7. PGWBI Italian population and study sample

	PGWBI values in population studies							
	Italian Pop.		Parents sample		Italian adolescent pop.		Siblings sample	
	Mean Score	SD	Mean Score	SD	Mean Score	SD	Mean Score	SD
Anx	17.3	4.96	17.2	4.4	18.5	4.68	15.9	1.70
Dep	12.4	2.69	12.3	2.4	12.7	2.73	12.0	5.41
Pos WB	11.8	4.02	11.3	3.6	13.2	4.03	11.2	3.42
Self Cont.	11.8	2.69	10.7	2.6	12.0	2.49	9.8	2.58
G Health	11.1	3.07	11.6	2.4	12.4	2.57	10.7	2.37
Vitality	13.4	4.0	12.4	3.4	14.6	3.81	12.7	3.08
PGWBI Tot	78	17.89	74.61	15.8	83.5	16.95	71.8	12.9

Levels of Depressive and Anxiety Symptoms in siblings

One-third (33%) of siblings reported depressive symptoms at or above the clinical cut-off score of 16 on the CES-D (Radloff 1977) and were identified as potentially at-risk siblings, while only 2 out of 15 (13%) reported high anxious symptoms on SAS.

Siblings psychological well-being appeared strongly influenced by style of attachment: those with secure attachment style (high level of "Confidence") had a higher level of perceived well-being (Pearson = .645), while siblings with Anxious-Resistant attachment (high levels of "Preoccupation with relationship") or Anxious-Avoidant attachment (high levels of "Discomfort with closeness") had a lower well-being level (Pearson = -.62, Pearson = -.75). Therefore, it appears that relational style seems to influence psychological well-being.

Attachment, Mindfulness and Coping Strategies

In parents Anxious-Resistant attachment or Anxious-Avoidant attachment appeared to be inversely correlated to the parent's ability to be consciousness/mindful about self mental states (Pearson = -0.527, Pearson = -0.331). Furthermore, results show that parents with Anxious-Resistant attachment have a high sense of self attributed guilt and use coping strategies of avoidance, while parents with the level of attribution in parents with Anxious-Avoidant is external (others or partner).

Relationship between Psychological Dimension, Severity of ASD and Demographic Variables

Unexpectedly, in both parents of ASD children, there is no correlation between ASD severity and magnitude of distress (Pearson = -0.127; Pearson = -0.299). No significant differences were found between perceived stress or psychological well-being when comparing gender or family size both in siblings and parents sample.

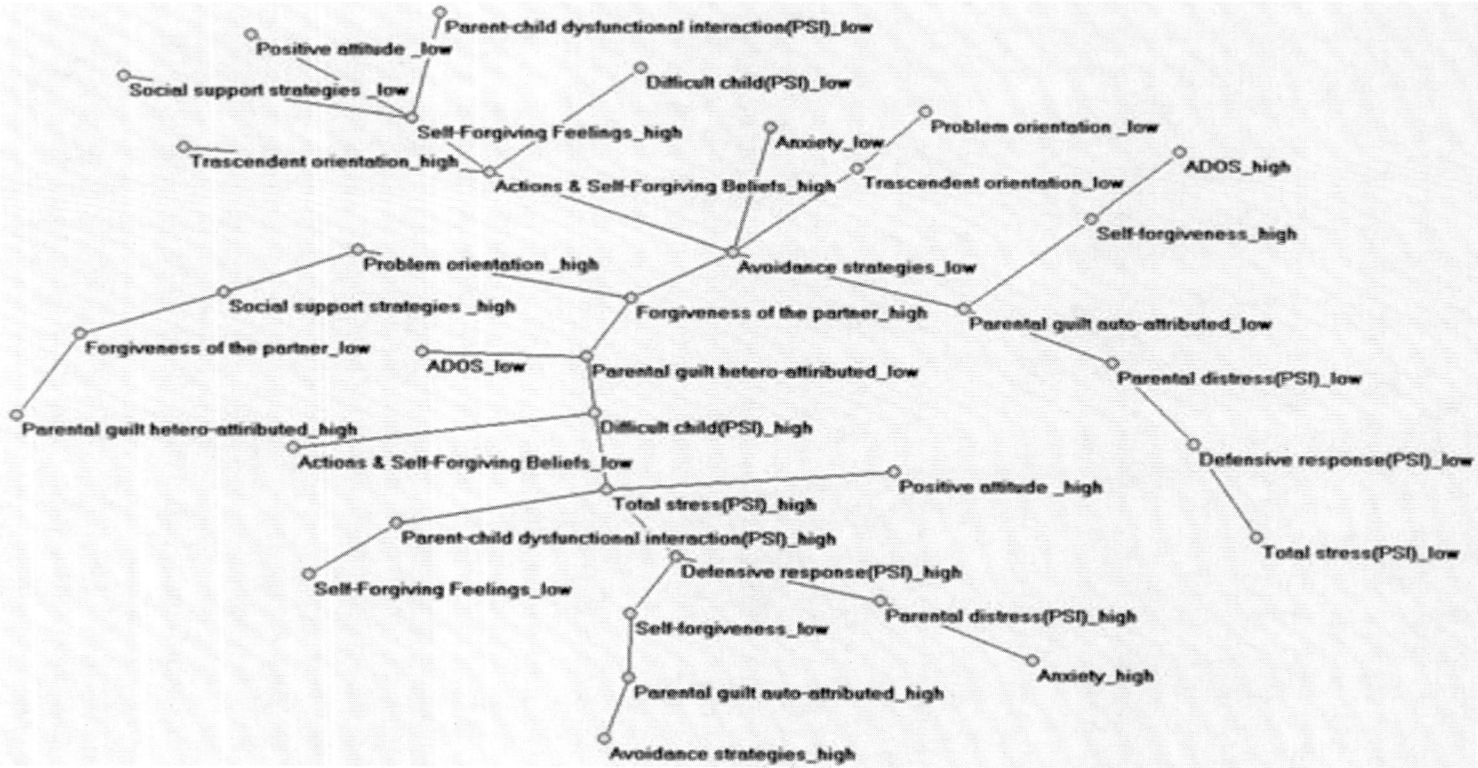

Figure 1. Semantic connectivity map of variables under study obtained by Auto-CM system.

Self Forgiveness, Guilty, Coping Strategies and Distress in Parents

Parents data regarding parental distress, coping styles, self-forgiveness ability and guilt, have been analyzed by Auto-CM system.

Associations, linear or non linear, are visualized as links by transforming the weights determined by Auto-CM into physical distances and applying a simple mathematical (minimum spanning tree) to the matrix of distances. The graph obtained allows a very intuitive visual mapping of the complex web of connection schemes among variables, and greatly eases the detection of the variables that play a key role in the schemes, i.e., that turn out to be "hubs" of the graph generally located in the central part. Auto-CM has been successfully applied in many complex chronic degenerative diseases, since is able to identify consistent trends and associations among variables creating a semantic connectivity map. The matrix of connections, visualized through minimum spanning tree filter, considers nonlinear associations among variables and captures connection schemes among clusters.

As Figure 1 shows, the variables connection scheme of psychological dimensions is remarkably complex with many branches, hubs and interconnections.

Predominant dimensions in families of children with ASD are: low feelings of guilt for themselves, high levels of forgiveness of themselves, and low levels of maladaptive coping responses. These three main dimensions are strictly related among themselves. Different severity (low or high) of psychological dimensions work in different way. High parental mental stress is strictly related to high parental distress subscales (Parental Distress, Difficult Child, Parent-Child Dysfunctional Interaction, Defensive Responding), high maladaptive coping styles, and low self-forgiveness ability. Conversely, low mental stress appears to be marginal in relation to the other psychological dimensions. The severity of the ASD does not seem to be related to parental psychological dimensions. The ADOS- 2 scores, both low and high, are in fact marginal in relation to the other dimensions.

Discussion

Several studies have demonstrated that parents of children diagnosed with ASD experience greater amounts of anxiety, depression, stress, and strained martial relationships than parents of typically developing children or parents of children with other types of developmental delays (Dumas, Wolf, Fisman, and Culligan, 1991; Plant and Sanders, 2007).

Parents and siblings of children with ASD experience significantly more parenting stress than parents of children with no psychological disorder, and this stress is directly related to characteristics of the children. As indicated by the elevated stress scores on the child domain of the Parental Stress Index, parents identified child behavioral factors such as hyperactivity, demandingness, and disturbed mood as contributing to stress within the family system.

It would be important to assess level of parental stress and family functioning and, if necessary, address those factors as part of an overall treatment plan.

This suggests that siblings need to be considered when planning intervention for ASD, as important units within a harmonious functioning of the whole family.

It's important consider siblings in order to identify those potentially at-risk.

In our sample, siblings of children with autism suffer from high distress irrespectively of ASD severity or family size. About one third of them are at risk of developing major depression.

Parents of autistic children tend to blame themselves for their child's disability. This dysfunctional explanation often leads to poorer resilience and health issues for parents. Recent research suggests that an effective way to mitigate the negative consequences of self-blaming is through self-forgiveness, the process whereby a person leaves self-resentment and self-criticism while admitting one's own possible mistakes and omissions. Self-forgiveness has been proven to promote better adjustment in people who blame themselves for life stressors like a medical illness.

The present study intends to examine whether self-forgiveness moderates the negative association between parents' self-blame for their child disability and their well-being.

39 parents of autistic children receiving treatment at a day care center reported their degree of self-blame and self-forgiveness for their children's autism as well as their level of personal well-being and parental distress across a number of dimensions.

Results indicate that self-blame is significantly related to personal well-being and parental distress only for parents reporting lower levels of self-forgiveness. The present findings suggest that interventions promoting self-forgiveness may help parents with reducing negative outcomes that are associated with self-blame.

The interplay of psychological factors related to stress in parents of ASD children is clearly complex. Due to the complexity of these relationships and the lack of symmetry between associations of the same dimension when high or low, the approach with advanced neural networks is essential for a beneficial relationship pattern analysis.

Understanding these relationships is the starting point to activating and enhancing parental resources essential to the wellbeing of both children and caregivers.

Parental resources and skills should be carefully considered in order to guarantee comprehensive and effective support and treatment for the whole family.

Given the high rate of psychological distress and its significant effects on the entire family's quality of life and mental health as well as on child development, it is essential that medical services provide support programs in order to assist parents and siblings in their difficult role in every phase of life's path.

Treatment shouldn't focus only on the child or adolescent with the disease, its impairment and restrictions, but target the entire family as a system, in order to reduce dysfunctional parenting styles (Parental over-reactivity, verbosity, conflict), parental and siblings stress, depression, anxiety, parental and siblings self-blame.

Early intervention aimed at improving adaptive parenting styles (parental confidence, satisfaction, self-efficacy), parental, siblings and children psychological wellbeing and quality of life, children problem behaviours as well as parental mindfulness can facilitate harmonious family functioning and positive changes in the child's ASD symptoms and related behaviors.

Psychological treatment for siblings and parents of ASD children should be provided in preventive programs that promote general wellbeing before the onset of psychological symptoms. This would reduce medical costs in psychopharmacology and long-term psychotherapeutic treatment.

REFERENCES

Abbeduto, L., Seltzer, M. M., Shattuck, P., Krauss, M. W., Orsmond, G. and Murphy, M. M. (2004). Psychological well-being and coping in mothers of youths with autism, Down syndrome, or fragile X syndrome. *Am J Ment Retard,* 109(3), 237-254.

Abidin, R. R. (1995). Parenting Stress Index: Professional Manual (3rd ed.). Odessa, FL: Psychological Assessment Resources, Inc.

American Psychiatric Association. (2013). Diagnostic and statistical manual of mental disorders-5. Washington, DC: American Psychiatric Association.

Baer, R. A., Smith, G. T., Hopkins, J., Krietemeyer, J. and Toney, L. (2006). Using self-report assessment methods to explore facets of mindfulness. *Assessment,* 13, 27-45.

Bagenholm A, Gillberg C (1991). Psychosocial effects on siblings of children with autism and mental retardation: A population-based study. *Journal of Mental Deficiency Research.;* 35:291–307.

Baker-Ericzn, M. J., Brookman-Frazee, L. and Stahmer, A. C. (2005). Stress Levels and Adaptability in Parents of Toddlers With and Without Autism Spectrum Disorders. *Research and practice for persons with severe disabilities,* 30(4), 194-204.

Bayat M., (2007). Evidence of resilience in families of children with autism, *Journal of Intellectual Disability Research,* vol. 51, no. 9, pp. 702–714.

Benderix Y. and Sivberg B. (2007), “Siblings’ experiences of having a brother or sister with autism and mental retardation: a case study of 14 siblings from five families,” *Journal of Pediatric Nursing,* vol. 22, no. 5, pp. 410–418, 2007.

Blacher, J. and McIntyre, L. L. (2006). Syndrome specificity and behavioural disorders in young adults with intellectual disability: Cultural differences in family impact. *Journal ofIntellectual Disability Research,* 50(3), 184-198.

Bouma, R. and Schweitzer, R. (1990). The impact of chronic childhood illness on family stress: A comparison between autism and cystic fibrosis. *Journal of clinical psychology,* 46(6), 722-730.

Buscema M (2007) Squashing Theory and Contractive Map Network, Semeion Technical Paper #32, Rome.

Buscema M, Grossi E (2008) The semantic connectivity map: an adapting self-organising knowledge discovery method in data bases. Experience in gastro-oesophageal reflux disease. *International Journal of Data Mining and Bioinformatics* 2: 362–404.

Buscema M, Grossi E, Ieee (2007) A novel adapting mapping method for emergent properties discovery in data bases: experience in medical field. *2007 IEEE International Conference on Systems, Man and Cybernetics,* Vols 1–8. New York: Ieee. pp. 1495–1501.

Buscema M, Grossi E, Snowdon D, Antuono P (2008) Auto-Contractive Maps: An Artificial Adaptive System for Data Mining. *An Application to Alzheimer Disease. Current Alzheimer Research* 5: 481–vii.

Buscema M, Grossi E, Snowdon D, Antuono P. (2008). Auto-Contractive Maps: an artificial adaptive system for data mining. *An application to Alzheimer disease. Curr Alzheimer Res.*;5(5):481-98.

Buscema M, Helgason C, Grossi E (2008) Auto Contractive Maps, H Function and Maximally Regular Graph: Theory and Applications, Special Session on “Artificial

Adaptive Systems in Medicine: applications in the real world. *Proceeding of North American Fuzzy Information Prcessing Society* (NAFIPS 2008), New York, USA.

Buscema M, Newman F, Massini G, Grossi E, Tastle WJ, and Liu AK (2013) Assessing Post-Radiotherapy Treatment Involving Brain Volume Differences in Children: An Application of Adaptive Systems Methodology, Chapter 1, pp 1-23, in W.J. Tastle (ed.), Data Mining Applications Using Artificial Adaptive Systems, Springer Science+Business Media New York.

Buscema MBM, Sacco PL (2010) Auto-contractive Maps, the H Function, and the Maximally Regular Graph (MRG): A New Methodology for Data Mining; Capecchi V, Buscema M, Contucci P, Damore B, editors. Dordrecht: *Springer.* 227–275 p.

Chassany, O., Dimenäs, E., Dubois, D., Wu, A. and Dupuy, H. (2004). The Psychological General Well-Being Index (PGWBI) User Manual. Lyon, France: MAPI Research Institute.

Compare A, Grossi E, Buscema M, Zarbo C, Mao X, Faletra F, Pasotti E, Moccetti T, Mommersteeg PM, Auricchio A. (2013). Combining personality traits with traditional risk factors for coronary stenosis: an artificial neural networks solution in patients with computed tomography detected coronary artery disease. *Cardiovasc. Psychiatry Neurol:* 814967.

Conner, C. M. and White, S. W. (2014). Stress in mothers of children with autism: trait mindfulness as a protective factor. *Research in Autism Spectrum Disorders,* 8(6), 617-624.

Coppedè F, Grossi E, Buscema M, Migliore L. (2013). Application of artificial neuralnetworks to investigate one-carbon metabolism in Alzheimer's disease and healthy matched individuals. *PLoS One*. 8(8):e74012.

Dabrowska, A. and Pisula, E. (2010). Parenting stress and coping styles in mothers and fathers of pre-school children with autism and Down syndrome. *Journal of Intellectual Disability Research,* 54, 266-280.

Dardas, L. A. and Ahmad, M. M. (2014). Psychosocial correlates of parenting a child with autistic disorder. *J Nurs Res,* 22(3), 183-191.

Davis, N. O., Carter, A. S. (2008). Parenting stress in mothers and fathers of toddlers with autism spectrum disorders: Associations with child characteristics. *Journal of Autism and Developmental Disorders,* 38, 7, 1278–1291.

de Bildt, A., Oosterling, I. J., van Lang, N. D., Sytema, S., Minderaa, R. B., van Engeland, H., et al. (2011). Standardized ADOS scores: Measuring severity of autism spectrum disorders in a Dutch sample. *Journal of Autism and Developmental Disorders,* 41, 311–319.

Deater-Deckard, K. (1998). Parenting stress and child adjustment: Some old hypotheses and new questions. *Clinical Psychological Science and Practice,* 5: 314–332.

Dierker LC, Albano AM, Clarke GN, Heimberg RG, Kendall PC, Merikangas KR, et al. (2001) Screening for anxiety and depression in early adolescence. *Journal of the American Academy of Child and Adolescent Psychiatry;* 40:929–936.

Donnenberg, G. and Baker, B. L. (1993). The impact of young children with externalizing behaviors on their families. *Journal of abnormal child psychology,* 21(2), 179-198.

Dumas, J. E., Wolf, L. C., Fisman, S. N. and Culligan, A. (1991). Parenting stress, child behavior problems, and dysphoria in parents of children with autism, down syndrome, behavior disorders, and normal development. *Exceptionality,* 2(2), 97- 110.

Dupuy, H. J. (1990). The Psychological General Well-being (PGWB) index. In N. K. Wenger, M. E. Mattson, C. D. Furburg, and J. Elinson (Eds.), Assessment of quality of life in clinical trials of cardiovascular therapies (pp. 170–183). New York: Le Jacq Publishing.

Estes, A., Munson, J., Dawson, G., Koehler, E., Zhou, X. H. and Abbott, R. (2009). Parenting stress and psychological functioning among mothers of preschool children with autism and developmental delay. *Autism,* 13(4), 375-387.

Estes, A., Olson, E., Sullivan, K., Greenson, J., Winter, J., Dawson, G. and Munson, J. (2013). Parenting-related stress and psychological distress in mothers of toddlers with autism spectrum disorders. *Brain Dev,* 35(2), 133-138.

Feeney J., Noller P. and Hanrahan (1994). Assessing adult attachment. In Berman W and Sperling M. (eds), Attachment in adults: Clinical and Developmental perspectives, Gulford Press, New York.

Fredman ML, Willard DE (1990) Trans-dichotomous algorithms for minimum spanning trees and shortest paths; pp. 719–725 vol.712.

Gallucci M, Zanardo A, Bendini M, Di Paola F, Boldrini P, Grossi E. (2014) Serum folate, homocysteine, brain atrophy, and auto-CM system: The Treviso Dementia (TREDEM) study. *J Alzheimers Dis.;*38(3):581-7.

Gatzoyia, D., Kotsis, K., Koullourou, I., Goulia, P., Carvalho, A. F., Soulis, S. and Hyphantis, T. (2014). The association of illness perceptions with depressive symptoms and general psychological distress in parents of an offspring with autism spectrum disorder. *Disabil Health J,* 7(2), 173-180.

Giovagnoli, G., Postorino, V., Fatta, L. M., Sanges, V., De Peppo, L., Vassena, L., Mazzone, L. (2015). Behavioral and emotional profile and parental stress in preschool children with autism spectrum disorder. *Res Dev Disabil,* 45-46, 411-421.

Gold N (1993). Depression and social adjustment in siblings of boys with autism. *Journal of Autism and Developmental Disorders.* 23:147–163.

Gotham, K., Pickles, A. and Lord, C. (2009). Standardizing ADOS scores for a measure of severity in autism spectrum disorders. *Journal of Autism and Developmental Disorders,* 39, 693–705.

Gray D.E. (1998), Autism and the Family: Problems, Prospects, and Coping With the Disorder, Charles Thomas, Springfield, Ill, USA, 1998.

Grossi, E., Mosconi, P., Groth, N., Niero, M. and Apolone, G. (2005). Questionario 'Psychological General Well-Being Index.' *Versione Italiana.* Milan: Istituto di Ricerche Farmacologiche Mario Negri.

Guralnick, M. J. (2006). Family influences on early development: Integrating the science of normative development, risk and disability, and intervention. *Blackwell handbook of early childhood development*, 44-61.

Hastings RP (2007). Longitudinal relationships between sibling behavioral adjustment and behavior problems of children with developmental disabilities. *Journal of Autism and Developmental Disorders;* 37:1485–1492.

Hastings RP, Kovshoff H, Brown T, Ward NJ, degli Espinosa F, Remington (2005). Coping strategies in mothers and fathers of preschool and school-age children with autism. *Autism.* B9:377–391.

Hastings, R. P. and Brown, T. (2002). Behavior problems of children with autism, parental selfefficacy, and mental health. *American Journal on Mental Retardation,* 107(3).

Hastings, R. P. and Johnson, E. (2001). Stress in UK families conducting intensive home-based behavioral intervention for their young child with autism. *Journal of Autism and Developmental Disorders*, 31(3), 327-336.

Hayes, S. and Watson, S. (2013). The Impact of Parenting Stress: A Meta-analysis of Studies Comparing the Experience of Parenting Stress in Parents of Children With and Without Autism Spectrum Disorder. *Journal of autism and developmental disorders,* 43(3), 629-642.

Hill-Chapman, C., Herzog, T. and Maduro, R. (2013). Aligning over the child: Parenting alliance mediates the association of autism spectrum disorder atypicality with parenting stress. *Research in Developmental Disabilities,* 34, 1498-1504.

Jones, L., Hastings, R. P., Totsika, V., Keane, L. and Rhule, N. (2014). Child behavior problems and parental well-being in families of children with autism: the mediating role of mindfulness and acceptance. *Am J Intellect Dev Disabil,* 119(2), 171-185.

Kaminsky L, Dewey D. (2002). "Psychosocial adjustment in siblings of children with autism. *Journal of Child Psychology and Psychiatry and Allied Disciplines,* vol. 43, no. 2, pp. 225–232.

Kruskal JB Jr (1956) On the Shortest Spanning Subtree of a Graph and the Traveling Salesman Problem. *Proceedings of the American Mathematical Society* 7: 48–50.

Kugler, K. and Jones, W. H. (1992). On conceptualizing and assessing guilt. *Journal of Personality and Social Psychology*, 62, 318-327.

Kuusikko-Gauffin, S., Pollock-Wurman, R., Mattila, M. L., Jussila, K., Ebeling, H., Pauls, D. and Moilanen, I. (2013). Social anxiety in parents of high-functioning children with autism and Asperger syndrome. *J Autism Dev Disord*, 43(3), 521-529.

Lewinsohn PM, Joiner TE Jr, Rohde P. (2001) Evaluation of cognitive diathesis-stress models in predicting major depressive disorder in adolescents. *Journal of Abnormal Psychology;* 110:203–215.

Licastro F, Porcellini E, Chiappelli M, Forti P, Buscema M, et al. (2010) Multivariable network associated with cognitive decline and dementia. *Neurobiol Aging* 31: 257-269.

Lord, C., Rutter, M., DiLavore, P. C., Risi, S., Gotham, K. and Bishop, S. (2012). Autism diagnostic observation schedule, second edition. Torrance, CA: Western Psychological Services.

Macks R. J. and Reeve R. E. (2007), "The adjustment of non-disabled siblings of children with autism," *Journal of Autism and Developmental Disorders*, vol. 37, no. 6, pp. 1060–1067.

Mates T.E. (1990). Siblings of autistic children: Their adjustment and performance at home and in school. *Journal of Autism and Developmental Disorders;* 20:545–553.

Moyson T. and Roeyers H. (2011), The quality of life of siblings of children with autism spectrum disorder, *Exceptional Children*, vol. 78, pp. 41–55.

Opperman S. and E. Alant E. (2003), The coping responses of the adolescent siblings of children with severe disabilities, *Disability and Rehabilitation,* vol. 25, no. 9, pp. 441–454.

Orsmond G. I. and Seltzer M. M. (2007), Siblings of individuals with autism spectrum disorders across the life course, *Mental Retardationand Developmental Disabilities Research Reviews,* vol. 13, no. 4, pp. 313–320.

Osborne, L. A., McHugh, L., Saunders, J. and Reed, P. (2008). Parenting stress reduces the effectiveness of early teaching interventions for autistic spectrum disorder. *Journal of Autism and Developmental Disorders,* 38, 1092–1103.

Osborne, L.A. and Reed, P. (2009). The relationship between parental stress and behavior problems of children with autistic spectrum disorders. *Exceptional Children,* 76, 54-73.

Pilowsky T., Yirmiya N., Doppelt O., Gross-Tsur V., and Shalev R. S. (2004). Social and emotional adjustment of siblings of children with autism, *Journal of Child Psychology and Psychiatry andAllied Disciplines*, vol. 45, no. 4, pp. 855–865.

Plant, K. M. and Sanders, M. R. (2007). Predictors of care-giver stress in families of preschool-aged children with developmental disabilities. *Journal of Intellectual Disability Research*, 51(2), 109-124.

Radloff LS (1977). The CES-D scale: A self-report depression scale for research in the general population. *Applied Psychological Measurement;* 1:385–401.

Radloff LS (1991). The use of the center for epidemiologic studies depression scale in adolescents and young adults. *Journal of Youth and Adolescence;* 20:149–166.

Rivard, M., Terroux, A., Parent-Boursier, C. and Mercier, C. (2014). Determinants of stress in parents of children with autism spectrum disorders. *Journal of Autism and Developmental Disorders*, 44(7), 1609–1620.

Rivers J. W. and Z. Stoneman Z. (2003), Sibling relationships when a child has autism: marital stress and support coping, *Journal of Autism and Developmental Disorders,* vol. 33, no. 4, pp. 383–394.

Rodrigue J. R., Geffken G. R., and Morgan S. B. (1993). Perceived competence and behavioral adjustment of siblings of children with autism, *Journal of Autism and Developmental Disorders,* vol. 23, no. 4, pp. 665–674.

Rodrigue, J. R., Morgan, S. B. and Geffken, G. (1990). Families of autistic children: Psychological functioning of mothers. *Journal of clinical child psychology,* 19(4), 371-379.

Roeyers H, Mycke K (1995). Siblings of a child with autism, with mental retardation and with normal development. *Child: Care, Health and Development.* 21:305–319

Ross P. and Cuskelly M. (2006). Adjustment, sibling problems and coping strategies of brothers and sisters of children with autistic spectrum disorder, *Journal of Intellectual and Developmental Disability*, vol. 31, no. 2, pp. 77–86.

Ruiz-Robledillo, N., De Andres-Garcia, S., Perez-Blasco, J., Gonzalez-Bono, E. and Moya-Albiol, L. (2014). Highly resilient coping entails better perceived health, high social support and low morning cortisol levels in parents of children with autism spectrum disorder. *Res Dev Disabil,* 35(3), 686-695.

Schoenbach VJ, Kaplan BH, Grimson RC, Wagner EH (1982). Use of a symptom scale to study the prevalence of a depressive syndrome in young adults. *American Journal of Epidemiology;* 116:791–800.

Sica C, Magni M, Ghisi M, Altoè G, Sighinolfi C, et al. (2008) Coping Orientation to Problems Experienced-Nuova Versione Italiana (COPE-NVI): uno strumento per la misura degli stili di coping. *Psicoterapia Cognitiva e Comportamentale* 14: 27–53.

Smith, L. E., Seltzer, M. M., Tager-Flusberg, H., Greenberg, J. S. and Carter, A. S. (2008). A comparative analysis of well-being and coping among mothers of toddlers and mothers of adolescents with ASD. *Journal of Autism and Developmental Disorders,* 38(5), 876-889.

Steinhausen HC, Haslimeier C, Metzke CW (2006). The outcome of episodic versus persistent adolescent depression in young adulthood. *Journal of Affective Disorders* 2006;96:49–57.

Vert´e S., Roeyers H., and Buysse A (2003), Behavioural problems, social competence and self-concept in siblings of children with autism, *Child,* vol. 29, no. 3, pp. 193–205.

Whitehead, K., Dorstyn, D. and Ward, L. (2015). Psychological Adjustment in Families Affected by Autism Spectrum Disorder. *Journal of Developmental and Physical Disabilities,* 27(5), 703-717.

Wohl, M. J. A., DeShea, L. and Wahkinney, R. L. (2008). Looking within: Measuring state self-forgiveness and its relationship to psychological wellbeing. *Canadian Journal of Behavioural Science,* 40, 1-10.

Yamada, A., Suzuki, M., Kato, M., Suzuki, M., Tanaka, S., Shindo, T. Furukawa, T. A. (2007). Emotional distress and its correlates among parents of children with pervasive developmental disorders. *Psychiatry Clin Neurosci,* 61(6), 651-657.

Zimmerman M, Coryell W (1994). Screening for major depressive disorder in the community: A comparison of measures. *Psychological Assessment;* 6:71–74.

Zung, W.W. (1971). A rating instruments for anxiety disirders. *Psichosomatics*; 12: 371-379.

In: Psychological Distress
Editors: A. Compare, C. Elia, A. G. Simonelli et al.
ISBN: 978-1-63485-405-4

Chapter 8

The Role of Stress, Psychological Distress and Coping Strategies in the Etiology and Prognosis of Cardiac Diseases

Cristina Zarbo [1] ***and Angelo Compare*** [1]
[1]University of Bergamo, Department of Human and Social Science,
Bergamo (BG), Italy

Abstract

The World Health Organization states that cardiac diseases are the major cause of death worldwide. Evidence suggests that several psychosocial factors, including psychological distress and maladaptive coping strategies, may influence etiology and prognosis of cardiac diseases. Prolonged psychological distress may result in physiological dysregulations that, in turn, can promote the onset of a cardiac disease or negatively influence its prognosis. Moreover, psychological distress may lead to maladaptive behavioral coping responses (e.g., smoking, alcohol drinking, not adherence to medical treatments, etc.), which can indirectly be linked to the onset or worse prognosis of a cardiac disease. The importance to take into account these psychosocial factors in order to prevent their onset and improve the effectiveness of cardiologic rehabilitation programs will be discussed.

Keywords: stress, psychological distress, cardiac disease, coping

Introduction

The World Health Organization states that cardiac diseases are the first cause of death in the world, causing approximately 7.2 million deaths every year (World Health Organization 2002). Studies over the last decades have focused on the risk factors of the onset and negative prognosis of cardiac diseases and have found that, over the traditional risk factors (e.g., smoking, familiarity, lifestyle, diabetes, etc.), a key role play also psychological and social factors (e.g., mental health, social support, personality traits, psychological distress, and coping styles) (Kop and Gottdiener 2012, Sher 2005, Hansen 2003, Kamarck and Jennings 1991, Sowden and Huffman 2009, Mitchell and Lawrence 2011, Kirk-Gardner and Crossman 1991, Steptoe and Kivimaki 2012). Moreover, a non nonlinear and simultaneous pathway between traditional risk factors for cardiac disease and personality traits has been found (Compare, Grossi, et al. 2013). Evidence has demonstrated that stress as well as several psychosocial factors (e.g., psychological distress, personality, sleep disorder, social isolation, low economic status) increase the risk of cardiac disorders, impair subjective quality of life, and contribute to poorer Health-Related Quality of Life (HRQoL) and prognosis in patients with established cardiac disorder (Gallagher, Parenti, and Doyle 2015, Pogosova et al. 2015).

Moreover, coping behaviors seem to play mediating role of stress on blood sugar, heart rate, and blood pressure (Cox and Gonder-Frederick 1992, Fontana and McLaughlin 1998). Stress and coping responses have been linked to the onset and prognosis outcomes of several medical diseases, such as cardiovascular conditions, cancer, colds, asthma, irritable bowel syndrome, arthritis, respiratory diseases, skin disorders and diabetes (Cox and Gonder-Frederick 1992, Schnall et al. 1998, Cohen and Rabin 1998, Cohen et al. 1998, Wright, Rodriguez, and Cohen 1998, Bennett et al. 1998, Straub et al. 2005, Crofford, Jacobson, and Young 1999, Nielsen et al. 2008, Lebwohl and Tan 1998).

This chapter resumes the concepts of stress, psychological distress and coping strategies as well as summarizes how stress could affect both the etiology and prognosis of a cardiac disease. Moreover, major findings about the role of psychological distress and coping strategies in both etiology and prognosis of cardiac diseases are discussed. Finally, a section shows the most efficient evidence-based interventions to reduce psychological distress as well as improve coping strategies and quality of life of cardiac patients.

STRESS, PSYCHOLOGICAL DISTRESS AND COPING STRATEGIES

Stress is a response that occurs when a person perceives that environmental requests (called "stressors") exceed his/her own supposed coping abilities (Selye 1956). Stress involves both behavioral and physiological mechanisms activated to cope with the stressful situation and return to normality. Mechanisms activated to deal with stressors are called coping responses, including the activation of sympathetic nervous system, the mobilization of the immune system, the secretion of stress hormones as well as behavioral reactions (Selye 1956).

According to Selye (1956), stress involves a specific response pattern, known as General Adaptation Syndrome (GAS), that aims at returning to homeostasis through three stages (alarm, resistance, and exhaustion). It has been shown that if GAS is prolonged over time or really severe, it could lead to psychological and medical diseases (Selye 1956). Stressful events persisting over time or stress experienced continuously have been considered toxic as they have been linked to risk of psychological distress as well as the onset and negative prognosis of several medical diseases (Cohen, Kessler, and Gordon 1995, McEwen 1998). The subsequent psychological distress could be defined as a state of emotional suffering characterized by symptoms of depression and anxiety, sometimes related to somatic symptoms (Drapeau, Marchand, and Beaulieu-Prévost 2012).

Literature is full of evidence about the role of chronic stressors, stress, and psychological distress on the onset and prognosis of medical and mental disorders. It has been shown that several chronic stressors (e.g., caregiving, PTSD, job strain, depressive or anxiety symptoms) could elicit a chronic low-grade hypercoagulable state that could be dangerous for vascular health (Austin, Wissmann, and von Kanel 2013). Moreover, stress has been related to immune system dysfunction, viral infection, broncho-constriction, diabetes mellitus, ulcer, atherosclerosis, chronic fatigue syndrome and cancer (Salleh 2008, Kato et al. 2006).

However, it should be highlighted that stress doesn't necessarily lead to psychological or medical diseases. There is a subjective difference in vulnerability of stress, due to genetic and psychological factors. Indeed, subjects cope differently with stressful situations (Antonovsky 1979). Coping strategies are the constantly cognitive and/or behavioral efforts to manage environmental or internal demands, including efforts to avoid, tolerate, minimize, change or accept stressful stimuli (Lazarus and Folkman 1984). Coping strategies could be problem-focused (i.e., direct actions) or emotion-focused (i.e., palliative actions). Problem-focused coping strategies aim to modify some characteristics of the environment or of the subject itself and could involve various strategies like define the problem, found possible solutions, weight benefits and costs of all solutions, act to change the changeable and, if it is possible and necessary, learn new skills (Lazarus and Folkman 1984). Conversely, emotion-focused coping strategies, usually used when events aren't changeable, aim to decrease emotional distress, through strategies of selective attention, blaming, minimizing, distancing, avoiding, wishful thinking, venting emotions, seeking social support, exercising and meditating (Lazarus and Folkman 1984). Other common coping strategies, that involve elements of both emotion-focused and problem-focused strategies, are seeking social support, religiosity and making meaning to stressful demands. In particular, support seeking involve asking for aid and advices, as well as emotional and concrete support (Thoits 1986). Moreover, it has been shown that coping strategies, as well as traditional risk factors, social supports and functional impairments, predict psychological disorders and distress in cardiac patients (Dew and DiMartini 2005).

Literature has shown that different coping strategies are related to specific psychobiological stress responses and some psychological conditions (Villada et al. 2014). It has been shown that fewer positive coping resources predict higher levels of depression and both predict worse mental status (Di Benedetto et al. 2014).

Coping strategies as well as traditional risk factors, social supports and functional impairments, predict psychological disorders and distress in cardiac patients (Dew and DiMartini 2005). However, coping styles seem to affect mental and physical health indirectly, through depression (Di Benedetto et al. 2014).

Defensive coping enhances cardiac risk, especially in patients with lower cortisol level (de Kock et al. 2015). However, coping strategies seem to be related to personality traits (Connor-Smith and Flachsbart 2007). In particular, problem-solving and cognitive restructuring are predicted by extraversion and conscientiousness traits, as well as neuroticism trait predicts dysfunctional coping strategies (e.g., withdrawal, emotion-focused coping); Support seeking is predicted by extraversion and neuroticism traits (Connor-Smith and Flachsbart 2007).

How does Stress Affect Cardiac Disease?

Literature has shown that stress influences the onset of medical diseases causing negative affective states that, in turn, affect biological mechanisms and behavioral patterns that play a key role on the risk and maintenance of a disease (Cohen, Kessler, and Gordon 1995). Biological and behavioral mechanisms affecting cardiac disease etiology are described below.

Biological Mechanisms

Literature has suggested that stress involves the activation of two endocrine response systems, that are the hypothalamic-pituitary-adrenocortical axis (HPA) and the sympathetic-adrenal-medullary (SAM) systems. HPA and SAM systems involve respectively cortisol and catecholamines relapse, that are both involved in several physiological processes (e.g., anti-inflammatory, gluconeogenesis, cardiovascular, pulmonary, hepatic, and immune responses) (Cohen, Kessler, and Gordon 1995, McEwen 1998). Repeated or prolonged activation of these systems can result in increased risk for psychiatric and medical disorders (Cohen, Kessler, and Gordon 1995, McEwen 1998). In addition, stress may influence the risk of a disease affecting other systems, within the most important for cardiac diseases are the impairment of cardiac vagal tone and of the regulation of immune and inflammatory processes (Porges 1995, Kiecolt-Glaser et al. 2002).

Behavioral Patterns

Perceived stress affects behavioral patterns leading to maladaptive coping responses to stressors, like smoking, drinking alcohol, lack of physical exercises, unhealthy diet, and poor sleep quality. This behavioral pattern may affect the risk of the onset of several medical diseases (Cohen, Kessler, and Gordon 1995, McEwen 1998). Moreover, unhealthy lifestyles decrease adherence to medical treatment (Pogosova et al. 2015) and account for about 63% of deaths (Kushner and Sorensen 2013).

Stress, Psychological Distress and Coping Strategies in Cardiac Diseases

Stress, psychological distress and coping strategies affect the risk of the onset of a cardiac disease, as well as its prognosis and mortality rate. Major evidence about these patterns will be discussed in the following paragraphs.

Risk of Cardiac Disease Onset in Healthy Subjects

Stress and Psychological Distress

Literature has demonstrated a strict link between psychological distress in health subjects and following cardiovascular morbidity and mortality, as well as its potential involvement in pathogenic processes in both healthy and cardiac patients (Rozanski, Blumenthal, and Kaplan 1999, Krantz and McCeney 2002). Strictly related to myocardial infarction events is moreover the anxiety-anger trait (Chorot and Sandin 1993).

Stressful events like natural disasters and war, experience of traumatic events (e.g., bereavement or abuse) increase the risk of cardiovascular disease onset in health subjects (Krantz and McCeney 2002, Rozanski, Blumenthal, and Kaplan 1999, Dong et al. 2004, Li et al. 2002). Among stressful stimuli, high levels of work stress have been particularly associated to following coronary infarction (Chorot and Sandin 1993) and 50% increase of cardiovascular risk (Kivimaki et al. 2006).

Moreover, cardiac patients before the onset of the disease show several psychosocial risk factors (e.g., hostility, social isolation, stress at work) (Fritzsche et al. 2014). Also poor quality of life seems to be a significant risk factor for other cardiovascular risk factors and cardiovascular diseases development (Siegrist 1987).

Coping Strategies

Evidence has shown that some coping strategies can be considered cardiovascular risk factors (Fritzsche et al. 2014, Martin et al. 2013). For example, repressive or defensive coping, that is the capacity to make events and feeling inaccessible to consciousness, has been related to elevated blood pressure levels, essential hypertension, and paroxysmal hypertension (Gleiberman 2007). As well, greater use of Seeking Social Support (SSS) seems to be a risk factor for cardiovascular disease, through atherothrombotic mechanisms activation (e.g., elevated inflammation and coagulation activity) (von Kanel et al. 2012). Conversely, social support existence has been suggested to be a protective factor of cardiovascular risk (Buckley et al. 2010) and a moderating factor between Type D personality and HRV (Martin et al. 2011).

Prognosis of Patients with Cardiac Disease

Stress and Psychological Distress

A large number of patients with a cardiac disease show depressive and anxiety disorders (Fritzsche et al. 2014, Dew and DiMartini 2005). If compared to healthy subjects, patients with hypertension report more stressful life events and distress (Lal, Ahuja, and Madhukar 1982). Patients with Myocardial Infarction (MI) show higher work stressors, acute life changes and lack of social support than healthy subjects, as well as higher exposure to several chronic and acute social risks that are strictly related to the recurrence of cardiac symptoms (Siegrist et al. 1982).

Some evidence has suggested that psychological outcomes can predict health outcomes in cardiac patients (Dew and DiMartini 2005). Stressful events have a significant negative impact on patients with cardiovascular diseases (Lesman-Leegte, Jaarsma, and van Veldhuisen 2006). In particular, high levels of perceived life stress, marital distress, social isolation, anxiety and job overload have been linked to increased recurred cardiovascular events and higher mortality rate in cardiac patients (Rozanski, Blumenthal, and Kaplan 1999, Roest et al. 2014). Moreover, higher levels of distress and depressive symptoms, independently of medical and background characteristics, have been associated with increased mortality 6 months after a cardiac surgery (Smith et al. 2015).

However, life satisfaction of patients with coronary heart disease could positively affect emotional distress (in term of anxiety and depression) in the short and long term (Sanjuán, Ruiz, and Pérez 2011).

Coping Strategies

Several studies have focused on the role of different coping strategies on both the prognosis of heart diseases and psychological outcomes in patients with established disease. Among cardiac patients, depressive coping has been found to be a predictor of low quality of life and emotional wellbeing (Fritzsche et al. 2007). Conversely, less emotional distress and better quality of life seem to be predicted by the employment of a broad range of coping strategies (Fritzsche et al. 2007).

Higher task-oriented coping strategies has been related to less hazard of adverse cardiac events in a sample of acute coronary syndrome patients, independently of demographic, clinical and behavioural data (Messerli-Burgy et al. 2015). Conversely, lower task-oriented coping strategies combined with high depressive symptoms seem to be strictly related to adverse outcomes in the same sample (Messerli-Burgy et al. 2015).

Moreover, Maladaptive coping styles (e.g., denial, focusing and venting of emotions) could be markers of emotional distress (depression) of cardiac patients that are candidates to heart transplant (Burker et al. 2005). Moreover, less use of problem-focused and frequent use of maladaptive coping strategies predict poor or no attendance of Cardiac Rehabilitation (CR) (Whitmarsh, Koutantji, and Sidell 2003). Eye contact and low-aggressiveness behavioural levels are associated to worse mood; displacement behaviour levels are positively related to pre-test anxiety levels, and negatively related to HR stress response; submissive behaviour instead is negatively related to cortisol levels (Villada et al. 2014). Moreover patients with hypertension have higher risk for repressive coping strategies (Mund and Mitte 2012). High approach coping in cardiac patients has been related to subsequent less levels of anxiety and depression, as well as high wellbeing (van Elderen, Maes, and Dusseldorp 1999).

Literature has suggested that social support is a coping strategy that buffers against distress: social support in cardiac patients is related to lower anxiety levels, both state and trait (Hughes et al. 2004). Social support in cardiac men patients predicts life satisfaction (Pérez-García et al. 2011). Conversely, low social support/being unmarried and depression are independent risk factors for poor cardiac prognosis (Compare, Zarbo, et al. 2013). However, evidence has suggested that the function of social support could be moderated by its quality, sustained by the presence of intimacy, good communication, secure attachment and empathy (Zarbo et al. 2013).

It should be highlighted that coping strategies in cardiac patients seem to be significantly related to gender and personality. Men in fact seem to use more adaptive strategies and benefit mostly of protective effects of social support (Pérez-García et al. 2011). Less negative cardiac events are reported by men with higher level of social support when compared to men with low social support (Pérez-García et al. 2011). Neuroticism personality trait in cardiac patients is associated, through problem-focused coping, with the occurrence of post-traumatic stress disorder and general psychological distress, as well as problem-focused coping (Chung et al. 2011).

Psychological Interventions to Reduce Psychological Distress and Improve Coping Strategies in Cardiac Patients

Due to the significant role of stress, distress and coping strategies in cardiac disease onset and prognosis, several studies have focused on the efficacy of Cardiac Rehabilitation (CR) programs and psychological interventions to improve them.

The World Health Organization states that CR is "the sum of activities required to influence favourably the underlying cause of the disease, as well as the best possible, physical, mental and social conditions, so that they (people) may, by their own efforts preserve or resume when lost, as normal a place as possible in the community. Rehabilitation cannot be regarded as an isolated form or stage of therapy but must be integrated within secondary prevention services of which it forms only one facet" (World Health Organization 1993). CR usually includes baseline assessment of patients, physical activity training and counselling, nutritional counselling, management of risk factors (e.g., dyslipidemia, hypertension, obesity, diabetes mellitus, and smoking), as well as psychosocial interventions and counseling (Balady et al. 2007).

Psychosocial interventions denote programs focused on psychological or social factors (e.g., health education, social activities) rather than on biological factors. Evidence has shown that psychological distress could be improved by multicomponent psychosocial strategies that focus on the reduction of risk factors and improvement of coping resources (Dew and DiMartini 2005). Moreover, it has been shown that psychosocial interventions (in particular social activities) for older adults have positive effect on quality of life, life satisfaction and mental health (i.e., reduction of depressive symptoms) (Forsman, Nordmyr, and Wahlbeck 2011). Nevertheless, to be effective the intervention should last at least 3 months (Forsman, Nordmyr, and Wahlbeck 2011).

Multidisciplinary CR has been demonstrated effective in reduce depressive symptoms, type A behaviour pattern, and improve physical and mental health status, job satisfaction levels, internal locus of control and coping strategy "involvement" up to 12 months later (Fiabane et al. 2015). CR program has been related to significant changes in both somatic and cognitive complaints in distressed patients and, if compared to usual care, it has been demonstrated to be more effective in improve functional and psychological morbidity (Hevey, McGee, and Horgan 2007). Multidisciplinary cardiac rehabilitation programmes improve patients' quality of life, exercise capacity, lipid profile, body mass index, body weight, blood pressure, resting heart rate, survival rate, mortality rate, decreased MI risk factors, depression and anxiety (Eshah and Bond 2009). However, Cardiac rehabilitation seems to be more effective in women than in men regarding social inhibition and less effective with regard to vital exhaustion (Barth et al. 2009). It has been suggested that the effectiveness of CR may be due to the interdependence of body and mind, due to the strict link between psychosocial risk factors and cardiovascular diseases onset and prognosis (Pogosova et al. 2015). Moreover, literature has shown that interventions aimed at using action and coping planning strategies are effective in improve adherence to drug treatment (Lourenco et al. 2014).

Finally, it has been shown that web-based distress management program for patients with an implantable cardioverter-defibrillator (WEBCARE), a 12-week fixed behavioral treatment based on the problem-solving principles of cognitive behavioral therapy, isn't effective to reduce anxiety, depression, shock anxiety, and ICD-related concerns or to improve health-related quality of life and device acceptance (Habibovic et al. 2014). It has been shown that a web-based distress management program, if compared to usual care of ICD patients, isn't more effective in improve psychological outcomes (Kroenke 2014).

CONCLUSION

This chapter has provided a brief overview of the link between stress, psychological distress and coping strategies with the onset and prognosis of cardiac diseases (see table 1 for a summary). Due to this strict relation, take into account distress and coping strategies seems to be relevant in order to prevent the onset of a cardiac disease in healthy at risk subjects, and negative prognosis/mortality in cardiac patients. In this setting, psychologists play a key role in helping the medical team to support patients, as well as their families, in the onset, the course, and the rehabilitation of a heart disease (Compare, Zarbo, and Bonaiti 2015). The prevention of negative outcomes due to distress and maladaptive coping strategies, as well as the promotion of wellbeing through supportive psychological, educational and medical programmes could results in a reduction of sanitary costs due to the onset of a medical disease as well as recurrent events and long-term pharmacological treatments.

Table 1. Key points summary

The role of stress, psychological distress and coping strategies on the etiology and prognosis of cardiac diseases: a key points summary

- Traditional risk factors (e.g., smoking, familiarity, lifestyle, diabetes, etc.) psychological and social factors (e.g., mental health, social support, personality traits, psychological distress, coping styles) are related to the onset and prognosis of cardiac diseases. A key role is played by stress, psychological distress and coping strategies.
- Stress influences the onset of medical diseases causing negative affective states that, in turn, affect biological mechanisms (e.g., HPA and SAM systems activation) and behavioral patterns (e.g., maladaptive coping responses) that influence the risk of a disease.
- Stress doesn't necessarily lead to psychological or medical diseases: subjects cope differently with stressful situation. Coping strategies (problem-focused or emotion-focused) include efforts to manage environmental or internal demands.
- Coping strategies that negatively affect cardiac diseases onset and prognosis are: defensive coping, seeking social support, depressive coping, denial, and focusing and venting of emotions.
- Coping strategies that positively affect cardiac diseases onset and prognosis are: task-oriented coping, approach-coping, social support availability, and religiosity.
- Multidisciplinary cardiac rehabilitations and psychosocial interventions as well as action and coping planning strategies interventions have been demonstrated effective to improve depressive symptoms, type A behaviour pattern, physical and mental health status, job satisfaction levels, internal locus of control, coping strategy "involvement", functional and psychological morbidity, quality of life, anxiety, and adherence to drug treatments.

REFERENCES

Antonovsky, A. 1979. Health, stress and coping. San Francisco: Jossey-Bass; 1979: Jossey-Bass.

Austin, A. W., T. Wissmann, and R. von Kanel. 2013. "Stress and hemostasis: an update." *Semin. Thromb Hemost.*, 39 (8):902-12. doi: 10.1055/s-0033-1357487.

Balady, G. J., M. A. Williams, P. A. Ades, V. Bittner, P. Comoss, J. M. Foody, B. Franklin, B. Sanderson, D. Southard, Cardiac Rehabilitation American Heart Association Exercise, the Council on Clinical Cardiology Prevention Committee, Nursing American Heart Association Council on Cardiovascular, Epidemiology American Heart Association Council on, Prevention, Physical Activity American Heart Association Council on Nutrition, Metabolism, Cardiovascular American Association of, and Rehabilitation Pulmonary. 2007. "Core components of cardiac rehabilitation/secondary prevention programs: 2007 update: a scientific statement from the American Heart Association Exercise, Cardiac Rehabilitation, and Prevention Committee, the Council on Clinical Cardiology; the Councils on Cardiovascular Nursing, Epidemiology and Prevention, and Nutrition, Physical Activity, and Metabolism; and the American Association of Cardiovascular and Pulmonary Rehabilitation." Circulation 115 (20):2675-82. doi: 10.1161/ CIRCULATIONAHA.106.180945.

Barth, J., A. Volz, J. P. Schmid, S. Kohls, R. von Kanel, H. Znoj, and H. Saner. 2009. "Gender differences in cardiac rehabilitation outcomes: do women benefit equally in psychological health?" *J. Womens Health (Larchmt),* 18 (12):2033-9. doi: 10.1089/jwh.2008.1058.

Bennett, E. J., C. C. Tennant, C. Piesse, C. A. Badcock, and J. E. Kellow. 1998. "Level of chronic life stress predicts clinical outcome in irritable bowel syndrome." *Gut,* 43 (2):256-61.

Buckley, T., S. McKinley, G. Tofler, and R. Bartrop. 2010. "Cardiovascular risk in early bereavement: a literature review and proposed mechanisms." *Int. J. Nurs. Stud.,* 47 (2):229-38. doi: 10.1016/j.ijnurstu.2009.06.010.

Burker, E. J., D. M. Evon, M. Marroquin Loiselle, J. B. Finkel, and M. R. Mill. 2005. "Coping predicts depression and disability in heart transplant candidates." *J. Psychosom. Res.,* 59 (4):215-22. doi: 10.1016/ j.jpsychores.2005.06.055.

Chorot, P., and B. Sandin. 1993. "Life events and stress reactivity as predictors of cancer, coronary heart disease and anxiety disorders." *International journal of psychosomatics: official publication of the International Psychosomatics Institute*, 41 (1-4):34-40.

Chung, M. C., I. Dennis, Z. Berger, R. Jones, and H. Rudd. 2011. "Posttraumatic stress disorder following myocardial infarction: personality, coping, and trauma exposure characteristics." *Int. J. Psychiatry Med.,* 42 (4):393-419.

Cohen, S., R. C. Kessler, and U. L. Gordon. 1995. "Strategies for measuring stress in studies of psychiatric and physical disorder." In Measuring Stress: A Guide for Health and Social Scientists, edited by Cohen S., Kessler R. C. and Gordon U. L., 3-26. New York, NY: Oxford University Press.

Cohen, S., E. Frank, W. J. Doyle, D. P. Skoner, B. S. Rabin, and J. M. Gwaltney, Jr. 1998. "Types of stressors that increase susceptibility to the common cold in healthy adults." *Health Psychol.,* 17 (3):214-23.

Cohen, S., and B. S. Rabin. 1998. "Psychologic stress, immunity, and cancer." *J. Natl. Cancer Inst.*, 90 (1):3-4.

Compare, A., E. Grossi, M. Buscema, C. Zarbo, X. Mao, F. Faletra, E. Pasotti, T. Moccetti, P. M. Mommersteeg, and A. Auricchio. 2013. "Combining personality traits with traditional risk factors for coronary stenosis: an artificial neural networks solution in patients with computed tomography detected coronary artery disease." *Cardiovasc. Psychiatry Neurol.*, 2013:814967. doi: 10.1155/2013/814967.

Compare, A., C. Zarbo, and A. Bonaiti. 2015. "Psychocardiology and the Role of the Psychologist in Acquired and Congenital Heart Disease." In Clinical Psychology and Congenital Heart Disease, edited by E. Callus and E. Quadri, 133-146. Milan: Springer.

Compare, A., C. Zarbo, G. M. Manzoni, G. Castelnuovo, E. Baldassari, A. Bonardi, E. Callus, and C. Romagnoni. 2013. "Social support, depression, and heart disease: a ten year literature review." *Front. Psychol.*, 4:384. doi: 10.3389/fpsyg.2013.00384.

Connor-Smith, J. K., and C. Flachsbart. 2007. "Relations between personality and coping: a meta-analysis." *J. Pers. Soc. Psychol.*, 93 (6):1080-107. doi: 10.1037/0022-3514.93.6.1080.

Cox, D. J., and L. Gonder-Frederick. 1992. "Major developments in behavioral diabetes research." *J. Consult. Clin. Psychol.*, 60 (4):628-38.

Crofford, L. J., J. Jacobson, and E. Young. 1999. "Modeling the involvement of the hypothalamic-pituitary-adrenal and hypothalamic-pituitary-gonadal axes in autoimmune and stress-related rheumatic syndromes in women." *J. Womens Health,* 8 (2):203-15.

de Kock, A., L. Malan, M. Hamer, M. Cockeran, and N. T. Malan. 2015. "Defensive coping and renovascular disease risk - Adrenal fatigue in a cohort of Africans and Caucasians: The SABPA study." *Physiol. Behav.,* 147:213-9. doi: 10.1016/j.physbeh.2015.04.033.

Dew, M. A., and A. F. DiMartini. 2005. "Psychological disorders and distress after adult cardiothoracic transplantation." *J. Cardiovasc. Nurs.,* 20 (5 Suppl.):S51-66.

Di Benedetto, M., H. Lindner, H. Aucote, J. Churcher, S. McKenzie, N. Croning, and E. Jenkins. 2014. "Co-morbid depression and chronic illness related to coping and physical and mental health status." *Psychol. Health Med.*, 19 (3):253-62. doi: 10.1080/13548506.2013.803135.

Dong, M., W. H. Giles, V. J. Felitti, S. R. Dube, J. E. Williams, D. P. Chapman, and R. F. Anda. 2004. "Insights into causal pathways for ischemic heart disease: adverse childhood experiences study." *Circulation,* 110 (13):1761-6. doi: 10.1161/01.CIR.0000143074.54995.7F.

Drapeau, A., A. Marchand, and D. Beaulieu-Prévost. 2012. "Epidemiology of psychological distress." In Mental Illness. Understanding, Prediction and Control, edited by L. D'Abate, 105-134. INTECH Open Access Publisher.

Eshah, N. F., and A. E. Bond. 2009. "Cardiac rehabilitation programme for coronary heart disease patients: an integrative literature review." *Int. J. Nurs. Pract.*, 15 (3):131-9. doi: 10.1111/j.1440-172X.2009.01738.x.

Fiabane, E., I. Giorgi, S. M. Candura, and P. Argentero. 2015. "Psychological and Work Stress Assessment of Patients following Angioplasty or Heart Surgery: Results of 1-year Follow-up Study." *Stress Health,* 31 (5):393-402. doi: 10.1002/smi.2564.

Fontana, A., and M. McLaughlin. 1998. "Coping and appraisal of daily stressors predict heart rate and blood pressure levels in young women." *Behav. Med.,* 24 (1):5-16. doi: 10.1080/08964289809596376.

Forsman, A. K., J. Nordmyr, and K. Wahlbeck. 2011. "Psychosocial interventions for the promotion of mental health and the prevention of depression among older adults." *Health Promot. Int.,* 26 Suppl. 1:i85-107. doi: 10.1093/heapro/dar074.

Fritzsche, K., F. Forster, A. Schweickhardt, H. Kanwischer, A. Drinkmann, S. Rabung, G. Bergmann, A. Geibel, and C. Herrmann-Lingen. 2007. "Depressive coping is a predictor for emotional distress and poor quality of life in a German-Austrian sample of cardioverter-defibrillator implant recipients at 3 months and 1 year after implantation." *Gen. Hosp. Psychiatry,* 29 (6):526-36. doi: 10.1016/j.genhosppsych.2007.07.003.

Fritzsche, K., S. D. Monsalve, G. Frahm, H. A. Zanjani, F. Goli, and F. K. Y. Chen. 2014. "Psycho-Cardiology." In Psychosomatic Medicine. New York: Springer.

Gallagher, J., G. Parenti, and F. Doyle. 2015. "Psychological Aspects of Cardiac Care and Rehabilitation: Time to Wake Up to Sleep?" *Curr. Cardiol. Rep.*, 17 (12):111. doi: 10.1007/s11886-015-0667-8.

Gleiberman, L. 2007. "Repressive/defensive coping, blood pressure, and cardiovascular rehabilitation." *Curr. Hypertens. Rep.*, 9 (1):7-12.

Habibovic, M., J. Denollet, P. Cuijpers, V. R. Spek, K. C. van den Broek, L. Warmerdam, P. H. van der Voort, J. P. Herrman, L. Bouwels, S. S. Valk, M. Alings, D. A. Theuns, and S. S. Pedersen. 2014. "E-health to manage distress in patients with an implantable cardioverter-defibrillator: primary results of the WEBCARE trial." *Psychosom. Med.,* 76 (8):593-602. doi: 10.1097/PSY.0000000000000096.

Hansen, S. 2003. "Mental health issues associated with cardiovascular disease in women." *Psychiatr. Clin. North Am.*, 26 (3):693-712.

Hevey, D., H. M. McGee, and J. Horgan. 2007. "Relationship of initial level of distress to changes in health-related quality of life during cardiac rehabilitation or usual care." *Psychosom. Med.,* 69 (8):793-7. doi: 10.1097/PSY.0b013e318156bcd2.

Hughes, J. W., A. Tomlinson, J. A. Blumenthal, J. Davidson, M. H. Sketch Jr., and L. L. Watkins. 2004. "Social support and religiosity as coping strategies for anxiety in hospitalized cardiac patients." *Annals of Behavioral Medicine,* 28 (3):179-185.

Kamarck, T., and J. R. Jennings. 1991. "Biobehavioral factors in sudden cardiac death." *Psychol. Bull.,* 109 (1):42-75.

Kato, K., P. F. Sullivan, B. Evengard, and N. L. Pedersen. 2006. "Premorbid predictors of chronic fatigue." *Arch. Gen. Psychiatry,* 63 (11):1267-72. doi: 10.1001/archpsyc.63.11.1267.

Kiecolt-Glaser, J. K., L. McGuire, T. F. Robles, and R. Glaser. 2002. "Emotions, morbidity, and mortality: new perspectives from psychoneuroimmunology." *Annu. Rev. Psychol.,* 53:83-107. doi: 10.1146/annurev.psych.53.100901.135217.

Kirk-Gardner, R., and J. Crossman. 1991. "Cardiac risk factors of smoking, hypertension, obesity and family history: a review of the literature." *Can. J. Cardiovasc. Nurs.*, 2 (1):9-14.

Kivimaki, M., M. Virtanen, M. Elovainio, A. Kouvonen, A. Vaananen, and J. Vahtera. 2006. "Work stress in the etiology of coronary heart disease--a meta-analysis." *Scand. J. Work Environ. Health*, 32 (6):431-42.

Kop, W. J., and J. S. Gottdiener. 2012. "The interaction between psychologic distress and biobehavioral processes in cardiovascular disease." In Psychiatry and Heart Disease: The Mind, Brain, and Heart, 1-17. John Wiley and Sons.

Krantz, D. S., and M. K. McCeney. 2002. "Effects of psychological and social factors on organic disease: a critical assessment of research on coronary heart disease." *Annu. Rev. Psychol.,* 53:341-69. doi: 10.1146/ annurev.psych.53.100901.135208.

Kroenke, K. 2014. "Distance therapy to improve symptoms and quality of life: complementing office-based care with telehealth." *Psychosom. Med.,* 76 (8):578-80. doi: 10.1097/PSY.0000000000000111.

Kushner, R. F., and K. W. Sorensen. 2013. "Lifestyle medicine: the future of chronic disease management." *Curr. Opin. Endocrinol. Diabetes Obes.,* 20 (5):389-95. doi: 10.1097/01.med.0000433056.76699.5d.

Lal, N., R. C. Ahuja, and Madhukar. 1982. "Life events in hypertensive patients." *J. Psychosom. Res.,* 26 (4):441-5.

Lazarus, R. S., and S. Folkman. 1984. Psychological stress and the coping process. New York, NY: Springer.

Lebwohl, M., and M. H. Tan. 1998. "Psoriasis and stress." *Lancet,* 351 (9096):82. doi: 10.1016/S0140-6736(05)78153-8.

Lesman-Leegte, I., T. Jaarsma, and D. J. van Veldhuisen. 2006. "Psychological distress and cardiovascular disease." *Eur. Heart J.,* 27 (9):1123. doi: 10.1093/eurheartj/ehi798.

Li, J., D. Hansen, P. B. Mortensen, and J. Olsen. 2002. "Myocardial infarction in parents who lost a child: a nationwide prospective cohort study in Denmark." *Circulation,* 106 (13):1634-9.

Lourenco, L. B., R. C. Rodrigues, M. A. Ciol, T. M. Sao-Joao, M. E. Cornelio, R. A. Dantas, and M. C. Gallani. 2014. "A randomized controlled trial of the effectiveness of planning strategies in the adherence to medication for coronary artery disease." *J. Adv. Nurs.,* 70 (7):1616-28. doi: 10.1111/ jan.12323.

Martin, L. A., J. W. Critelli, J. A. Doster, C. Powers, M. Purdum, M. R. Doster, and P. L. Lambert. 2013. "Cardiovascular risk: gender differences in lifestyle behaviors and coping strategies." *Int. J. Behav. Med.,* 20 (1):97-105. doi: 10.1007/s12529-011-9204-3.

Martin, L. A., J. A. Doster, J. W. Critelli, M. Purdum, C. Powers, P. L. Lambert, and V. Miranda. 2011. "The 'distressed'personality, coping and cardiovascular risk." *Stress and Health,* 27 (1):64-72.

McEwen, B. S. 1998. "Protective and damaging effects of stress mediators." *N. Engl. J. Med.,* 338 (3):171-9. doi: 10.1056/NEJM199801153380307.

Messerli-Burgy, N., G. J. Molloy, L. Poole, A. Wikman, J. C. Kaski, and A. Steptoe. 2015. "Psychological coping and recurrent major adverse cardiac events following acute coronary syndrome." *Br. J. Psychiatry,* 207 (3): 256-61. doi: 10.1192/bjp.bp.114.154419.

Mitchell, A. J., and D. Lawrence. 2011. "Revascularisation and mortality rates following acute coronary syndromes in people with severe mental illness: comparative meta-analysis." *Br. J. Psychiatry,* 198 (6):434-41. doi: 10.1192/bjp.bp.109.076950.

Mund, M., and K. Mitte. 2012. "The costs of repression: a meta-analysis on the relation between repressive coping and somatic diseases." *Health Psychol.,* 31 (5):640-9. doi: 10.1037/a0026257.

Nielsen, N. R., T. S. Kristensen, P. Schnohr, and M. Gronbaek. 2008. "Perceived stress and cause-specific mortality among men and women: results from a prospective cohort study." *Am. J. Epidemiol.,* 168 (5):481-91; discussion 492-6. doi: 10.1093/aje/kwn157.

Pérez-García, A. M., M. Ruiz, P. Sanjuán, and B. Rueda. 2011. "The association of social support and gender with life satisfaction, emotional symptoms and mental adjustment in patients following a first cardiac coronary event." *Stress and Health*, 27 (3):252-260.

Pogosova, N., H. Saner, S. S. Pedersen, M. E. Cupples, H. McGee, S. Hofer, F. Doyle, J. P. Schmid, R. von Kanel, Prevention Cardiac Rehabilitation Section of the European Association of Cardiovascular, and Cardiology Rehabilitation of the European Society of. 2015. "Psychosocial aspects in cardiac rehabilitation: From theory to practice. A position paper from the Cardiac Rehabilitation Section of the European Association of Cardiovascular Prevention and Rehabilitation of the European Society of Cardiology." *Eur. J. Prev. Cardiol.*, 22 (10):1290-306. doi: 10.1177/ 2047487314543075.

Porges, S. W. 1995. "Cardiac vagal tone: a physiological index of stress." *Neurosci. Biobehav. Rev.*, 19 (2):225-33.

Roest, A. M., A. Heideveld, E. J. Martens, P. de Jonge, and J. Denollet. 2014. "Symptom dimensions of anxiety following myocardial infarction: associations with depressive symptoms and prognosis." *Health Psychol.*, 33 (12):1468-76. doi: 10.1037/a0034806.

Rozanski, A., J. A. Blumenthal, and J. Kaplan. 1999. "Impact of psychological factors on the pathogenesis of cardiovascular disease and implications for therapy." *Circulation*, 99 (16):2192-217.

Salleh, M. R. 2008. "Life event, stress and illness." *Malays. J. Med. Sci.*, 15 (4):9-18.

Sanjuán, P., Á. Ruiz, and A. Pérez. 2011. "Life satisfaction and positive adjustment as predictors of emotional distress in men with coronary heart disease." *Journal of Happiness Studies*, 12 (6):1035-1047.

Schnall, P. L., J. E. Schwartz, P. A. Landsbergis, K. Warren, and T. G. Pickering. 1998. "A longitudinal study of job strain and ambulatory blood pressure: results from a three-year follow-up." *Psychosom. Med.*, 60 (6):697-706.

Selye, H. 1956. The stress of life. New York: McGraw-Hill.

Sher, L. 2005. "Type D personality: the heart, stress, and cortisol." *QJM*, 98 (5):323-9. doi: 10.1093/qjmed/hci064.

Siegrist, J. 1987. "Impaired quality of life as a risk factor in cardiovascular disease." *Journal of Chronic Diseases*, 40 (6):571-578.

Siegrist, J., K. Dittmann, K. Rittner, and I. Weber. 1982. "The social context of active distress in patients with early myocardial infarction." *Soc. Sci. Med.*, 16 (4):443-53.

Smith, P. J., J. A. Blumenthal, E. P. Trulock, K. E. Freedland, R. M. Carney, R. D. Davis, B. M. Hoffman, and S. M. Palmer. 2015. "Psychosocial Predictors of Mortality Following Lung Transplantation." *Am. J. Transplant.*, doi: 10.1111/ajt.13447.

Sowden, G. L., and J. C. Huffman. 2009. "The impact of mental illness on cardiac outcomes: a review for the cardiologist." *Int. J. Cardiol.*, 132 (1):30-7. doi: 10.1016/j.ijcard.2008.10.002.

Steptoe, A., and M. Kivimaki. 2012. "Stress and cardiovascular disease." Nat. *Rev. Cardiol.*, 9 (6):360-70. doi: 10.1038/nrcardio.2012.45.

Straub, R. H., F. S. Dhabhar, J. W. Bijlsma, and M. Cutolo. 2005. "How psychological stress via hormones and nerve fibers may exacerbate rheumatoid arthritis." *Arthritis Rheum.*, 52 (1):16-26. doi: 10.1002/ art.20747.

Thoits, P. A. 1986. "Social support as coping assistance." *J. Consult. Clin. Psychol.*, 54 (4):416-23.

van Elderen, T., S. Maes, and E. Dusseldorp. 1999. "Coping with coronary heart disease: a longitudinal study." *J. Psychosom. Res.*, 47 (2):175-83.

Villada, C., V. Hidalgo, M. Almela, F. Mastorci, A. Sgoifo, and A. Salvador. 2014. "Coping with an acute psychosocial challenge: behavioral and physiological responses in young women." *PLoS One*, 9 (12):e114640. doi: 10.1371/journal.pone.0114640.

von Kanel, R., B. T. Mausbach, J. E. Dimsdale, P. J. Mills, T. L. Patterson, S. Ancoli-Israel, M. G. Ziegler, S. K. Roepke, M. Allison, and I. Grant. 2012. "Ways of coping and biomarkers of an increased atherothrombotic cardiovascular disease risk in elderly individuals." *Cardiovasc. Psychiatry Neurol.*, 2012:875876. doi: 10.1155/2012/875876.

Whitmarsh, A., M. Koutantji, and K. Sidell. 2003. "Illness perceptions, mood and coping in predicting attendance at cardiac rehabilitation." *Br. J. Health Psychol.*, 8 (Pt 2):209-21. doi: 10.1348/135910703321649178.

World Health Organization. 1993. "Needs and action priorities in cardiac rehabilitation and secondary prevention in patients with CHD." World Health Organization. Available from http://whqlibdoc.who.int/euro/-1993/EUR_ICP_CVD_125.pdf.

World Health Organization. 2002. "The world health report 2002 - reducing risks, promoting healthy life." World Health Organization.

Wright, R. J., M. Rodriguez, and S. Cohen. 1998. "Review of psychosocial stress and asthma: an integrated biopsychosocial approach." *Thorax,* 53 (12):1066-74.

Zarbo, C., A. Compare, E. Baldassari, A. Bonardi, and C. Romagnoni. 2013. "In Sickness and in Health: a Literature Review about Function of Social Support within Anxiety and Heart Disease Association." *Clin. Pract. Epidemiol. Ment. Health,* 9:255-62. doi: 10.2174/1745017901309010255.

In: Psychological Distress
Editors: A. Compare, C. Elia, A. G. Simonelli et al.
ISBN: 978-1-63485-405-4

Chapter 9

Assessment of Physiological Patterns of Acute Stress Responses: The Role of Near-Infrared Spectroscopy

Agostino Brugnera[1,*], Kaoru Sakatani[2] and Angelo Compare[1]
[1]Department of Human and Social Sciences, University of Bergamo, Bergamo, Italy
[2]NEWCAT Research Institute, Department of Electrical and Electronic Engineering, College of Engineering, Nihon University, Japan

Abstract

Near-Infrared Spectroscopy (NIRS) is a functional neuroimaging technique based on the properties of light that allows a non-invasive measurement of concentration changes in cortical hemoglobin. Developed in the last 40 years, NIRS can be used to detect
non-invasively the activation patterns of cerebral cortex. Its use in the field of psychophysiology has constantly increased over time, thanks to some intrinsic advantages over other neuroimaging techniques.

Even so, one of the areas understudied using NIRS technology is stress responses. The exposure to both acute and chronic psychosocial stressors can lead to unfavorable health outcomes. Moreover, literature collected and meta-analyzed over time shows that the exposition to stressors hyperactivates right frontal areas of the cortex as well as neuroendocrine systems. Interestingly, these findings have been partly replicated by few NIRS studies, even though a number of methodological and practical issues have been raised.

The resolution of these problems could allow in future NIRS studies, to better explore the neurophysiological underpinnings of stress responses and even contribute to study the protective/risk factors of those physical and mental diseases exacerbated by stress.

Keywords: NIRS, stress responses, psychosocial stress, ANS, HPA, right prefrontal cortex

---

* Corresponding author: Agostino Brugnera. Email: agostino.brugnera@unibg.it.

Introduction

Stress responses and stressors are probably one of the most investigated areas in neurophysiology, medicine and psychology due to the profound effects on physical and mental health: stress for example, is widely considered one of the main risk factors for the onset/worsening of cardiovascular diseases (Backé et al. 2012).

Stress can be defined as a modality of reaction to social, cognitive or physiological events (commonly called stressors), that alters the physiological homeostatic process of the body, and it is critical to the adaptation of the organism to its environment (Kogler et al. 2015). Typically, stress responses are dichotomized as acute or chronic basing on their total length, while stressors are categorized in physiological (e.g., pain, hunger) and psychosocial (e.g., social exclusion, achievement situations) basing on their characteristics (Kogler et al. 2015).

Clinical and experimental researches showed a correlation between both chronic and acute stress and the development of various diseases (Backé et al. 2012). From a physiological point of view, a stress response leads to the activation of neuroendocrine systems and of various cerebral areas (Rutters et al. 2014, Kogler et al. 2015) that – if acutely or chronically hyperactivated- could result in negative consequences on physical health (Rutters et al. 2014). Long-lasting stress conditions could even induce anatomical volume changes in the brain and neural reorganization (Kogler et al. 2015).

Therefore, functional studies on stress are essential to understand the pathophysiology of various morbid conditions linked to it and to explore some of the questions still open in literature, especially if using hi-tech instruments such as near-infrared spectroscopy (NIRS).

This chapter will focus on acute physiological responses to psychosocial stressors that are more easily investigated in psychophysiology, using both laboratory and ecological settings. This area has been understudied with NIRS, a relatively new neuroimaging technique based on scattering and absorption properties of near-infrared light.

Initially we will discuss stress responses, from both autonomic and cerebral point of view, and how they're linked with anxiety. In the following paragraphs, after a short summary on various neuroimaging technologies, we will introduce NIRS technology, its principles of functioning as well as pros and cons.

Finally, we will discuss the NIRS literature on prefrontal cortical and neuroendocrine reactivity to psychosocial stressors. Indeed, the sympathetic branch of autonomic nervous system, the hypothalamic-pituitary-adrenocortical axis and right areas of prefrontal cortex share common elements: during acute stress tasks, they evidence a hyperactivity which correlate to, or is detected by near-infrared spectroscopy, as extensively discussed in the latest paragraphs of this chapter.

Neuroendocrine Systems and Stress Responses

Stressful events lead to the activation of subcortical areas (e.g., brainstem nuclei, hypothalamic paraventricular nucleus and amygdala) that subsequently trigger two neuroendocrine systems. These systems automatically work together to modulate responses to acute stressors with the aim of preserving the physiological integrity of the organism (Ulrich-Lai and Herman 2009).

The first is the hypothalamic-pituitary-adrenocortical axis (HPA): when activated by stress responses, HPA induces a cascade of endocrine changes that leads to glucorticoids (especially cortisol) release approximately ten minutes after the initiation of the stress (Ulrich-Lai and Herman 2009, Herman and Cullinan 1997).

The cortisol, considered the prototypical stress hormone, has profound effects on body, acutely altering metabolic and immune functions of the organism.

The second is the autonomic nervous system (ANS), which is composed of two antagonistic branches, namely the sympathetic and the parasympathetic nervous system. The former is involved in excitatory "fight-or-flight" responses, while the latter in inhibitory "rest-and-digest" responses.

The sympathetic branch provides immediate responses to stress exposure through the activation of the sympatho-adrenomedullary axis (SAM): the activation of this axis leads to i) the release of adrenaline and noradrenaline, and ii) to acute increases of heart rate and blood pressure by exciting the cardiovascular system (Ulrich-Lai and Herman 2009).

The latter outcome, called cardiac reactivity, has been extensively studied in laboratory settings: indeed, individuals showing greater cardiovascular shifts during a psychosocial stress task suffer of high rates of long-term mortality (Carroll et al. 2012). A greater cardiovascular reactivity is characterized by higher blood pressure status that (over time) could increase the risk of mortality due to i) the harmful effect of hypertension and atherosclerosis or ii) an acute triggering effect of cardiovascular events (Carroll et al. 2012).

Changes in HPA axis activity are commonly detected evaluating cortisol concentrations over time, or using indirect methods such as the evaluation of sebaceous hyperplasia (Tanida, Katsuyama, and Sakatani 2007).

Changes in ANS activity are typically examined through the analysis of Heart Rate and Heart Rate Variability: evidence suggests that stress stimuli result in parasympathetic withdrawal and increased sympathetic activity (Tanida, Katsuyama, and Sakatani 2007), leading to higher heart rates and lower High Frequencies (For a review on HRV and its indexes, see for example Cardiology and Cardiology 1996). Interestingly, both neuroendocrine responses can be modulated or even inhibited by neuronal circuitry that originate in prefrontal cortex (Herman and Cullinan 1997).

Cerebral (De)Activation Patterns of Stress Responses

Acute responses to psychosocial stress tasks are characterized by complex activation/ deactivation patterns of various cerebral structures, as reviewed in a recent meta-analysis (Kogler et al. 2015).

Psychosocial stress increases the activity of i) right fronto-temporal areas, such as the right superior temporal gyrus (STG) and the right inferior frontal gyrus (IFG), and ii) ventral/anterior part of the insula (Kogler et al. 2015).

The STG region, located in the temporal lobe, seems to be involved in cognitive control of emotions and attentional processes, therefore its activation during psychosocial stress tasks could be explained as a result of "enhanced attention processing and regulation of emotional arousal," which enables the subjects to implement goal-directed and focused behaviors (Kogler et al. 2015).

The IFG region, which corresponds to the ventrolateral prefrontal cortex, seems to be involved, again, in cognitive control (i.e., suppressing) of emotions and in the regulation/processing of negative affective states, therefore its involvement during psychosocial stress could suggest an active processing of negative experiences, accompanied by inhibition of behavioral impulses such as potential flight reactions (Kogler et al. 2015).

Finally, the insula, a cerebral region that seems to mediate affective and sensorial processing, is probably activated during psychosocial stress to encode "affective and autonomic features of the current state" (Kogler et al. 2015).

As regards the cerebral deactivation patterns, psychosocial stress is associated with a hypoactivation of subcortical telencefalic structures, such as left caudate nucleus and the putamen.

The former region is involved in motivation and reward processing suggesting that psychosocial stress impact the motivational system (e.g., decreasing motivation, positive reinforcement processing, and inducing anhedonia). The latter region is involved in motor processes, pain sensation and intensity discrimination, suggesting that psychosocial stress lead to reduced motor responses and decreased pain-related stimuli properties (Kogler et al. 2015).

From a conceptual point of view, the asymmetry in prefrontal cortical areas (i.e., in the IFG) during stress responses can also be explained by approach-withdrawal hypothesis, developed by Davidson in the late 80's (1992, 2002, 1990, 1999). Davidson observed that left and right prefrontal lesions produce different emotional reactions in patients, and from a number of ECG studies, that left prefrontal regions have a greater involvement in positive emotions, while right prefrontal regions in negative ones (Wheeler, Davidson, and Tomarken 1993).

Therefore, considering that emotional circuitries involve a number of brain regions (i.e., PFC, anterior cingulate cortex, hippocampus, insular cortex and amygdala) he advanced the hypothesis that different forms of motivations and emotions are mediated by two basic systems, namely the approach and the withdrawal system (Wheeler, Davidson, and Tomarken 1993, Davidson and Irwin 1999).

"The approach system facilitates appetitive behavior and generates certain types of positive affect that are approach-related (e.g., enthusiasm). This form of positive affect is usually generated in the context of moving toward a desired goal. The withdrawal system facilitates the withdrawal of an individual from sources of aversive stimulation and generates certain forms of negative affect (e.g., fear and disgust) that are withdrawal-related" (Davidson and Irwin 1999).

Davidson (1999) considered that these systems are implemented in partially separable and lateralized neural circuits, and that the lateralization is more evident in PFC.

Indeed, left prefrontal regions have specialized circuitry to mediate approach-related behaviors, while the right ones mediate withdrawal-related behaviors (Wheeler, Davidson, and Tomarken 1993). Using this hypothesis as a framework, stressors lead to withdrawal-related behaviors (which generate negative emotions) and consequently to an activation of the right side of prefrontal cortex.

Anxiety Leads to an Hyperactivation of Right PFC during Stressful Tasks

A typical emotion associated with withdrawal behaviors is anxiety, which increases the distance between the organism and a source of aversive stimulation and, thus, leads to a hyperactivation of right anterior cortical areas (Davidson and Irwin 1999). This hyperactivation is noticeable even during acute psychosocial stress tasks, as evidenced by previous studies (see for example Tanida et al., 2007).

As suggested in the previous paragraph, two key areas of emotional responses are the prefrontal cortex (PFC) and the amygdala. The latter is a subcortical structure crucial for emotional learning (such as fear conditioning) and for the expression of cue-specific fear (Davidson 2002). Amygdala, along with PFC, plays an important role in governing various aspects of anxiety (Davidson 2002). Both structures share extensive bidirectional connections; for example, PFC efferents have an inhibitory input to the amygdala to extinguish aversive responses (Davidson 2002).

Moreover, these connections are subjected to a lateralization, with the left PFC that seems to inhibit the amygdala, and the right PFC to increase the metabolic activity in the amygdala (Davidson 2002). Anxiety, characterized by an increased vigilance toward harmful stimuli "to stop ongoing behavior and re-orient processing capacity to address a perceived threat," elicits therefore higher neuronal activity in right sectors of prefrontal cortex and, correspondingly, in the amygdala (Davidson 2002).

Neuroimaging Methods and Cerebral Stress Responses

Researchers can use various functional neuroimaging techniques to evaluate cerebral responses during stress tasks, such as electroencephalography (EEG), magnetoencephalography (MEG), positron emission tomography (PET), single-positron emission computed tomography (SPECT) and functional magnetic resonance imaging (fMRI).

As reviewed by Strangman, Boas and Sutton (2002) the aforementioned techniques can provide direct or indirect information about cerebral activity.

EEG, event-triggered EEG (called event related potentials; ERP) and MEG are considered direct methods, as they monitor the brain electromagnetic activity (Strangman, Boas, and Sutton 2002). PET, SPECT and fMRI are considered indirect methods, as they indirectly monitor the hemodynamic changes resulting from the brain electrical activity (Strangman, Boas, and Sutton 2002). Each of these techniques has some advantages and limitations.

EEG, ERP and MEG suffer from a limited spatial resolution, while having a strong temporal sensitivity; PET, SPECT and fMRI, instead, have stronger spatial resolution but suffer from a reduced temporal sensitivity (Strangman, Boas, and Sutton 2002).

However, both direct and indirect techniques are limited by high management costs, they require specialized personnel for their management, and the equipment (such in the case of fMRI) is extremely expensive. Moreover, all the indirect techniques, as well as fMRI, require the subjects to sit or lie still in a very narrow and noisy environment (such in the case of fMRI) or in shielded experimental rooms (Dieler, Tupak, and Fallgatter 2012).

Among the neuroimaging techniques, NIRS constitutes a more recent but less widespread indirect technology: due to its advantages, described in the paragraphs below, NIRS constitutes a promising tool in the field of neuroscience and in the real-time evaluation of stress responses.

NIRS: What It Is and Principles of Functioning

NIRS is a light-based technology that allows a non-invasive measurement and monitoring of in-vivo concentration changes in cortical oxygenated (O-Hb), deoxygenated (H-Hb) and total (T-Hb = O-Hb + H-Hb) hemoglobin (Soul and du Plessis 1999, Pellicer and del Carmen Bravo 2011). Before the late '70 it was considered impossible–using spectroscopic techniques- to retrieve information from the cortical layers of the brain due to apparent optical limits, such as the presence of strong scattering phenomena or the relative opacity of skull (Strangman, Boas, and Sutton 2002, Scholkmann et al. 2014). However, in 1977 Jobsis was the first to demonstrate the feasibility of a continuous and non-invasive monitoring of hemoglobin concentration changes in the brain, using near-infrared light (Jobsis 1977, Scholkmann et al. 2014), opening up a new research area.

NIRS is used to investigate cerebral functions in humans, allowing to monitor cortical activity simply using light applied to and detected from the scalp (Strangman, Boas, and Sutton 2002). Cerebral activity, indeed, increases oxygen consumption in that specific brain area, leading to increased cerebral blood flow (rCBF) and therefore to concentration changes of local O-Hb and H-Hb (Scholkmann et al. 2014). This phenomenon, called neurovascular coupling, leads to a decrease of H-Hb accompanied with a two or threefold increase in magnitude of O-Hb, and it is detected non-invasively by NIRS (Scholkmann et al. 2014, Ferrari, Mottola, and Quaresima 2004). Interestingly, NIRS monitors primarily venous blood, because in the cerebral tissues hemoglobin is distributed in a proportion of ~70% venous and ~30% arterial (Murkin and Arango 2009).

NIRS is based on the principles that i) biological tissues are relatively transparent to light in the near-infrared range (700-1000 nm), and ii) the propagation of light through these tissues depends mainly on scattering and absorption phenomena (Soul and du Plessis 1999, Pellicer and del Carmen Bravo 2011). The crucial point is that the main absorbing molecules (the so-called chromophores) of NIR light in biological tissues are oxy- and deoxy-hemoglobin, and that each of these chromophores absorb NIR light of different wavelengths (Strangman, Boas, and Sutton 2002).

An optical law (the modified Beer-Lambert law) can describe the relationship between absorption of NIR light by chromophore at a specific wavelength, and the chromophore's concentration in tissue (Soul and du Plessis 1999).

Thus, simply applying the aforementioned law, NIRS is capable of measuring the concentration changes -in the cortical tissue- of intravascular oxygenated, deoxygenated and total hemoglobin and, therefore, increases (or decreases) in brain activity (Soul and du Plessis 1999).

In summary NIR light, injected in the scalp through specific emitters, penetrates forehead skin and skull, reaching the underlying cortex for some centimeters, and it is either scattered (deviated from its trajectory) or absorbed by chromophores (Strangman, Boas, and Sutton 2002, Ferrari, Mottola, and Quaresima 2004).

Most of the commercially available NIRS devices use the so-called Reflectance Mode, in which "receiving optodes are placed ipsilateral to the transmitter and exploit the fact that photons transmitted through a sphere will traverse an elliptical [often referred as banana-shaped] path in which the mean depth of penetration is proportional to the transmitter and receiver optode separation" (Murkin and Arango 2009).

Typologies of NIRS Devices

In the last 40 years, technical and technological advancements allowed to realize three different NIRS techniques, namely the continuous wave (CW), the time-domain (TD) and frequency domain (FD) ones (Scholkmann et al. 2014). Each of these devices can have up to 16-24 channels, or even more (such as some CW systems).

CW devices were the first type of near-infrared technology to be ever built, after the discovery of Jobsis. CW instruments simply inject NIR light on the scalp, and then measure the intensity of the re-emerging light, applying the aforementioned modified Beer-Lambert law (Scholkmann et al. 2014). The main limit of CW devices is that they can only measure relative concentration changes of OHb and HHb in the tissues, which are evaluated with respect to an arbitrary zero (Scholkmann et al. 2014). That is, CW devices assume that scattering is constant over time, and that the changes in absorption are only due to blood (Pellicer and del Carmen Bravo 2011).

On the other hand, CW devices are extremely small, portable and relatively cheap.

Interestingly, it is possible to arrange CW instruments to realize a spatially resolved spectroscopy (SRS), capable of measuring the absolute values of OHb and HHb in tissues, but a description of SRS goes beyond the scope of this chapter (for a review, see for example Pellicer and del Carmen Bravo 2011).

TD and FD are far more complex devices; they were developed more recentlyand they measure the intensity of re-emerging light and also the time of flight of photons, enabling to compute the absolute concentration changes of oxy- and deoxy-hemoglobin (Scholkmann et al. 2014).

The main problems of TD and FD technology are i) device cost, which is higher compared to CW, ii) device weight, which is significant even for 2-channel instruments and iii) reduced temporal sensibility (i.e., TD devices can acquire only 1 sample per second). However, the main advantage is their capability to evaluate the absolute (and not the relative) concentration changes of chromophores.

Advantages and Limitations of Near-Infrared Spectroscopy

When compared to other neuroimaging techniques, NIRS can provide excellent temporal sensitivity (up to 61 Hz for CW devices), even though lower than ERP, MEG and EEG, and a reasonable spatial sensitivity, even though lower than fMRI (Strangman, Boas, and Sutton 2002).

As aforementioned, the main advantage of NIRS consists in its capability to provide continuous and in-vivo measurements of intravascular hemodynamics of both adults and infants (Soul and du Plessis 1999), providing therefore real time information about cortical activity. Near-Infrared technology is also harmless (it simply uses proprieties of light), non-invasive and noise-resistant (i.e., individuals undergoing evaluation can speak; electromagnetic interferences are minimal) and it is less sensitive to external noise sources (e.g., movements). NIRS can be used with subjects in any position (e.g., lying in bed or sitting still), without requiring particular laboratory rooms (e.g., faraday cages). It requires less time and burden (both physical and psychological) for the preparation of the subjects and the application of the probes.

Finally, some CW devices, such as 2-channel ones, are extremely portable, potentially opening their use in natural settings (i.e., during natural experiments characterized by high ecological validity).

As regards the limits, one of the main problems is the penetration depth of the NIRS signal, which allows to measure only hemodynamic responses of the most superficial layers of the cortex (Dieler, Tupak, and Fallgatter 2012). Therefore, NIRS is unsuitable to evaluate the activity of subcortical structures. Other limits are i) the interference of skull thickness and hairs in the penetration of light in the brain, ii) the difficulty in predicting the origin of NIRS signal (e.g., brain or scalp blood flow), and iii) the lack of standard procedures in signal processing, data analysis and instrumentation (for more information on limits, see Dieler, Tupak, and Fallgatter 2012, Ferrari, Mottola, and Quaresima 2004).

The Evaluation of PFC Activity during Stress Responses: The Use of NIRS

As reviewed before, one of the cerebral areas most involved in stress responses is the right prefrontal cortex (PFC). The meta-analysis of Kogler and colleagues (2015), indeed, evidenced that a specific right sector of frontal areas, called right inferior frontal gyrus (IFG), has an important role in cognitive processing of emotions and in the regulation/experience of negative affects. Furthermore, the approach-withdrawal hypothesis suggests a main role of right prefrontal cortex in mediating withdrawal behaviors and negative emotions, as commonly experienced during stress responses.

Therefore, NIRS technology seems a valuable tool to evaluate prefrontal activity during acute stress responses, in accordance with the aforementioned hypotheses of Davidson (1990, 1992) and the results of the meta-analysis of Kogler (2015). Unfortunately, due to its limited depth resolution, NIRS cannot evidence activation patterns in the insula or deactivations in telencefalic structures. Even temporal activity (i.e., in the inferior frontal gyrus) is more challenging to evaluate as compared to the PFC one, due to the presence of melatonin in the hairs that can absorb and therefore limit the propagation of NIR light. Nevertheless, PFC is typically one of the main focused areas in studies about stress responses.

As regards the paradigm, NIRS studies typically use a mathematical task, considered a form of psychosocial stressor. Indeed, this cognitive task is considered an achievement situation that requires goal-directed performances, with social pressure induced by the presence of experimenters. A limit of the literature is that many scientists (Hoshi and Tamura

1993, Fujimaki, Takemoto, and Morinobu 2014) have not searched for functional hemispheric differences using statistical methods (such as analysis of variance, ANOVA) or a laterality index ([right – left]/[right + left]).

Therefore, a number of potentially valuable studies were excluded from this review due to the absence of analyses on asymmetrical PFC activity during stress tasks. Despite some methodological and practical limitations, and the paucity of researches on this field, some studies have evidenced an asymmetric right PFC activity during stress responses. Interestingly, this activity was stronger in subjects with higher anxiety.

Tanida and colleagues (2004) evaluated the cortical responses of 16 adult females to an arithmetic task, which consisted in subtracting 2-digit number from a 4-digit number as quickly as possible for 60s. Authors used a 2-channel CW-NIRS device, located over the left and right PFC. Based on the HR reactivity to the stress task, the 16 female participants were divided in 2 groups, High- and Low-HR. In the High-HR group, the laterality score evidenced an asymmetrical right PFC activity during the task, while in the Low-HR group results were opposite (laterality scores showed negative values). The lack of manipulation checks of the stress induction, however, did not allow to draw more robust conclusions.

In the 2007, Tanida, Katsuyama and Sakatani specifically studied stress responses on 20 young female adults, using the same paradigm of the previous paper (Tanida et al. 2004). The 2-channel spatially resolved CW-NIRS system was positioned on the left and right PFC (over the dorsolateral and frontopolar area). This study evaluated HR, HRV, PFC activities and also the level of sebaceous secretion and P. acne populations. Indeed, the HPA axis hyperactivity, commonly observed during acute stress responses, can cause sebaceous hyperplasia and aggravate acne. As regards the results, the task elicited stress responses in participants, as evidenced by the STAI state scores that were significantly different from the baseline to the post-task. That is, a manipulation check was implemented. Correlational analyses evidenced that individuals with right-dominant laterality index (i.e., those with an increased activity of the right PFC during the task), experienced larger increases of HR, a decrease of parasympathetic activity (evidenced by HRV analyses), and an increase in sebum levels and in acne population (Tanida, Katsuyama, and Sakatani 2007).

Yang and colleagues (2009), in a study focused on gender-differences, examined hemodynamic responses of 30 young university adults (15 males, 15 females) using 2 mathematical tasks with different difficulties (First task: subtractions of 1-digit number from a 3-digit number. Second task: subtractions of 2-digit number from a 3-digit number). The 16-channel CW-NIRS device used in this research was positioned on prefrontal areas. However, an ANOVA with also channels and hemisphere as factors evidenced no significant effect. It should be noted that stress responses were not the main focus of this study: no cardiac data were collected and no manipulation checks for stress induction were used.

In 2010, Sakatani and colleagues explored the physiological differences in cortical and autonomous reactivity among 24 young and 11 middle-aged adult females during the same psychosocial stress task used in the previous papers of Tanida and colleagues (2004, 2007). Researchers used a 2 channel spatially resolved CW-NIRS system, that was positioned on the left and right PFC (over the dorsolateral and frontopolar area). After selecting the participants who showed a contemporary increase of Oxy-Hb and a decrease of Deoxy-Hb during the tasks, further analyses evidenced as expected, a correlation between right-dominant laterality index and increased HR in both young and middle-aged adults. Interestingly, the hemodynamic and cardiac responses were a function of age (i.e., responses were flattered in older adults, when compared to the ones of young adults).

Takizawa and colleagues published in 2014 a paper on NIRS and stress responses. Authors administered to 70 healthy individuals (45 males, 25 females) the Uchida-Kraepelin test (UKT), a standardized serial arithmetic test capable of elicit psychosocial stress (for more detail about, see Takizawa et al. 2014), recording fronto-temporal activity using a 24-channel CW-NIRS system. NIRS probes evidenced an increase in Oxy-Hb in all the PFC channels during the task, but no hemispheric differences were evaluated (using, for example a laterality index or an ANOVA). However, results showed a correlation between the right lateral PFC, state/trait anxiety (evaluated through the STAI questionnaire) and performances. State anxiety, indeed, was associated with a greater increase in Oxy-Hb in right frontopolar and dorsolateral PFC, while trait anxiety was associated with a smaller decrease in Deoxy-Hb in the same regions. Finally, performance during the tasks positively correlated with a greater increase in Oxy-Hb in right ventrolateral PFC. Therefore, authors evidenced a clear dissociation between right PFC subregions and their role in association with anxiety and performance, and used the attentional control theory of Eysenck (2007) as framework to interpret the findings (Takizawa et al. 2014).

Finally, additional studies on a different but equally interesting topic should be mentioned. Starting from 2013 some research groups (Sato et al. 2013, Ishikawa et al. 2014) used machine-learning algorithms to examine the spontaneous oscillations of oxyhemoglobin concentrations in the bilateral PFC at rest in normal adults, using a 2-channel CW-NIRS device. Results evidenced that higher STAI State (a questionnaire to evaluate state anxiety) scores collected before the experiment predicted an increased right PFC activity at rest, compared to the left one.

Sympathetic and HPA Activities Are Associated with Right PFC Oxy-Hb Increases

An interesting result of some of the previously mentioned researches is the positive association between neuroendocrine responses and right prefrontal activity; these findings are in line with the approach-withdrawal hypothesis and they were even confirmed by previous EEG studies (Yu et al. 2009).

Among other NIRS studies, Sakatani and Tanida (Sakatani, Tanida, and Katsuyama 2010, Tanida, Katsuyama, and Sakatani 2007, Tanida et al. 2004) correlated the laterality index during a mental arithmetic task to various autonomic and endocrine indexes, constantly reporting significant results. Increased heart rate, vagal withdrawal (i.e., reduced parasympathetic influence on cardiac activity) and sebaceous secretions as well as levels of P. acne populations, are associated as expected with an increased right-frontal activity.

As regards the HPA axis, it is well known that PFC neurons project to medial hypothalamus, the cerebral region where the HPA response starts (Tanida, Katsuyama, and Sakatani 2007). A hypothesis is that the right prefrontal cortex could be responsible of the increased activation of HPA axis during stress responses, as shown by previous correlational or lesion studies (Tanida, Katsuyama, and Sakatani 2007): more investigations are needed to better clarify these findings.

Finally, even the ANS activity seems to be associated to left and right PFC responses: indeed, right prefrontal cortex activation correlates with an increased heart rate or a reduced HRV (e.g., reduced High Frequencies), suggesting a hyperactivation of sympathetic arm of autonomous nervous system (Sakatani, Tanida, and Katsuyama 2010, Tanida et al. 2004, Tanida, Katsuyama, and Sakatani 2007, Yu et al. 2009). Yu and colleagues (2009) explained these results stating that "the right-sided innervations of sympathetic fibers exert a greater influence on the sinoatrial node than do the left- sided innervations, leading to a greater influence on HR."

Conclusion and Future Directions

As should be clear from the previous paragraphs, NIRS technology has some advantages over other neuroimaging techniques that could be exploited in future researches on stress responses. These studies, for example, could be performed in more ecological settings, permitting to analyze stress responses in real-world situations. Moreover, it was previously mentioned in this study, papers on the prediction of an increased right PFC activity at rest in highly anxious subjects, using machine-learning algorithms (Sato et al. 2013, Ishikawa et al. 2014). Future NIRS studies could use questionnaires on perceived stress to evaluate if their scores predict a specific pattern of cortical activation. Potential results could lead to unexpected developments in the area of predictive medicine as well as in the early detection of stress responses.

However, current findings are partly limited by methodological problems. It is not clear, for example, if stress responses lead per se, to an asymmetrical right PFC activity. Most of the studies calculated a Laterality Index and then correlated it to other physiological parameters, while different statistical analyses (such as ANOVA) could have provided information about a hemispheric effect, simply putting the left/right channels as a factor in the analyses. Another concern is raised about the control of PFC over ANS and HPA axis; the contemporary increase in activity of cortical areas and neuroendocrine systems during stress tasks does not imply a causation.

Moreover, it is unclear if the results in studies which used Laterality Index could be explained by different dispositional affective styles of the subjects. Sakatani, Tanida and colleagues (2010, 2004, 2007) evidenced that individuals with increased right PFC activity during a stress task experience a hyperactivity of SNA and HPA, but approach-withdrawal hypothesis suggests that some subjects can have greater relative metabolism in the right PFC and in the amygdala (Davidson 2002, Davidson and Irwin 1999) which simply depends on pre-existing characteristics (e.g., their affective style).

Finally, the role of anxiety should be clarified: does state anxiety explain the lateralization effects during stress tasks? Or individuals with higher state anxiety experience more intense stress responses? Can trait anxiety modulate these responses? Further studies are required to elucidate these concerns.

Probably, the main limitation lies in the protocol used to induce psychosocial stress, which did not include a control condition. A simple mathematical task (e.g., subtracting 2-digit number from a 4-digit number, or the UKT) lacks of additional psychosocial pressure sources that are relevant in studies focused mainly on stress responses. Therefore, future researches should use better suited protocols, such as the Montreal Imaging Stress Task (MIST), proposed by Dedovic and colleagues (2005). MIST is a standardized and computerized psychosocial stress protocol that allow to investigate separately the effect of stress and mental arithmetic tasks. As stated in the paper, "in the control condition, a series of mental arithmetic tasks are displayed on the computer screen, and subjects submit their answers by means of a response interface. In the experimental condition, the difficulty and time limit of the tasks are manipulated to be just beyond the individual's mental capacity" (Dedovic et al. 2005).

Therefore, during the experimental condition participants continue to solve arithmetic tasks, but a new variable in added, namely the psychosocial stress (Dedovic et al. 2005).

The Montreal Imaging Stress Task was extensively and proficiently used in well-conducted fMRI experiments, so that many of the studies on psychosocial stress responses that were meta-analyzed by Kogler and colleagues (2015) used exactly this protocol. As reviewed before, this meta-analysis evidenced right PFC lateralization patterns (i.e., IFG hyperactivation) only during the experimental condition of MIST (Kogler et al. 2015), leading to the hypothesis that the increased right PFC activity could be observed even with NIRS technology. However, it should be noted that the right inferior frontal gyrus, part of the ventrolateral prefrontal cortex, is roughly beyond the area observed by 2-channel NIRS devices (which evaluates dorsolateral and frontopolar areas). Even so, results obtained in previous studies (Sakatani, Tanida, and Katsuyama 2010, Tanida et al. 2004, Tanida, Katsuyama, and Sakatani 2007) showed that some individuals, when facing psychosocial stressors, experienced a hyperactivity in the right PFC that correlates positively with autonomous data. These inconsistencies are difficult to explain without further investigations in this topic, even though it is possible that stress responses lead to a recruitment of even more right PFC areas than expected.

Future NIRS studies on this topic should be able to answer some of the theoretical concerns raised before. Well-performed experiments (e.g., using standardized and controlled protocols to induce psychosocial stress) could allow to explore psychophysiological responses to acute stressors and more generally even contribute to study the protective/risk factors of those physical and mental diseases that are exacerbated by stress.

REFERENCES

Backé, Eva-Maria, Andreas Seidler, Ute Latza, Karin Rossnagel, and Barbara Schumann. 2012. "The role of psychosocial stress at work for the development of cardiovascular diseases: a systematic review." *International archives of occupational and environmental health* 85 (1):67-79.

Cardiology, Task Force of the European Society of, and Task Force of the European Society of Cardiology. 1996. "the North American Society of Pacing and Electrophysiology. Heart rate variability: standards of measurement, physiological interpretation and clinical use." *Circulation* 93 (5):1043-1065.

Carroll, Douglas, Annie T Ginty, Geoff Der, Kate Hunt, Michaela Benzeval, and Anna C Phillips. 2012. "Increased blood pressure reactions to acute mental stress are associated with 16-year cardiovascular disease mortality." *Psychophysiology* 49 (10):1444-1448.

Davidson, Paul Ekman, Clifford D Saron, Joseph A Senulis, and Wallace V Friesen. 1990. "Approach-withdrawal and cerebral asymmetry: Emotional expression and brain physiology: I." *Journal of personality and social psychology* 58 (2):330.

Davidson, Richard J. 1992. "Anterior cerebral asymmetry and the nature of emotion." *Brain and cognition* 20 (1):125-151.

Davidson, Richard J. 2002. "Anxiety and affective style: role of prefrontal cortex and amygdala." *Biological psychiatry* 51 (1):68-80.

Davidson, Richard J, and William Irwin. 1999. "The functional neuroanatomy of emotion and affective style." *Trends in cognitive sciences* 3 (1):11-21.

Dedovic, Katarina, Robert Renwick, Najmeh Khalili Mahani, Veronika Engert, Sonia J Lupien, and Jens C Pruessner. 2005. "The Montreal Imaging Stress Task: using functional imaging to investigate the effects of perceiving and processing psychosocial stress in the human brain." *Journal of Psychiatry and Neuroscience* 30 (5):319.

Dieler, AC, SV Tupak, and AJ Fallgatter. 2012. "Functional near-infrared spectroscopy for the assessment of speech related tasks." *Brain and language* 121 (2):90-109.

Eysenck, Michael W, Nazanin Derakshan, Rita Santos, and Manuel G Calvo. 2007. "Anxiety and cognitive performance: attentional control theory." *Emotion* 7 (2):336.

Ferrari, Marco, Leonardo Mottola, and Valentina Quaresima. 2004. "Principles, techniques, and limitations of near infrared spectroscopy." *Canadian journal of applied physiology* 29 (4):463-487.

Fujimaki, Koichiro, Hidenori Takemoto, and Shigeru Morinobu. 2014. "Association between Sub-Threshold Affective Symptoms and Prefrontal Activation in Non-Clinical Population—An NIRS Study." *Psychology* 5 (09):1024.

Herman, James P, and William E Cullinan. 1997. "Neurocircuitry of stress: central control of the hypothalamo–pituitary–adrenocortical axis." *Trends in neurosciences* 20 (2):78-84.

Hoshi, Yoko, and Mamoru Tamura. 1993. "Detection of dynamic changes in cerebral oxygenation coupled to neuronal function during mental work in man." *Neuroscience letters* 150 (1):5-8.

Ishikawa, Wakana, Masakaze Sato, Yukikatsu Fukuda, Takashi Matsumoto, Naohiro Takemura, and Kaoru Sakatani. 2014. "Correlation between asymmetry of spontaneous oscillation of hemodynamic changes in the prefrontal cortex and anxiety levels: a near-infrared spectroscopy study." *Journal of biomedical optics* 19 (2):027005-027005.

Jobsis, Frans F. 1977. "Noninvasive, infrared monitoring of cerebral and myocardial oxygen sufficiency and circulatory parameters." *Science* 198 (4323):1264-1267.

Kogler, Lydia, Veronika I Müller, Amy Chang, Simon B Eickhoff, Peter T Fox, Ruben C Gur, and Birgit Derntl. 2015. "Psychosocial versus physiological stress—Meta-analyses on deactivations and activations of the neural correlates of stress reactions." *NeuroImage* 119:235-251.

Murkin, JM, and M Arango. 2009. "Near-infrared spectroscopy as an index of brain and tissue oxygenation." *British journal of anaesthesia* 103 (suppl. 1):i3-i13.

Pellicer, Adelina, and María del Carmen Bravo. 2011. "Near-infrared spectroscopy: a methodology-focused review." *Seminars in Fetal and Neonatal Medicine*.

Rutters, Femke, Stefan Pilz, Anitra D Koopman, Simone P Rauh, Saskia J Te Velde, Coen D Stehouwer, Petra J Elders, Giel Nijpels, and Jacqueline M Dekker. 2014. "The association between psychosocial stress and mortality is mediated by lifestyle and chronic diseases: The Hoorn Study." *Social Science and Medicine* 118:166-172.

Sakatani, Kaoru, Masahiro Tanida, and Masako Katsuyama. 2010. "Effects of aging on activity of the prefrontal cortex and autonomic nervous system during mental stress task." In: *Oxygen Transport to Tissue XXXI*, 473-478. Springer.

Sato, Masakaze, Wakana Ishikawa, Tomohiko Suzuki, Takashi Matsumoto, Takeo Tsujii, and Kaoru Sakatani. 2013. "Bayesian STAI anxiety index predictions based on prefrontal cortex NIRS data for the resting state. " In: *Oxygen Transport to Tissue XXXIV*, 251-256. Springer.

Scholkmann, Felix, Stefan Kleiser, Andreas Jaakko Metz, Raphael Zimmermann, Juan Mata Pavia, Ursula Wolf, and Martin Wolf. 2014. "A review on continuous wave functional near-infrared spectroscopy and imaging instrumentation and methodology." *Neuroimage* 85:6-27.

Soul, Janet S, and Adré J du Plessis. 1999. "Near-infrared spectroscopy." *Seminars in pediatric neurology*.

Strangman, Gary, David A Boas, and Jeffrey P Sutton. 2002. "Non-invasive neuroimaging using near-infrared light." *Biological psychiatry* 52 (7):679-693.

Takizawa, Ryu, Yukika Nishimura, Hidenori Yamasue, and Kiyoto Kasai. 2014. "Anxiety and performance: the disparate roles of prefrontal subregions under maintained psychological stress." *Cerebral Cortex* 24 (7):1858-1866.

Tanida, Masahiro, Masako Katsuyama, and Kaoru Sakatani. 2007. "Relation between mental stress-induced prefrontal cortex activity and skin conditions: a near-infrared spectroscopy study." *Brain research* 1184:210-216.

Tanida, Masahiro, Kaoru Sakatani, Ruriko Takano, and Keiko Tagai. 2004. "Relation between asymmetry of prefrontal cortex activities and the autonomic nervous system during a mental arithmetic task: near infrared spectroscopy study." *Neurosci Lett* 369 (1):69-74.

Ulrich-Lai, Yvonne M, and James P Herman. 2009. "Neural regulation of endocrine and autonomic stress responses." *Nature Reviews Neuroscience* 10 (6):397-409.

Wheeler, Robert E, Richard J Davidson, and Andrew J Tomarken. 1993. "Frontal brain asymmetry and emotional reactivity: A biological substrate of affective style." *Psychophysiology* 30 (1):82-89.

Yang, Hongyu, Ying Wang, Zhenyu Zhou, Hui Gong, Qingming Luo, Yiwen Wang, and Zuhong Lu. 2009. "Sex differences in prefrontal hemodynamic response to mental arithmetic as assessed by near-infrared spectroscopy." *Gender medicine* 6 (4):565-574.

Yu, Xiaolin, Jianbao Zhang, Dongdong Xie, Jue Wang, and Chong Zhang. 2009. "Relationship between scalp potential and autonomic nervous activity during a mental arithmetic task." *Autonomic Neuroscience* 146 (1):81-86.

In: Psychological Distress
Editors: A. Compare, C. Elia, A. G. Simonelli et al.
ISBN: 978-1-63485-405-4

Chapter 10

Predictive and Preventive Psychological Assessments for Women in Outpatient Integrated Care Clinic

Maddalena Ischia[1], Sara Zanelli[1], Maurizio Gerolamo Biraghi[1], Rodolfo Milani[1,2], Nadia Bernocchi[1], Rossella Dal Bo'[1], Chiara Carzaniga[1], Silvia Briganti[1] and Angelo Compare[1,3]

[1]Service of Clinical Psychology and Sexology, CAM Lei, Viale Elvezia ang, Monza, Italy

[2]Università Milano-Bicocca, Milano, Italy

[3]Università degli Studi di Bergamo, Bergamo BG, Italy

Abstract

Clinical Psychologists working in outpatient integrated care clinics can deal with particular psychological disorders including: psychological distress caused by infertility, premenstrual syndrome and premenstrual dysphoric disorder, postpartum depression, emotion dysregulation and eating disorder symptoms.

The present chapter will examine the role of psychologists in the assessment and treatment of these disorders.

Keywords: clinical psychology, psychological assessment, infertility, premenstrual syndrome, postpartum depression, emotion dysregulation, emotional eating, psychological treatment

1. The Role of the Psychologist in Infertility

1.1. Infertility: A Definition

According to World Health Organization, infertility is defined as the inability to achieve clinical pregnancy after 12, or more, months of unprotected sexual intercourse. This reproductive problem affects approximately 10% of the worldwide population [1, 2]. Approximately 40% of infertility problems are attributable to the female, 40% to the male, and 20% to both partners or of unknown etiology [3].

Infertility has various medical and nonmedical causes. Medical causes include anatomical reasons, autoimmune disorders, and hormonal problems. Nonmedical causes include lifestyle factors such as delayed child bearing, not exercising or exercising excessively, obesity, inappropriate diet, psychological stress, smoking and alcohol consumption [4-8].

Due to its multifactorial origin, Jing, Botao, and Min (2014) [9] suggest that the prevention and treatment of infertility requires biomedical science research, as well as efforts in the fields of psychology and sociology. Therefore, a Psychologist is essential to treatment of the biopsychosocial nature of infertility.

1.2. Psychological Distress as a Cause and Consequence of Infertility

For decades, clinicians have believed that some infertility was caused by stress [10].

Several studies, in fact, suggest that certain psychological variables such as distress can predict infertility [11].

Psychological stress may interfere with hypothalamic-pituitary axis function, thereby altering gonadotropin secretion and inhibiting ovulation [8].

Social and psychological factors can also interfere with sperm quality. For example, Vellani, Colasante, Mamazza et al. (2013) [12] suggested that increased levels of state and trait anxiety were associated with lower semen volume, sperm concentration and count, reduced sperm motility, and increased sperm DNA fragmentation in in vitro fertilization (IVF) patients.

An additional study conducted by Hjollund et al. (1999) [13], found that high levels of distress were significant predictors of lower odds of conception per cycle, particularly between women with long (>35 days) menstrual cycles.

Although extreme environmental stress appears to be associated with hormonal disruptions (such as women with concentration-camp amenorrhea) [14], most researchers believe that psychological distress is a consequence, rather than a cause, of infertility and its treatment [3].

According to Cwikel, Gidron, and Sheiner (2004) [11], fertility treatment, ranging from medical monitoring, to hormonal remedies, and in vitro fertilization (IVF), carry physical, economical and emotional burden on women and their partners. A couple that is trying to conceive will experience, in fact, a feeling of frustration and disappointment if a pregnancy is not easily achieved. However, if the difficulties persist and the man or woman are labelled as having fertility problems, this may result in a severe attack to self-esteem, body image, and self-assessed masculinity or femininity.

For example, Freeman et al. (1985) [15], in their study of 200 couples consecutively seen at a pretreatment consultation in an IVF and embryo transfer program, found that half of the women and 15% of the man reported that infertility is the most upsetting experience of their lives.

Infertile women are significantly more depressed than their fertile counterparts, with depression and anxiety levels equivalent to women with heart disease, cancer, or HIV-positive status. Eleven percent of infertile women met the criteria for a current major depressive episode [16].

Kainz (2001) reports that sexual dysfunction may also be either a cause or a result of conception difficulties [10]. Vaginismus may occur only during the ovulatory period, when anxiety about success or failure of conceiving is high. In the male, problems in achieving or maintaining erections, and ejaculatory competence must be assessed. However, while sexual difficulties may contribute to infertility problems, the most common situation is for sexual problems to arise after a prolonged period of unsuccessful attempts at pregnancy. This can be caused by the fact that sex performed on demand is very different from recreational sex. In fact, often husbands may feel "like a machine," losing the pleasure of intercourse [14]. Sexual urgency around ovulation may also interfere with the wife's attainment of orgasm. Both women and men may share feelings of shame during same-morning post-coital exams. For these and other reasons, it is often recommended that the couple take a periodic "vacation" from infertility treatments to relax, regroup, and focus on other areas of life and their relationship that give them meaning and pleasure [10].

In their review of the studies examining the relationship between psychological factors and infertility, Cwikel, Gidron e Sheiner (2004) suggested that the psychological consequences of infertility may affect the outcome of fertility treatments [11]. In this regard, for example, they reported that Thiering et al. (1993) found that there was a significant difference between the level of depressive symptoms observed among women entering IVF for the first treatment and repeat cycle women. Among the first cycle women, those with symptoms of depression were less likely to achieve a pregnancy than non-depressed women [17].

Due to the fact that psychological factors such as depression, anxiety, and stress-induced are predictive of a decreased probability to achieving a viable pregnancy in various types of infertility and fertility treatments, Cwikel, Gidron e Sheiner (2004) affirmed that screening for psychological stress markers in women experiencing difficulties achieving pregnancy may allow practitioners to channel interventions to those at greatest need for psychological assistance [11].

In addition, they suggested that treatments could combine hormone and psychological measurements with biofeedback and cognitive behavioral therapy techniques for the alteration of psychological and psycho-physiological risk factors of infertility for the optimization of successful conception.

1.3. Assisting Couple with Infertility

When assisting couples with infertility, it is useful to consider the stages of the infertility crisis [14, 18]. In particular, we can identify three stages: when the couple wants to begin the assisted reproductive's path ("initial consultation/psychological evaluation"), when the couple undergoes assisted reproductive treatments and when the couple decides to end infertility treatment. We will discuss the role of the psychologist in these different stages.

Initial Consultation/Psychological Evaluation

In general, Klock (1998) believes that infertility should be considered a couples' issue, with the couple seen together for the initial consultation [3].

According to Kainz (2001), the goal of the psychological evaluation or initial consultation is "to prepare patients for the treatment that they are about to experience, to raise emotional and ethical treatment issues that the individuals may not have considered, to screen for those who may benefit from further psychological treatment, and to screen for the rare case where psychopathology would preclude infertility treatment. Other situations to be watchful for are when one partner is coercing the other to proceed with treatment, or when a legal history relevant to child endangerment or abuse is discovered" [10].

Leiblum (1998) affirms that the behavioral counselor can offer assistance to those couples in which there is conflict regarding reproductive options. "Taking the time to explore each partner's fears and misgivings, to correct misconceptions, and to consider the relative risks and benefits of each reproductive option may help avert a marital crisis" [14].

Kainz (2001) underlines that there are more psychological demands placed on the patients in the case of IVF and donor gamete treatments. For these reason, specific issues such as the couple's religious, cultural, and moral beliefs should be discussed, to determine how they feel about options such as cryopreservation of embryos, multifetal pregnancy reduction, nongenetic parenting via donor sperm, and possible legal entanglements over the custody of created embryos [10].

For therapists working with couples using third-party reproduction, it is also essential to help the couple to decide how they will handle a number of different issues, including privacy and disclosure to family, friends, and the child. According to Klock (1996) [19], the following points should be considered:

- Examining the pros and cons of both disclosure and privacy in the context of the couple's specific social milieu;
- Examining the couple's beliefs about what makes a parent;
- Discussion of the relative contribution of genetics and environment in parenting
- For those couples planning to tell the child, a discussion of when and how to tell;
- For those couples planning not to tell the child, a discussion regarding limiting the number of people to whom is told;
- If there is disagreement between partners, it is important not to let infertility treatment begin until some consensus can be reached.

Nowadays, there is no evidence in literature that there is a "best" option for all couples. Therefore, the therapist should remain neutral help the couple come to their own decision regarding disclosure. The clinician should also suggest to the couple that their decision may change in the future and they may want to periodically reassess their decision over time.

As mentioned above, couples frequently perceive infertility and its treatment as stressful. Therefore, couples may need a variety of psychosocial services to help them cope with infertility-related distress [20].

As reported by Jing, Botao and Min, some authors argued that patient vulnerability can be tackled by implementing pretreatment evidence-based screening for psychological distress, providing appropriate referral for support, eliminating barriers to acceptance of psychosocial support, and identifying specific treatment stages when psychosocial support should be provided [9, 21]. Read et al. (2014) suggested that The Fertility Quality of Life (FertiQOL) Questionnaire may be a good method for assessing psychosocial support needs and patient's level of distress, thus providing important and detailed information to guide treatment intervention and determine the compliance of patients, both of which can be used to direct patients to the appropriate resources [20]. In addition, some authors suggest that the FertiQoL should be used in conjunction with the Short Form 36 (SF36) to investigate quality of life among patients undergoing assisted reproductive technologies [22].

It is important to notice that various general and specific questionnaire have been tailored for assessing different aspects of quality of life in infertile men, women, or couples. Mousavi, Masoumi, Keramat, Pooralajal and Shobeiri (2013) perform a systematic review on the tools used for assessing quality of life in infertile couples [23]. The results of their review are shown in Table 1 at page 9.

As the readers can see in Table 1, these questionnaires specifically assess the different life's dimensions that can be impaired when undergoing assisted reproductive technologies: mental, psychological and physical health; anxiety, depression and somatic symptoms; social and sexual relationship; marital satisfaction and personality issues.

Therefore, healthcare providers should properly evaluate the medical and emotional states of couples, in order to tailor psychosocial services to individual infertility patients [9].

In addition, Read et al. (2014), suggested that when considering which psychosocial services would be most helpful for infertile couples, clinicians and researchers must ask patients whether they want support, as well as why [20].

Finally, Kainz (2001) underlines that, "if contact with a trained mental health professional is provided in the early stages of an infertility workup, the stage is set for the patient to see this professional as a resource in the future if problems develop or if infertility treatment ends and counseling regarding adoption or child-free living is needed" [10].

Psychological Interventions during Infertility Treatment

As previously discussed, the initial psychological evaluation should allow the psychologist to identify the infertile couple's needs and propose them the most appropriate psychological intervention.

Different treatment stages should be taken into account during psychological intervention. For example, some authors underline that women with recurrent pregnancy loss after IVF have different experiences that those with recurrent implantation failure [24, 25].

In 2014, Jing Li, Botao Liu, and Min Li reviewed the most important and interesting articles published regarding infertility, including those describing psychological treatments [9].

In their review, they reported that infertile individuals may be less open and have less psychological flexibility to their painful inner mental states. For these reasons, some researchers suggest that they may benefit from training for emotion regulation processes, such as psychological flexibility or acceptance, self-efficacy, and self-compassion. Furthermore, interventions that target emotion-regulation skills, such as acceptance and commitment therapy, mindfulness-based cognitive therapy, and compassion-focused therapy, may improve the effectiveness of psychotherapeutic interventions [26].

Galhardo et al. (2013) carried out a research in which 55 infertile women completed a mindfulness-based program for infertility (MBPI) and found that by the end of the intervention, the MBPI women showed a significant decrease in depressive symptoms, internal and external shame, entrapment, and defeat and significant improvement in mindfulness skills and self-efficacy to deal with infertility [27]. Women in the control group did not show significant changes in psychological measures, except for a decrease in self-judgment. Their study indicated that increasing mindfulness and acceptance skills seem to help women experience negative feelings in new ways, which allowed them do decrease psychological distress. Therefore, they argued that the MBPI is an effective psychological intervention for women experiencing infertility.

Kim et al. (2014) also demonstrated that mind-body therapy effectively alleviated uncertainty and anxiety in infertile women with unknown cause who where preparing for a second IVF treatment [28].

Another mind-body approach for fertility is the fertile body method (FBM), which consider six areas of treatment: solution-oriented focus, the restoration of balance and cultivation of inner and outer resources, the resolution of relevant problems, visualization and guided imagery, adequate mental preparation, and good emotional support. In their study, Wurlitzer et al. (2013) showed that using FBM to prepare for IVF is of great benefit. In particular, reducing stress before treatment may reduce the number of treatments [29].

Summarizing the abovementioned, we can affirm that psychological interventions focusing on mindfulness and acceptance skills seem to be the most effective way in reducing psychological distress related to infertility.

When the Couple Decides to End Infertility Treatment

Deciding to end infertility treatment may be a difficult decision.

This decision, in fact, can be complicated by conflicting emotions and information, and pressures from partners, parents, or cultural expectation. When a couple decides to end treatment, it may be to go on to alternative parenthood options, such as adoption, surrogacy, or donor gametes, or may result in the difficult decision to remain childfree.

Regardless of what course of action is taken, the decision to stop is, in the end, tied to the individual's ability to surrender the hope and dream of having his or her own genetic child.

While society provides rituals for dealing with actual death, there is usually little help given to individuals who are grieving the loss of their fertility.

For this reason, the psychologist should pay particular attention to these conditions, providing a supportive, neutral and introspective environment for patients to examine their feelings, as well as the options open to them. The final step is acceptance-building other life plans or considering other parent-hood options.

Braverman (1996) states that "The two most relevant issues when beginning therapy with individuals and couples who are considering ending infertility treatment are: (a) what not having a biological child means to them; and (b) how that makes them feel. It is only by determining what individual meaning this decision holds for the client that the therapist can begin to formulate a hypothesis and treatment plan" [30].

Table 1. The general and specific instruments for assessing quality of life in infertile couples

Instrument	Feature	Dimension	Item
SF-36	Generic	Physical functioning Vitality/energy Physical role limitation Bodily pain Mental health Change in health Emotional role limitation Health perception Social functioning	36
WHOQOL-BREF	Generic	General health Physical health Psychological health Social relationship Environment	26
SF-12	Generic	All aspects of quality of life	12
GHQ-28	Generic	Somatic symptoms Anxiety/insomnia Social dysfunction Depression	28
Quality of wellbeing scale	Generic	Social and self-care activities Physical activity Mobility	80
Enrich Inventory	Generic	Marital satisfaction Personality issues Communication Conflict resolution Financial management Leisure activities Sexual relationship Children and parenting Family and friends Equalitarian roles Religious orientation Marital cohesion Marital change	125
QLQ (C30-version 2)		Physical Role Cognitive Emotional Social	30
Quality of life Index	Generic	Functioning Socio-economic Psychological/spiritual family	26

Table 1. (Continued)

Instrument	Feature	Dimension	Item
The Hopkines Symptom checklist (SCL-90-R)		Somatization Obsessive-compulsive Interpersonal sensivity Paranoid ideation Anxiety Depression Psychoticism Phobia Aggression	90
Impact profile the sickness	Generic	Emotional Behavior	136
Fertility Problem Inventory	Specific for infertility	Emotional Relational Sexual concern Rejection of child-free lifestyle	46
fertiQOL	Specific for infertility	Emotional Relational Mind/body Social Environment Tolerability treatment	36

Cognitive therapy can be also helpful to restructure thoughts such as "I'm a failure," or "I'll never be happy again." As Braverman (1996) states, the main objective of the therapist should be to "accompany the client on this journey through the grief and into an uncertain future. Ultimately, the therapist helps the client to hope and to build" [30].

2. Premenstrual Syndrome and Premenstrual Dysphoric Disorder

2.1. Definition

According to Biggs and Demuth (2011), Premenstrual Syndrome (PMS) is defined as recurrent moderate psychological and physical symptoms that occur during the luteal phase of the menstrual cycle (one week before menstruation) and resolve with menstruation [31]. This condition affects 20 to 32 percent of premenopausal women [32].

In Premenstrual Dysphoric Disorder (PMDD), more severe and debilitating affective and somatic symptoms impact the patient's relationship and social and occupational realms. This disorder affect 3 to 8 percent of premenopausal women [32].

Physical symptoms associated with PMS and PMDD include: abdominal bloating, body aches, breast tenderness, cramps, fatigue, headaches, nausea, weigh gain [31].

On the other hand, psychological and behavioral symptoms are: anger, irritability, anxiety, changes in appetite, changes in libido, depressed mood, decreased concentration, mood swings, poor sleep or increased need for sleep, tension, and withdrawal from usual activities.

PMS and PMDD symptoms may reoccur with each ovulatory cycle until menopause, although the severity and frequency of different symptoms may vary over time [33, 34].

The average duration of symptoms each month is six days, with the peak of severity anywhere from two days before to the first day of the menstrual flow [32].

Biggs and Demuth report that the etiologies of PMS and PMDD are not definitive, but several theories are postulated. In particular, proposed etiologies include increased sensitivity to normal cycling levels of estrogen and progesterone, increased aldosterone and plasma renin activity, and neurotransmitter abnormalities, particularly serotonin [31].

Independently of the causes of these disorders, both PMS and PMDD have been shown negatively affect relationship, work attendance, productivity and health care costs and utilization [35]. For these reasons, the diagnosis and treatment of these conditions becomes crucial.

2.2. Screening and Diagnosis (Assessment Measures)

Steiner (2000) asserts that "there are no objective diagnostic tests for PMS and PMDD." Therefore, a complete medical and psychiatric history must be elicitated [36].

According to Steiner, screening should also include a complete review of physical systems and medical disorders, and a detailed review of heritable disorders, including psychiatric disorders, in the patient's family. In fact, before making a diagnosis of PMS or PMDD, concurrent major mental disorders, personality disorders and medical conditions must be excluded [36]. For example, affective disorders such as depression and anxiety may have premenstrual cyclic worsening, but do not have the symptom-free interval during the mid-follicular phase (days 6 through 10 of the menstrual cycle), needed for the clinical diagnosis of PMS or PMDD. At the same time, some medical or gynecologic conditions such as hypothyroidism, anemia, endometriosis, or physiologic ovarian cysts may replicate physical symptoms of PMS. To exclude these diagnosis, clinicians should check thyroid function or hemoglobin levels respectively [31].

The American College of Obstetrician and Gynecologists suggests diagnosing PMS based on prospective diaries [37]. One instrument to chart symptoms associated with PMS and PMDD is the Daily Record of Severity of Problems [38]. The instrument is composed by a list of item (symptoms). The patient has to record the score, for each item/symptom, on each day, using a scale ranging from 1 ("not at all") to 6 ("extreme"). It is possible to add the scores in the column for the first day of menses. If the total score is less than 50, the authors suggest to consider a diagnosis other than premenstrual syndrome. If the total score is greater than 50, it is necessary to record two cycles of symptoms. If more than three item have an average score of more than 3 (mild) during the luteal phase, add the scores of five-day intervals during the luteal and follicular phases. A luteal phase score that is 30 percent greater than the follicular phase score indicates a diagnosis of premenstrual syndrome.

The psychiatric, medical and psychosocial screens, together with verification of the timing of symptoms, enable the clinician to make a diagnosis [36]. Possible diagnoses after screening include: PMS or PMDD; another psychiatric or medical illness only; PMS or PMDD coexisting with another illness; premenstrual exacerbation/magnification of an underlying psychiatric or medical illness; or no diagnosis (situational, psychosocial stressors) [39].

Steiner (2000) reports that a woman may have a psychiatric or medical disorder as well as PMS or PMDD [36]. In such cases, the premenstrual symptoms are distinct from other disorder, and arise during the luteal phase and remit during the follicular phase. Patients can also demonstrate premenstrual exacerbation or magnification of an underlying psychiatric or medical illness. In these cases, the symptoms (such as dysphoria, fatigue, panic, anxiety) persist throughout the menstrual cycle but worsen premenstrually. Finally, women who do not meet the criteria for any diagnosis may subjectively sense disruptive symptoms as a result of psychosocial stressors and likely benefit from charting and conservative interventions.

2.3. Treatment

The goal of treatment of PMS and PMDD is symptom relief, addressing the physiologic causes of symptoms, such as ovulatory hormonal cyclicity of menstruation and the central nervous system neurotransmitter which affect mood (serotonin) [31].

Biggs and Demuth categorize treatments of PMS and PMDD in nonpharmacologic and pharmacologic.

Nonpharmacologic Treatments of PMS and PMDD

Nonpharmacologic treatments of PMS and PMDD include: lifestyle modifications, cognitive behavior therapy, complementary and alternatives therapies.

Lifestyle Modifications

Although there are evidence that diet and exercise improve general health, no current evidence substantiates those recommendation for PMS symptom relief.

However, dietary calcium and vitamin D intake may play a role in the reduction of PMS and PMDD's symptoms. In this regard, Bertone-Johnson and colleagues (2005; 2010) report that women with high daily vitamin D intake were less likely to have PMS symptoms [40, 41].

In addition, Thys-Jacobs, Starkey, Bernestein, and Tian (1998) report that women whose calcium intake was supplemented with 1,200 mg of calcium carbonate per day for the duration of three menstrual cycles had significantly lower symptom scores for the second and third cycles of treatment compared with placebo [42].

Cognitive Behavioral Therapy

Because cognitive behavioral therapy is proved to be effective for affective and somatic disorders such as anxiety and pain, Biggs and Demuth (2011) suggest that it could be useful for PMS treatment [31].

Cognitive-behavioral therapy in the form of 12 weekly individual sessions significantly improved symptoms and functional impairment in women with PMS randomly assigned to the treatment, compared with those in the waiting-list control group [43].

Complementary and Alternative Therapies

Some studies suggest that chasteberry (a small tree or shrub grown in southern Europe) and vitamin B6 may reduce PMS symptoms [44].

In 2001, Schellenberg performed a study showing that women treated with 20 mg of chasteberry per day were more likely to have a decrease in PMS symptoms (irritability, mood swings, anger, headache, breast fullness) of more than 50 percent compared with placebo [45].

In their systematic review of the efficacy of vitamin B6 in the treatment of premenstrual syndrome, Wyatt, Dimmock, Jones and O'Brein (1999) conclude that doses of up to 100 mg daily are likely to be of moderate benefit in treating premenstrual symptoms and depression [46].

Pharmacologic Treatment of PMS and PMDD

Pharmacologic treatments of PMS and PMDD include serotonergic antidepressant, oral contraceptives and other medications.

Serotonergic Antidepressant

The first-line pharmacologic treatments for severe PMS and PMDD are medications affecting serotonin [37].

The selective serotonin reuptake inhibitors (SSRIs), such as citalopram, escitalopram, fluoxetine and sertraline, in fact, significantly decrease physical and psychological symptoms of PMS, compared with placebo [47].

However, nausea, insomnia, headache, and decreased libido are common adverse effects of SSRIs, and the benefit of symptom relief must be balanced against these potential effects [31].

Oral Contraceptives

Few data support the effectiveness of oral contraceptives in the treatment of PMS. In this regard, Lopez, Kaptein, and Helmerhorst (2009) notice that combined oral contraceptives that include drospirenone appear to improve PMS and PMDD symptoms, in comparison with placebo [48].

Other Medications

Other medications include, for example, alprazolam (Xanax). For those patients who report anxiety symptoms, physician may consider treatment with 0.25 mg of alprazolam (Xanax), intermittently up to three or four times per day during the luteal phase. However, its use should be limited to carefully selected patients because of its dependence, tolerance and potential abuse [49].

In summary, we can affirm that the treatment of PMS and PMDD is mainly medical and pharmacological. However, cognitive behavior therapy can be used, in conjunction with these treatments, to reduce anxiety and psychological pain related to these conditions.

3. Postpartum Depression

3.1. Definition

Postpartum depression (PPD) is a mental health problem that affects women and families in multiple ways. Its negative impact on women, children and families has been addressed in several studies, documenting the negative effects of mother's depression on child's functioning in multiple domains, such as cognitive, social and developmental [50, 51]. As Field pointed out in 2010, "postpartum depression limits a woman's ability to function effectively in the maternal role: depressed mothers provide less responsive caregiving, are more likely to discontinue breastfeeding early or have problems breastfeeding, are less likely to comply with recommended safety practices such as use of car seats, and their children have lower rates of preventive healthcare utilization and vaccination" [52].

As a psychiatric diagnosis, PPD presents specific symptoms and criteria that all clinicians should know in order to properly assess and treat women who suffer from this illness.

Post partum depression is part of a range of post partum affective disorders, along with postpartum blues (the most common, with a prevalence of 40% to 80%) and postpartum psychosis (with a prevalence rate of 0.1% to 0.2%). The prevalence of PPD has been found to be around 13% in Europe, with a range that varies from 2.1% in Zurich, Switzerland, to 31.6% in Bordeaux, France [53, 54].

PPD is defined in the psychiatric nomenclature as a major depressive disorder (MDD) with a specifier of postpartum onset within 1 month after childbirth [55]. To meet criteria for MDD, depressed mood or loss of interest in activities must be present for at least 2 weeks. In addition, may be present symptoms of sleep disturbance, appetite disturbance, loss of energy, feelings of worthlessness or guilt, diminished concentration, and thoughts of suicide. Clinicians must pay great attention to physical symptoms in PPD, because changes in sleep patterns, in appetite, and excessive fatigue are mostly common for women after delivery. For example, the lack of sleep in PPD is characterized by the incapacity of a woman to be able to sleep even when her baby is sleeping, or she may sleep excessively. Additional symptoms to look for include anxiety, intense irritability or anger, feelings of guilt, a sense of being overwhelmed, feelings of being a failure as a mother, and changes in libido more than expected.

As for risk factors in PPD, three meta-analyses reported from Robertson and colleagues in 2004, found that the strongest risk factors for postpartum depression are as follows: depression during pregnancy, anxiety during pregnancy, life events such as losing a job or divorce, and past history of psychiatric illness [56]. Moreover, inadequate social support, childcare-related stressors, and poor quality relationship with a partner have been considered consistent predictors of PPD, whereas low socioeconomic status and difficult infant temperament have not been upheld as consistent predictors [57].

Even though the causes of PPD are still source of debate, scientists agree in recognizing a mutifactorial model composed by three interrelated factors: hormones' fluctuation, situational risks, and life stresses [58]. *Hormones' fluctuation* refers to decreased levels of serotonin and estrogens after delivery; *situational risks* could be described as those social/environmental factors that could led to clinical depression, and *life stresses* that may also lead to the development of PPD include balancing career and motherhood, loss of former roles or freedoms, relationship stresses, and unresolved feelings about the pregnancy [58]. Others psychosocial risk factors for PPD include Mayor Depression Disorder during pregnancy, anxiety during pregnancy, previous nonpuerperal MDD, previous premenstrual dysphoria, stressful life events during pregnancy, poor social support, low income, immigrant status, and young maternal age [57].

3.2. Screening and Diagnosis (Assessment Measures)

Given this variety of symptoms, the task for the clinicians is to determine which symptoms are significant to formulate a diagnosis of PPD and which symptoms are connected to normal changes after delivery, in psychological or physiological sphere. Even though there is increasing awareness of the impact of PPD in women's life, some researches argue that the screening of depression is problematic, given the above cited nature of symptoms [59].

Screening tools have been designed to aid clinicians in this process, and are necessary to identify PPD as a mood disorder (major depressive, maniac, or mixed episode) according to the *Diagnostic and Statistical Manual of Mental Disorders*, 4th Edition (*DSM-IV*) [55]. It is important to remember that self-report instruments cannot provide a diagnosis for MDD, but they can identify women in need of further evaluation and/or women at high risk for developing PPD.

In this section, a list of screening tools for the assessment of PPD is provided, based on the review of self report depression measures conducted by Boyd and colleagues [60].

- The Beck Depression Inventory [61] presents 21 items with Likert scale in 4 step, and a score range between 0 and 63. It was originally created for assess depression severity, focusing in somatic symptoms. This characteristic has been criticized in the screening of PPD, because physical symptom are frequently similar to normal issues of postpartum condition. A second version, BDI-II [62], has been proposed in order to improve the degree of correspondence with DSM-IV criteria for MDD and confirming the bifactorial structure of the previous version (Cognitive-Affective and Somatic scale). Several researches have used BDI for PPD, and the instrument has been shown to have good specificity, sensitivity and moderate correlations with instruments for postpartum depression, depression, anxiety, and general distress.
- The Bromley Postnatal Depression Scale (BPDS) [63] has 10 items, including open-ended and yes/no questions, and a chart to indicate when postpartum depression began, how long it lasted, and when it was the worst. It allows women to report their own experience during pregnancy as for mood and behaviors, but it is needed a specific training to interpret results. Even though there are limited data on this instrument, the psychometric properties have shown to be acceptable [60].
- The Edinburgh Postnatal Depression Scale (EPDS) [64] is the most widely used instrument for assessing PPD. Composed by 10 items scored from 0 to 3, it measures cognitive and emotional features of PPD, excluding somatic symptoms of depression. With a maximum score of 30, a score greater than 12 identify most women with PPD. The EPDS demonstrates moderate to good reliability properties across samples

from a wide variety of countries and languages, even though different cut-off scores may be needed for different cultural groups [60].

- The Postpartum Depression Screening Scale (PDSS) [65] is a 35-item measure on a Likert scale of 1 to 5 that focuses on seven different dimensions of PPD: Sleeping/ Eating Disturbances, Anxiety/Insecurity, Emotional Lability, Cognitive Impairment, Loss of Self, Guilt/Shame, and Contemplating Harming Oneself. Score of 60 to 79 identifies women with a positive screen for minor depression, and a score of 80 or more represents a positive screen for major PPD. The validity information for the PDSS is also promising, with good sensitivity and specificity.

As seen above, there are different opportunities to recognize risk for PPD in clinical settings. It is always important to note whether a woman reports history of depression, being depression the strongest risk factor for PPD. Using brief self report instrument is also recommended to assess the severity of the woman's condition and the subsequent plan of intervention.

3.3. Treatment

Antenatal Interventions to Prevent Postnatal Depression

As stated in Sockol, 2013, "while the goal of treatment is to alleviate symptoms of a disorder already diagnosed, preventive interventions are intended to avoid the initial onset of symptoms," in order to reduce the human and economic costs associated with mental illness [66].

The recent meta-analytic review by Sockol et Alii, suggests that a wide range of interventions may be effective in the prevention of depression during the first 6 months postpartum, as they result in small but significant reduction of depressive symptoms and prevalence of depressive episodes [66]. Preventive interventions appear to be most efficacious when they are assessed early during the postpartum period and this positive effect is important to reduce distress in the relationship between mother and child in the early phases. Although the natural course of postpartum depression is for symptom severity to decrease over time, preventive interventions still remain necessary to safeguard initial interaction between mother and child.

Type of intervention (i.e., antidepressant medication, educational programs, dietary supplements, hormonal interventions, social support, therapy) has shown not to be related to the effectiveness of treatments for either reducing depressive symptoms or preventing depressive episodes [66]. For example, non specific social contact seems to contrast the "lack of social support" risk factor more than specific active elements of treatment, which seem to be less important. On the other hand, psychotherapy is the only type of intervention for which enough studies have assessed potential moderation of specific aspects of the intervention, such as therapeutic orientation, method of administration and number of sessions. Nevertheless, no categorical characteristics of psychotherapeutic interventions seem to be significant moderators of effectiveness.

Another recent review by Clatworthy [67] have examined effectiveness of antenatal interventions to prevent postnatal depression, trying also to explore whether specific types of intervention are more effective than others. In this review emerges that, over 11 studies that met criteria for inclusion, subjects were selected among those women who were experiencing symptoms of depression during pregnancy or had history of depression. At this regard, it seems that preventive antenatal interventions are more affective among women with higher level of depressive symptoms during pregnancy, whilst no effect has been found among women who didn't have depressive features during pregnancy [68, 69].

Another interesting result emerging from this review is that psychological preventive treatment seem to be more effective that educational type, because it focuses on indentifying and managing interpersonal and couple conflict [70]. Further research is needed to assess whether those treatments are useful for women who don't have partners.

The clinical implications of this review are that pregnant women experiencing symptoms of depression should be offered psychological intervention [67], but it is also important to acknowledge that not all women who develop postnatal depression will have experienced depression during the antenatal period. Therefore, postpartum depression treatment remains of great importance.

Treatments of Postpartum Depression

With regard to treatment of depression during postpartum, the meta-analysis conducted by Sockol in 2011 [71], assesses the efficacy of psychological and pharmacological interventions for perinatal depression, defined as the period encompassing pregnancy and the first 12 months postpartum.

In this review, studies including three types of psychological interventions are compared: pharmacological, psychological, and combined (pharmacological + psychological), showing no significant differences in effect sizes among the three major types of interventions. At a clinical level, this result confirms the need to combine both psychological and pharmacological interventions throw antidepressant [72]. Antidepressant treatment is in fact a critical topic, mostly with regard to pharmacological management for breast-feeding mothers, where "the benefits to the mother must be weighed against the harms that may be done to the child" [72]. This poses an ethical dilemma, which should be addressed in further researches.

It emerges also that individual settings are more likely to be effective than group ones and, considering differences in therapeutic orientation (Cognitive Behavioral Therapy and Interpersonal Therapy), both seem to be effective with a superiority of IPT to CBT.

Interpersonal Therapy is reported to be associated with greater decrease in symptoms from pretreatment to posttreatment, confirming the idea that the focus on interpersonal areas, particularly on role transitions and interpersonal disputes, may be indicated to solve the problems women experience during the perinatal period [73].

Given the possibility that other aspects of the mentioned study design may have been confounded with the therapeutic orientation of the interventions included in the different studies, these results regarding the superiority of IPT to CBT should be interpreted with caution [71]. Other researches have shown that CBT appear to be cost-effective in primary care [74] and also helpful in preventing relapses [75].

Given the prevalence of postpartum depression and the negative outcomes associated with depressive symptoms during this period, the identification of effective and acceptable treatments for this population is vitally necessary.

4. Emotions and Eating Disorders

4.1. Emotion Regulation and Attitude towards Food

Relationship between emotions and food intake has been discussed in several papers and books. The aim of this paragraph is to draw attention to the concept of emotional eating and its relationship with psychological suffering and eating disorders in women who search for clinical help and support in different moment of their lives.

Food is, of course, important to our survival and the maintenance of good health, but it is also connected to our social and psychological dimensions. Emotions in particular seem to have an important role in the way we approach the "eating" attitude. In particular, a concept that is important to fully understand is the "Emotional Eating," a specific attitude towards food that has been cited as a common problem by clinicians and researchers.

The concept of emotional eating has been defined by various scientists. According to Macht, "emotional eating theory postulates that negative emotions, such as anxiety, induce eating and in turn reduce and alleviate the negative emotion" [76]. In this definition, emotional eating is conceptualized as eating in response to a range of negative emotions such as anxiety, depression, anger, loneliness, and inadequate coping with negative affects. In other words, people who could be defined as "Emotional Eaters" consume foods to reduce the feeling of negative emotions.

Lluch and colleagues define Emotional Eating as "an expression of beliefs about the frequency of eating when being emotional" [77]. The focus, in this definition, is the maladaptive belief underlying a particular coping strategy, which, in turns, maintains and reinforces a dysfunctional behavior.

Emotional eating can be also defined as "an increase in food intake in response to negative emotions" [78], underlying that emotional *over*eating could be qualified as a form of emotion-focused coping strategy, which attempts to minimize, regulate and prevent emotional distress.

In his work, Macht notices that, despite a large amount of studies on this topic, the effect of emotion on eating in different groups of people is still difficult to explain, due to extreme variability. For example, emotions can push people to eat more or less as usual, and different emotions may increase or decrease the amount of food intake in people who belongs to the same group. Thus, the author offers an integrative model that considers both emotion features and individual characteristics in order to explain a twofold variability in emotional eating [76].

After identifying as antecedents a number of factors that make difference in emotion induced changes of eating (i.e., arousal/intensity, valence and food relatedness of emotions, restrained and emotional eating), Macht suggests that emotions affect eating in five basic ways, as shown below:

1. Emotions aroused in response to food stimuli affect food choice.
2. In this sense, appetitive food related stimuli can elicit a strong desire to eat or craving, that can itself be considered an emotional feature induced by food;
3. Highly intense emotions suppress eating stimulus due to incompatible emotional response.

4. In fact, intense emotions features are associated to physiological and behavioral patterns that inhibit the eating desire (i.e., intense sadness is related to deactivation and withdrawal, while intense fear motivates avoidance of stimuli);
   a) Mild intensity emotions affect eating depending on motivations to eat:
   b) In restrained eating, emotions (both positive and negative) could enhance food intake due to their ability to stop cognitive control: in fact, dieting requires a lot of cognitive control and emotions could act as distraction, leading to temporary cognitive impairment;
   c) In emotional eating, due to the tendency of controlling negative emotions by eating, an increase in emotions perception enhances intake of sweet and high fat food, as suggested in a previous study by Macht and Mueller [79];
   d) In normal eating, different emotions affect eating behavior in different ways, in accordance with their cognitive and motivational features. For instance, sadness is associated with slow cognitive processing and motor activation, while joy is connected with an increase of processing ability and readiness [80].

If emotional eating can be considered as a coping strategy to deal with emotions, it could be interesting to understand which emotions are more frequently associated with this kind of behavior. When dealing with people who eat food in search of comfort, it is easy to believe that mostly negative emotions are involved. On the contrary, at least one study tried to investigate the relationship between eating and emotions in everyday life, finding that there are four types of emotional states related to food intake: anger-dominance, tension/fear, relaxation/joy and an unemotional state [81].

The emotional stressors that can trigger emotional eating differ from person to person, as shown below.

Stress. Different researches recognize stress as a leading factor in changing health behavior, such as food choice and intake [82, 83]. Moreover, it seems that diet restraint may be the most important predictor of overeating during stress. Stress may also influence the kind of food chosen to eat: when stressed, people tend to choose more highly caloric foods and sweets, diminishing the intake of fruits and vegetables [82]. It is suggested that when under stress, individuals seek comfort foods that are highly palatable that, as a consequence, tend to produce further negative emotions such as post-consumption guilt. This is primarily associated with the female gender [84].

Boredom. As an eating trigger, this particular emotion has been investigated by many clinicians and researchers. Koball and colleagues [85] showed that students eat mostly in response to feeling bored, compared to other emotions. Further studies are needed to assess the boredom as a relevant emotion that precedes eating [85].

Depression. With this regard, a study found a significantly increased consumption of sweet soft drinks within depressed school children [83]. Another study suggests that emotional eating could be one factor explaining the association between depressive symptoms and consumption of sweet foods [86]. On the other hand, the findings that subjects with higher levels of depressive symptoms consumed more non-sweet foods and fewer vegetables/fruits irrespective of their level of emotional eating suggests that emotional eating is not the only factor accounting for the association of depressive symptoms with unhealthy food choices, supporting the hypothesis (Macht, 2008) that emotional eating is specifically related to the increased eating of sweets and high-fat foods.

Anger. Following Macht theory [76], we should consider emotions in their valence, intensity and arousal in order to understand different influence on eating behavior. In this sense, anger can be considered an high stimulation, negative valence emotion with specific cognitive and behavioral activation which could be linked to motivation to eat in both men and women. According to Appelhans and colleagues, anger itself does not impact on the amount of energy snacks intake, instead is the lack of distraction response strategies that has direct connection to overeating [87].

Happiness. Many researches show that women who report high restraint in their eating behavior eat less when exposed to food during positive moods. For example, Turner et al. [88] investigated the effects of positive emotions on food intake in restrained and non-restrained eaters, finding that positive emotions lead to lower food intake mostly among those who already practice effective self-control, and also showing the exact opposite result in the group with uncontrolled eating. These findings support the assumption that a general tendency to respond to emotional eating is related to food consumption indirectly, and more directly associated with uncontrolled eating style.

4.2. Emotion Dysregulation and Eating Disorder Symptoms

Even though the studies aforementioned seemed to agree in underlying that eating could reduce emotional distress, other studies suggested that this might not be true. For instance, Bennet and colleagues found that emotional eating sometimes does not reduce emotional distress but instead enhances emotional distress by "sparking feelings of intense guilt after an emotional eating session" [89].

In this sense, emotional eating could activate a vicious circle in which negative emotions lead to an increase of food intake, and, as a consequence, generate feelings of sadness and guilt, resulting in eating more food in an attempt to face and cope with these negative feelings (Figure 1) [90, 91]. Thus, not only is emotional eating a poor way to cope, but those individuals who frequently utilize emotional eating to cope with social or psychological stressors are more likely to develop eating disorders [78].

Negative emotions have been shown to result in overeating in obese individuals and in eating-disordered women [78]. Furthermore, deficits in emotion regulation processes are a common and widely used explanation for the development and maintenance of Binge Eating Disorder (BED). It is assumed that BED patients – as they have difficulty in regulating their negative emotions – use binge eating and emotional eating to deal with these emotions and to find relief.

In the DSM-5, BED is defined as a distinct Eating Disorder and characterized by recurrent binge eating episodes which are defined as "eating an unusually large amount of food someone else would not eat in the same period of time and in a similar setting while experiencing loss of control (LOC)" [92]. Further attributes of binge eating episodes are: eating faster than normal, eating until feeling uncomfortably full, eating without feeling of guilt or disgust afterwards. Binge eating episodes are also associated with distress and have to occur at least once a week over a period of three months. Explanation models of binge eating behavior in BED and overeating in obesity refer to self-regulation failure caused by intense emotions, following the idea that neurobiological processes concerning self-regulation, including control over eating behavior, are influenced by emotions [93].

From a behavioral point of view, different theories regarding emotion regulation and bingeing have been proposed [94]:

- The theory of emotional eating proposed by Bennett and already mentioned above [89], identifies binge eating as a form of - failing - coping strategy in response to negative affects;
- The escape theory by Heatherton and Baumeister [95] presumes an alleviation of aversive affect while bingeing, due to a form of escape from self awareness;
- The affect regulation theory [96], assume an improvement of affect after binge eating;

To subsume and comprehend more components, Leehr and colleagues propose the "emotion regulation theory," in an attempt to include two aspects of the binge eating behavior: (1) the presence of negative emotions as trigger to bingeing and (2) down regulation of negative emotions throw bingeing in short term or long term period of time [94]. More specifically, Leehr conducted a systematic review of experimental studies to investigate the two components (trigger component and relief component) in overweight/obese people with and without BED. In the studies that met criteria for the inclusion, samples were most composed by women.

The results of the review show that in individuals (mostly women) with BED, negative emotions may impair processes of self-regulation. As a consequence, "these subjects engage in binge eating and overeating as other, more efficient strategies cannot be used, as it may be the case for obese individuals without BED. One plausible reason to explain why states of negative emotion cause a self-regulation failure in people with BED, but not in obese people without BED, may be a lower emotion regulation capacity or the use of dysfunctional emotion regulation strategies" [94].

Furthermore, a lack of emotional clarity, or inability to determine what emotion is being felt, can be associated with emotional overeating in obese people with BED [97], underlying that being able to accurately identify the emotion felt by individuals is essential before being able to effectively cope with said emotions.

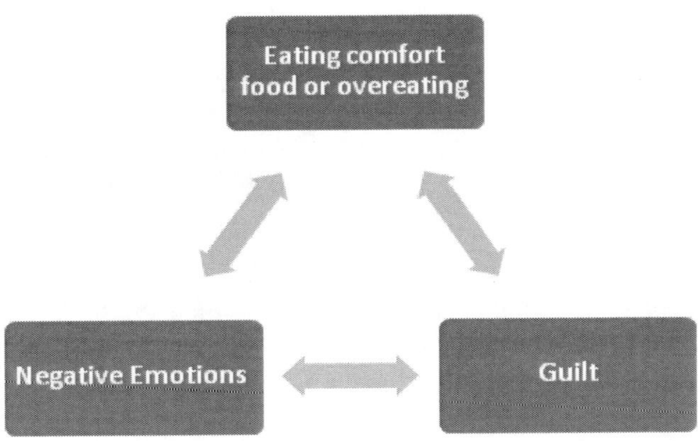

Figure 1. Vicious circle of emotional eating.

In this study, non acceptance of emotional responses and difficulties in engaging goal-directed behavior seemed to be the emotion regulation difficulties most strongly associated with eating pathology. It is possible that when individuals feel they are overwhelmed by negative affects and cannot concentrate or focus on other tasks, they engage in disordered eating as an attempt to mitigate or escape from these aversive emotional states [97].

In discussing such topic, seems relevant to mention the concept of alexithymia, which describes difficulties identifying feelings and differentiating between feelings and bodily sensations, difficulties communicating feelings, lack of fantasy, and a concrete cognitive style. This concept has been found to be related to eating disorders and disturbed eating, in fact a robust body of research illustrates that individuals with eating disorders show specific deficits in identifying and describing affective states compared to healthy community controls [98]. With this regard, at least one study suggests that different mechanisms might subtend to difficulties in identifying emotions for patients who restrict or engage in bingeing and purging behaviors. Specifically, while depression may directly induce difficulties in identifying and expressing emotions in patients who restrict, the emotional issues of patients with bingeing and purging behaviors may be influenced by high level of impulsivity and affective instability [99].

As for the role that alexithymia plays in the development of eating disorders, an interesting hypothesis comes from Ruggiero and colleagues [100], stating that perfectionism mediates the relation between alexithymia and eating disorders, such that alexithymia increases the risk of perfectionism, which in turn increases the risk of developing an eating disorder. In the particular case of binge eating, it is possible that coexistence of emotion intolerance, difficulties in impulse control and emotion dysregulation could led to bingeing in response to negative perceived emotions [101].

4.3. Treatment: Management of Emotions and Mindfulness Meditation

On the practical level, the challenge is how to help people to cope with these kinds of tendencies in order to prevent the onset of eating disorder symptoms and treat eating pathology.

Cognitive Behavior Therapy (CBT) is one of the most used therapies and its efficacy has been proved in several studies [102-104]. It focuses on teaching behavioral strategies to help patients restore normal eating, identifying and understanding triggers for their eating disorder behaviors and examining and modifying their cognitions related to food, shape and weight.

Another well established treatments for BED (Binge Eating Disorder) is Interpersonal Therapy (IPT), in conjunction with pharmacologic treatment [105].

Given the significant role of emotion dysregulation in eating disorders and the finding that alexithymia is a negative predictor of treatment outcome [98], a treatment approach that emphasizes identification of emotions and useful coping strategies, in combination with traditional CBT, may help in improving treatment efficacy.

Concerning the abovementioned, there have been promising results from studies examining Dialectical Behavioral Therapy, DBT [106]. Dialectical Behavioral Therapy specifically addresses emotion regulation by teaching adaptive skills to patients, in order to enhance their ability to cope with negative emotions.

Another type of psychological intervention which is specifically focused on emotions is inspired by mindfulness. The efficacy of the so-called Mindfulness Based Interventions (MBI) in binge eating and emotional eating has been recently reviewed by Katterman and colleagues [107].

Throw a systematic review of 14 studies, the authors suggest that mindfulness meditation effectively decreases binge eating and emotional eating in populations engaging in this behavior, without been diagnosed with BED or ED in general. The attention is drawn to evaluating the impact of mindfulness meditation in dysfunctional eating behavior in those subject with subclinical symptoms.

Mindfulness can be defined as "a state of nonjudgmental attention to the immediate experience and an acceptance of moment-to-moment experience" [108]. The rationale for the use of mindfulness meditation techniques in the treatment of eating disorders is the importance of cultivating awareness of internal experiences (emotions and physical sensations), facilitating self-acceptance, cognitive flexibility, compassion and forgiveness, and improving ability to cope adaptively with emotions, both positive and negative. The aim and purpose of this kind of intervention is to encourage patients to accept themselves, experience their emotions in a more integrated and non judgmental way.

Future research should continue examining these and other possible ways of helping people to deal with negative emotions in a more functional way.

REFERENCES

[1] Ombelet, W., Is global access to infertility care realistic? The Walking Egg Project. *Reprod Biomed Online*, 2014. 28(3): p. 267-72.

[2] Mormandi, E.A. et al., [Body weight increase and quality of semen: a controversial association]. *Endocrinol Nutr*, 2013. 60(6): p. 303-7.

[3] Klock, S., Obstetric and gynecological conditions. *Clinical handbook of health psychology*, 2004: p. 209-232.

[4] Abrao, M.S., L. Muzii, and R. Marana, Anatomical causes of female infertility and their management. *Int J Gynaecol Obstet*, 2013. 123 Suppl. 2: p. S18-24.

[5] Luciano, A.A., A. Lanzone, and A.J. Goverde, Management of female infertility from hormonal causes. *Int J Gynaecol Obstet*, 2013. 123 Suppl. 2: p. S9-17.

[6] Belloc, S. et al., How to overcome male infertility after 40: Influence of paternal age on fertility. *Maturitas*, 2014. 78(1): p. 22-29.

[7] Afeiche, M.C. et al., Dairy intake and semen quality among men attending a fertility clinic. *Fertil Steril*, 2014. 101(5): p. 1280-7.

[8] Petraglia, F., G.I. Serour, and C. Chapron, The changing prevalence of infertility. *Int J Gynaecol Obstet*, 2013. 123 Suppl. 2: p. S4-8.

[9] Jing, L., L. Botao, and L. Min, Coping with infertility: a transcultural perspective. *Current opinion in psychiatry*, 2014. 27(5): p. 320-325.

[10] Kainz, K., The role of the psychologist in the evaluation and treatment of infertility. *Womens Health Issues*, 2001. 11(6): p. 481-5.

[11] Cwikel, J., Y. Gidron, and E. Sheiner, Psychological interactions with infertility among women. *Eur J Obstet Gynecol Reprod Biol*, 2004. 117(2): p. 126-31.

[12] Vellani, E. et al., Association of state and trait anxiety to semen quality of in vitro fertilization patients: a controlled study. *Fertil Steril*, 2013. 99(6): p. 1565-72.

[13] Hjollund, N.H.I. et al., Distress and reduced fertility: a follow-up study of first-pregnancy planners. *Fertility and sterility*, 1999. 72(1): p. 47-53.

[14] Leiblum, S.R., Infertility, In: *Handbook of behavioral medicine for women*, E.A. Blechman and K.D. Brownell, Editors. 1988, Pergamon Press.

[15] Freeman, E.W. et al., Psychological evaluation and support in a program of in vitro fertilization and embryo transfer. *Fertil Steril*, 1985. 43(1): p. 48-53.

[16] Domar, A.D., Stress and infertility in women: Is there a relationship? In *Session: Psychotherapy in Practice*, 1996. 2(2): p. 17-27.

[17] Thiering, P. et al., Mood state as a predictor of treatment outcome after in vitro fertilization/embryo transfer technology (IVF/ET). *J Psychosom Res*, 1993. 37(5): p. 481-91.

[18] Greenfeld, D.A., The course of infertility: Immediate and long-term reactions. *In Session: Psychotherapy in Practice*, 1996. 2(2): p. 5-16.

[19] Klock, S.C., Privacy and disclosure in infertility treatment. *In Session: Psychotherapy in Practice*, 1996. 2(2): p. 55-71.

[20] Read, S.C. et al., Psychosocial services for couples in infertility treatment: what do couples really want? *Patient Educ Couns*, 2014. 94(3): p. 390-5.

[21] Gameiro, S., J. Boivin, and A. Domar, Optimal in vitro fertilization in 2020 should reduce treatment burden and enhance care delivery for patients and staff. *Fertil Steril*, 2013. 100(2): p. 302-9.

[22] Heredia, M. et al., Quality of life and predictive factors in patients undergoing assisted reproduction techniques. *Eur J Obstet Gynecol Reprod Biol,* 2013. 167(2): p. 176-80.

[23] Mousavi, S.A. et al., Assessment of questionnaires measuring quality of life in infertile couples: a systematic review. *J Reprod Infertil*, 2013. 14(3): p. 110-9.

[24] Dornelles, L.M. et al., 'Living each week as unique': maternal fears in assisted reproductive technology pregnancies. *Midwifery*, 2014. 30(3): p. e115-20.

[25] Coughlan, C. et al., A comparison of psychological stress among women with and without reproductive failure. *Int J Gynaecol Obstet*, 2014. 124(2): p. 143-7.

[26] Palomba, S. et al., Physical activity before IVF and ICSI cycles in infertile obese women: an observational cohort study. *Reprod Biomed Online*, 2014. 29(1): p. 72-9.

[27] Galhardo, A., M. Cunha, and J. Pinto-Gouveia, Mindfulness-Based Program for Infertility: efficacy study. *Fertil Steril*, 2013. 100(4): p. 1059-67.

[28] Kim, M. et al., Effect of a mind-body therapeutic program for infertile women repeating in vitro fertilization treatment on uncertainty, anxiety, and implantation rate. *Asian Nurs Res* (*Korean Soc Nurs Sci*), 2014. 8(1): p. 49-56.

[29] Wurlitzer, S.H., J. Evans, and S. Znidar, Psychological and emotional preparation for IVF brings numerous benefits including an improved likelihood of success--the fertile body method. *Australian Journal of Clinical Hypnotherapy and Hypnosis*, 2013. 35(1): p. 28-45.

[30] Braverman, A.M., Issues involved in the decision to end infertility treatment: When is enough enough? *In Session: Psychotherapy in Practice*, 1996. 2(2): p. 85-96.

[31] Biggs, W.S. and R.H. Demuth, Premenstrual syndrome and premenstrual dysphoric disorder. *American family physician*, 2011. 84(8).

[32] Yonkers, K.A., P.M. O'Brien, and E. Eriksson, Premenstrual syndrome. *Lancet*, 2008. 371(9619): p. 1200-10.

[33] Dennerstein, L. et al., Premenstrual symptoms -- severity, duration and typology: an international cross-sectional study. *Menopause Int*, 2009. 15(3): p. 120-6.

[34] Potter, J. et al., Premenstrual syndrome prevalence and fluctuation over time: results from a French population-based survey. *J Womens Health* (Larchmt), 2009. 18(1): p. 31-9.

[35] Rapkin, A.J. and S.A. Winer, Premenstrual syndrome and premenstrual dysphoric disorder: quality of life and burden of illness. *Expert Rev Pharmacoecon Outcomes Res*, 2009. 9(2): p. 157-70.

[36] Steiner, M., Premenstrual syndrome and premenstrual dysphoric disorder: guidelines for management. *J Psychiatry Neurosci*, 2000. 25(5): p. 459-68.

[37] Gynecologists, A.C.o.O.a., ACOG practice bulletin n 15:Premenstrual Syndrome, In: *Obstet Gynecol* 2000.

[38] Endicott, J., J. Nee, and W. Harrison, Daily Record of Severity of Problems (DRSP): reliability and validity. *Arch Womens Ment Health*, 2006. 9(1): p. 41-9.

[39] Steiner, M. and A. Wilkins, Diagnosis and assessment of premenstrual dysphoria. *Psychiatric Annals*, 1996. 26(9): p. 571-575.

[40] Bertone-Johnson, E.R. et al., Calcium and vitamin D intake and risk of incident premenstrual syndrome. *Archives of internal medicine*, 2005. 165(11): p. 1246-1252.

[41] Bertone-Johnson, E.R. et al., Dietary vitamin D intake, 25-hydroxyvitamin D3 levels and premenstrual syndrome in a college-aged population. *J Steroid Biochem Mol Biol*, 2010. 121(1-2): p. 434-7.

[42] Thys-Jacobs, S. et al., Calcium carbonate and the premenstrual syndrome: effects on premenstrual and menstrual symptoms. Premenstrual Syndrome Study Group. *Am J Obstet Gynecol*, 1998. 179(2): p. 444-52.

[43] Blake, F. et al., Cognitive therapy for premenstrual syndrome: a controlled trial. *J Psychosom Res*, 1998. 45(4): p. 307-18.

[44] Whelan, A.M., T.M. Jurgens, and H. Naylor, Herbs, vitamins and minerals in the treatment of premenstrual syndrome: a systematic review. *Can J Clin Pharmacol*, 2009. 16(3): p. e407-29.

[45] Schellenberg, R., Treatment for the premenstrual syndrome with agnus castus fruit extract: prospective, randomised, placebo controlled study. *BMJ*, 2001. 322(7279): p. 134-7.

[46] Wyatt, K.M. et al., Efficacy of vitamin B-6 in the treatment of premenstrual syndrome: systematic review. *BMJ*, 1999. 318(7195): p. 1375-81.

[47] Brown, J. et al., Selective serotonin reuptake inhibitors for premenstrual syndrome. *Cochrane Database Syst Rev*, 2009(2): p. CD001396.

[48] Lopez, L.M., A.A. Kaptein, and F.M. Helmerhorst, Oral contraceptives containing drospirenone for premenstrual syndrome. *Cochrane Database Syst Rev*, 2009(2): p. CD 006586.

[49] Freeman, E.W. et al., A double-blind trial of oral progesterone, alprazolam, and placebo in treatment of severe premenstrual syndrome. *JAMA*, 1995. 274(1): p. 51-7.

[50] Weissman, M.M. and P. Jensen, What research suggests for depressed women with children. *J Clin Psychiatry*, 2002. 63(7): p. 641-7.

[51] Goodman, S.H. and I.H. Gotlib, Risk for psychopathology in the children of depressed mothers: a developmental model for understanding mechanisms of transmission. *Psychol Rev*, 1999. 106(3): p. 458-90.

[52] Field, T., Postpartum depression effects on early interactions, parenting, and safety practices: a review. *Infant Behav Dev*, 2010. 33(1): p. 1-6.

[53] Wisner, K.L., B.L. Parry, and C.M. Piontek, Clinical practice. Postpartum depression. *N Engl J Med*, 2002. 347(3): p. 194-9.

[54] Gorman, L.L. et al., Adaptation of the structured clinical interview for DSM-IV disorders for assessing depression in women during pregnancy and post-partum across countries and cultures. *Br J Psychiatry* Suppl., 2004. 46: p. s17-23.

[55] Association, A.P., Diagnostic and statistical manual-text revision (DSM-IV-TR, 2000). 2000: American Psychiatric Association.

[56] Robertson, E. et al., Antenatal risk factors for postpartum depression: a synthesis of recent literature. *Gen Hosp Psychiatry*, 2004. 26(4): p. 289-95.

[57] Beck, C.T., Predictors of postpartum depression: an update. *Nurs Res*, 2001. 50(5): p. 275-85.

[58] Currie, M.L. and R. Rademacher, The pediatrician's role in recognizing and intervening in postpartum depression. *Pediatr Clin North Am*, 2004. 51(3): p. 785-801, xi.

[59] Rost, K. et al., The role of competing demands in the treatment provided primary care patients with major depression. *Arch Fam Med*, 2000. 9(2): p. 150-4.

[60] Boyd, R.C., H.N. Le, and R. Somberg, Review of screening instruments for postpartum depression. *Arch Womens Ment Health*, 2005. 8(3): p. 141-53.

[61] Beck, A.T. et al., An inventory for measuring depression. *Arch Gen Psychiatry*, 1961. 4: p. 561-71.

[62] Beck, A.T. et al., Comparison of Beck Depression Inventories -IA and -II in psychiatric outpatients. *J Pers Assess*, 1996. 67(3): p. 588-97.

[63] Stein, G. and O. Van den Akker, The retrospective diagnosis of postnatal depression by questionnaire. *J Psychosom Res*, 1992. 36(1): p. 67-75.

[64] Cox, J.L., J.M. Holden, and R. Sagovsky, Detection of postnatal depression. Development of the 10-item Edinburgh Postnatal Depression Scale. *Br J Psychiatry*, 1987. 150: p. 782-6.

[65] Beck, C.T. and R.K. Gable, Postpartum Depression Screening Scale: development and psychometric testing. *Nurs Res*, 2000. 49(5): p. 272-82.

[66] Sockol, L.E., C.N. Epperson, and J.P. Barber, Preventing postpartum depression: a meta-analytic review. *Clin Psychol Rev*, 2013. 33(8): p. 1205-17.

[67] Clatworthy, J., The effectiveness of antenatal interventions to prevent postnatal depression in high-risk women. *J Affect Disord*, 2012. 137(1-3): p. 25-34.

[68] Austin, M.P. et al., Brief antenatal cognitive behaviour therapy group intervention for the prevention of postnatal depression and anxiety: a randomised controlled trial. *J Affect Disord*, 2008. 105(1-3): p. 35-44.

[69] Cho, H.J., J.H. Kwon, and J.J. Lee, Antenatal cognitive-behavioral therapy for prevention of postpartum depression: a pilot study. *Yonsei Med J*, 2008. 49(4): p. 553-62.

[70] Grote, N.K. et al., A randomized controlled trial of culturally relevant, brief interpersonal psychotherapy for perinatal depression. *Psychiatr Serv*, 2009. 60(3): p. 313-21.

[71] Sockol, L.E., C.N. Epperson, and J.P. Barber, A meta-analysis of treatments for perinatal depression. *Clin Psychol Rev*, 2011. 31(5): p. 839-49.

[72] Pearlstein, T. et al., Postpartum depression. *Am J Obstet Gynecol*, 2009. 200(4): p. 357-64.

[73] Stuart, S. and M.W. O'Hara, Treatment of postpartum depression with interpersonal psychotherapy. *Arch Gen Psychiatry*, 1995. 52(1): p. 75-6.

[74] Churchill, R. et al., A systematic review of controlled trials of the effectiveness and cost-effectiveness of brief psychological treatments for depression. *Health Technol Assess*, 2001. 5(35): p. 1-173.

[75] Scott, J. et al., Use of cognitive therapy for relapse prevention in chronic depression. Cost-effectiveness study. *Br J Psychiatry*, 2003. 182: p. 221-7.

[76] Macht, M., How emotions affect eating: a five-way model. *Appetite*, 2008. 50(1): p. 1-11.

[77] Lluch, A. et al., Internal validation of a French version of the Dutch eating behaviour questionnaire. *Eur Psychiatry*, 1996. 11(4): p. 198-203.

[78] Spoor, S.T. et al., Relations between negative affect, coping, and emotional eating. *Appetite*, 2007. 48(3): p. 368-76.

[79] Macht, M. and J. Mueller, Immediate effects of chocolate on experimentally induced mood states. *Appetite*, 2007. 49(3): p. 667-74.

[80] Izard, C.E., and Ackerman, B. P., ed. Organizational and motivational functions of discrete emotions. Vol. M. L. J. M. Haviland (Ed.) *Handbook of emotions* (2nd ed.) 2000, New York: Guilford Press. 253–264.

[81] Macht, M. and G. Simons, Emotions and eating in everyday life. *Appetite*, 2000. 35(1): p. 65-71.

[82] Zellner, D.A. et al., Food selection changes under stress. *Physiol Behav*, 2006. 87(4): p. 789-93.

[83] Gibson, E.L., Emotional influences on food choice: sensory, physiological and psychological pathways. *Physiol Behav*, 2006. 89(1): p. 53-61.

[84] Wallis, D.J. and M.M. Hetherington, Emotions and eating. Self-reported and experimentally induced changes in food intake under stress. *Appetite*, 2009. 52(2): p. 355-62.

[85] Koball, A.M. et al., Eating when bored: revision of the emotional eating scale with a focus on boredom. *Health Psychol*, 2012. 31(4): p. 521-4.

[86] Konttinen, H. et al., Emotional eating, depressive symptoms and self-reported food consumption. A population-based study. *Appetite*, 2010. 54(3): p. 473-9.

[87] Appelhans, B.M. et al., Response style and vulnerability to anger-induced eating in obese adults. *Eat Behav*, 2011. 12(1): p. 9-14.

[88] Turner, S.A. et al., Emotional and uncontrolled eating styles and chocolate chip cookie consumption. A controlled trial of the effects of positive mood enhancement. *Appetite*, 2010. 54(1): p. 143-9.

[89] Bennett, J., G. Greene, and D. Schwartz-Barcott, Perceptions of emotional eating behavior. A qualitative study of college students. *Appetite*, 2013. 60(1): p. 187-92.

[90] Compare, A. et al., Emotionally focused group therapy and dietary counseling in binge eating disorder. Effect on eating disorder psychopathology and quality of life. *Appetite*, 2013. 71: p. 361-8.

[91] Compare, A. and E. Grossi, Stress e disturbi da somatizzazione: Evidence-Based Practice in psicologia clinica. 2012: Springer Science and Business Media.

[92] APA, Diagnostic and Statistical Manual of Mental Disorders. 2013, Washington, DC.: American Psychiatric Association.

[93] Heatherton, T.F. and D.D. Wagner, Cognitive neuroscience of self-regulation failure. *Trends Cogn Sci*, 2011. 15(3): p. 132-9.

[94] Leehr, E.J. et al., Emotion regulation model in binge eating disorder and obesity--a systematic review. *Neurosci Biobehav Rev*, 2015. 49: p. 125-34.

[95] Heatherton, T.F. and R.F. Baumeister, Binge eating as escape from self-awareness. *Psychol Bull*, 1991. 110(1): p. 86-108.

[96] Heatherton, T.F. et al., Self-awareness, task failure, and disinhibition: how attentional focus affects eating. *J Pers,* 1993. 61(1): p. 49-61.

[97] Gianini, L.M., M.A. White, and R.M. Masheb, Eating pathology, emotion regulation, and emotional overeating in obese adults with Binge Eating Disorder. *Eat Behav*, 2013. 14(3): p. 309-13.

[98] Nowakowski, M.E., T. McFarlane, and S. Cassin, Alexithymia and eating disorders: a critical review of the literature. *J Eat Disord*, 2013. 1: p. 21.

[99] Rozenstein, M.H. et al., Perception of emotion and bilateral advantage in women with eating disorders, their healthy sisters, and nonrelated healthy controls. *J Affect Disord*, 2011. 134(1-3): p. 386-95.

[100] Ruggiero, G.M. et al., The relationship between alexithymia and maladaptive perfectionism in eating disorders: a mediation moderation analysis methodology. *Eat Weight Disord*, 2011. 16(3): p. e182-7.

[101] Sassaroli, S. and G.M. Ruggiero, The role of stress in the association between low self-esteem, perfectionism, and worry, and eating disorders. *Int J Eat Disord*, 2005. 37(2): p. 135-41.

[102] Carter, J.C. and C.G. Fairburn, Cognitive–behavioral self-help for binge eating disorder: A controlled effectiveness study. *Journal of Consulting and Clinical Psychology*, 1998. 66(4): p. 616.

[103] Hofmann, S.G. et al., The efficacy of cognitive behavioral therapy: a review of meta-analyses. *Cognitive therapy and research*, 2012. 36(5): p. 427-440.

[104] Fairburn, C.G. and P.J. Harrison, Eating disorders. *The Lancet*, 2003. 361(9355): p. 407-416.

[105] Wilfley, D.E. et al., A randomized comparison of group cognitive-behavioral therapy and group interpersonal psychotherapy for the treatment of overweight individuals with binge-eating disorder. *Arch Gen Psychiatry*, 2002. 59(8): p. 713-21.

[106] Telch, C.F., W.S. Agras, and M.M. Linehan, Dialectical behavior therapy for binge eating disorder. *J Consult Clin Psychol*, 2001. 69(6): p. 1061-5.

[107] Katterman, S.N. et al., Mindfulness meditation as an intervention for binge eating, emotional eating, and weight loss: a systematic review. *Eat Behav*, 2014. 15(2): p. 197-204.

[108] Bishop, S.R. et al., Mindfulness: A proposed operational definition. *Clinical psychology: Science and practice*, 2004. 11(3): p. 230-241.

EDITORS' CONTACT INFORMATION

Dr. Angelo Compare, PhD
Professor in Clinical &Health Psychology and
Innovative ICT Solutions, University of Bergamo
Director of Applied Technology for Mental Health &
Psychological Well Being
Lab – Mediaclinics Ltd
Email: angelo.compare@unibg.it

Claudia Elia
Univesity of Bergamo
Email: c.elia1@studenti.unigb.it

Antonio Giulio Simonelli
University of Bergamo
Email: a.simonelli@studenti.unibg.it

Francesco Cattafi
University of Bergamo
Email: f_catta@virgilio.it

INDEX

A

B

C

D

N

O

P

Q

R

S

T

U

V

W